Newman Smyth

Old Faiths in New Light

Newman Smyth

Old Faiths in New Light

ISBN/EAN: 9783743348929

Manufactured in Europe, USA, Canada, Australia, Japa

Cover: Foto ©ninafisch / pixelio.de

Manufactured and distributed by brebook publishing software (www.brebook.com)

Newman Smyth

Old Faiths in New Light

OLD FAITHS IN NEW LIGHT

BY

NEWMAN SMYTH

AUTHOR OF "THE RELIGIOUS FEELING"

"THE HOLY SPIRIT OF EDUCATION."
Wisdom, 1:5.

NEW YORK
CHARLES SCRIBNER'S SONS
743-745 BROADWAY
1879

To the Memory

OF

AN HONORED FATHER AND A REVERED MOTHER,

WHO LEFT ME, AS THEIR HERITAGE,

THE OLD FAITHS

WHICH THEY NOW BEHOLD IN THE NEW LIGHT OF A BETTER WORLD,

THIS VOLUME,

THE RESULT OF THE ENDEAVOR TO KEEP THE BIRTHRIGHT OF A CHRISTIAN CHILDHOOD THROUGH THE DOUBTS AND QUESTIONINGS

OF AFTER YEARS,

IS DEDICATED

IN GRATEFUL REMEMBRANCE.

PREFACE.

John Ruskin has said that for the words, good and bad, we might almost substitute the words, makers and destroyers. While writing this book, I have seen workmen tearing down portions of the walls of a church whose beauty had vanished, like a dream, in the flames of an hour; but they tore down only so far as was necessary, in order to find firm points from which to build up again the crumbling arches. I have had thus, in a daily figure, before me the true object of any destructive criticism of old faiths. We are justified in pulling down as we cherish the purpose of building up. If to any my work shall seem at points to unsettle traditional beliefs which have become sacred in their eyes, I would ask them to read on, and wait to see whether, upon the old foundations, a better home for our religious faiths is not to be built up by the Christian scholarship of to-day.

"I do not, as a rule, find what I want in

the books where I naturally seek it;" so a friend writes to me, whose words I may perhaps be permitted to quote, as one sign among others of the failure of many cultivated and sincere minds to find what their faith craves in the standard treatises or stereotyped methods of religious thought. Modern research has gathered many truths which the people need for a living faith, but which lie scattered through numerous articles in reviews, or are hidden in philosophical phraseology, or remain inaccessible to most readers in voluminous German books. It has been my aim to meet what I believe to be a growing need of intelligent people, by gathering materials of faith which have been quarried by many specialists in their own departments of biblical study or scientific research, but which, to a large extent, have been left by them in a disconnected and fragmentary state; and by endeavoring to put these results of recent scholarship together, according to one leading idea, in a modern construction of old faiths. The science by which the works of the specialists are to be arranged in one order and harmony, is a science which needs now-a-days to be advanced and honored. Building firmly, on the one hand, upon the facts of nature and history, and, on the other, upon the moral and religious experience of the soul, its high office and endeavor is to spring from either side the arch which shall at last bring together the material and the spiritual, the natural and the supernatural, in one continuous and rounded whole of knowledge. The accomplishment of that task—the ultimate philosophy—seems indeed beyond the power of human reason, but we may at least pursue it as an ideal. My object, then, has been to make more popularly known results already gained in this direction by the labors of the learned, as well as to offer some contribution to this growing science of the sciences. I would read the old faiths, which I still believe, in the light of modern thought to which I cannot be blind. I would help others, if possible, walk still in the old ways which prophets and apostles have trod, but in the light of to-day.

The modern idea which seems to reopen old questions of faith, and the spirit in which renewed religious inquiries should be prosecuted, form the subject of the opening chapter. I have then dwelt in succession upon certain prominent points around which, as it seems to me, the Christian evidences need now-a-days to be worked up anew. The endeavor to single out these leading points, and to pursue a straightforward line of argument between them, has compelled me to give only a passing glance at many subjects which are deserving of thorough exploration, and to cross, often rapidly, over much debatable ground. While not wishing to burden my pages with the details of scientific investigations, or the minutiæ of critical discussions, I have occasionally, however, given references, in foot-notes, to authorities for statements which might seem to require further support than my plan would allow me to bring forward; and, so far as I am aware, I have indicated my obligations to writers whose suggestions I have found grown into my own thought. I am sensible, however, of more indebtedness than I can easily acknowledge by passing references, in theology, to the broad, but genuine, Protestantism of Prof. Dorner; in biblical history, to the always inspiring, but not always safe, leadership of Ewald; and, in metaphysics, to the profound spiritual thought of that master of physical science as well as of ideas, the sceptical believer, Lotze.

TABLE OF CONTENTS.

CHAPTER I.

THE IDEA OF DEVELOPMENT, AND THE NEW QUESTIONS ABOUT OLD FAITHS.

Separation between modern scholarship and the popular belief.—Prevalence of undefined unbelief.—Need of popularizing the results of the best Christian scholarship.—Evolution a revolutionary call to modern thought.—Old faiths in the light of the idea of development.—Supreme importance of these questions, and the temper of mind to be observed in their discussion.—The three epochs of modern thought.—The age of theological reconstruction.—The service of destructive criticism.—The need of resetting our faiths. 13-32

CHAPTER II.

THE HISTORICAL GROWTH OF THE BIBLE.

The historical development of revelation.—The nature of inspiration a secondary question.—Periods of the growth of the Bible.—Its materials.—The forces in its development.—The law of heredity, and the development of religion in Israel.—Signs of anti-historic evolution.—The higher law of selection in the canon.—The progress of revelation and its unity of design.—The broader view of revelation and its advantage. . . 33-61

1*

CHAPTER III.

THE COURSE OF MORAL EDUCATION AND PROGRESS OF REVELATION.

The educational method of God.—Three views of history.—The science of social statistics.—The idealistic philosophy of history.—The theology of history.—Revelation a progressive moral education of mankind.—The true moral test of a course of revelation.—The educational method of God in the Bible.—Its truths are forces of progress.—Moral leadership of the Scriptures.—Progress of doctrine.—Object-lessons.—Educational intent of the law.—Illustrated by the use of vows, the preparatory law of the Sabbath, the advance in the names for God.—Success of the divine method of education.—Its results. —The family.—The end of human sacrifices.—Abraham's offering an historical object-lesson, and its effect.—The abolition of slavery.—Growth of the hope of immortality.—Difficulties surmounted by this view of revelation.—Revelation its own final test.—The silence of Scripture.—The moral limitations of revelation.—Evidence in the course of revelation of a supernatural evolution. 62–127

CHAPTER IV.

THE ADVANCE OF KNOWLEDGE AND THE SCIENTIFIC TENDENCY OF THE BIBLE.

The same educational method in the scientific teaching of the Bible.—Elementary scientific virtues of the Bible.—Freedom from nature-myths.—Contrast between the Mosaic Genesis and its environment.—The biblical conception of law.—Optical accuracy of the Bible.—Genesis a first lesson.—Its object and point of view.—Its real service to science.—The alphabet of science in revelation.—The spiritual origin of material things.—Creation not magic.—The impossibility of being a materialist.—Matter, life, and mind from God.—The biblical teaching of the development of the creation.—The element of time left indefinite.—The scientific tendency of revelation the

main question.—Summary.—The Mosaic Genesis a providential elementary lesson in nature.—Moses' genius for teaching.
—Additional evidence of a supernatural course of history. 128–184

CHAPTER V.

THE CULMINATION IN THE CHRIST: I. THE UNIQUENESS OF JESUS.

Jesus the surprise of history.—Failure to account for his appearance by the laws of heredity.—Jesus not a Jew, nor a Gentile, nor the child of two races.—His teaching not eclecticism, nor a revival of an older prophetic spirit.—Uniqueness of Jesus shown in his doctrine, his moral ideal, his method and plan, and in the absence of certain common human traits.—The unique power of Jesus.—Peculiar moral quality of his miracles.—His power in history.—The new society.—Originality of Jesus' self-consciousness.—Originality of the idea of the Lord's Supper.—These characteristics independent of questions concerning the origin of the Gospels.—Conflict of the conclusion thus gained with the law of continuity.—The deeper question. 185–231

CHAPTER VI.

THE CULMINATION IN THE CHRIST: II. THE NATURALNESS OF CHRIST.

The naturalness of the life of Christ as a whole —Correspondence between being and influence.—The argument from prophecy.—The place of Christ in the divine order of history.—
The ascent of life.—The law of individualization.—Christ the end of the creation.—The moral interpretation of the creation.—The human need of the Messiah and its prophecy.—The moral necessity of the incarnation.—Its form determined by sin.—The incarnation a process.—The ideal truth of the incarnation. 232–288

CONTENTS.

CHAPTER VII.

THE UNFINISHED WORLD AND ITS COMPLETION.

Confirmation of foregoing reasonings by the signs of the future course of nature.—The unfinished world.—The unseen universe.—Evidence of another order of existence from the temporal origin of the world; the apparent waste of nature; the probable end of the present, visible creation; the spiritual significance of life, and the nature of mind.—Facts and theories. —Probabilities of science and teachings of revelation compared.—Relation of the two spheres of the one creation.—Influences of the unseen.—The final conservation and completion of the natural.—Where is heaven ?—Removal of difficulties. 289-348

CHAPTER VIII.

THE PROCESS OF RESURRECTION AND THE END.

The resurrection of Jesus a fact and a revelation to the disciples.— Circumstantial evidences of the fact.—Jesus' resurrection a special object-lesson illustrating a general law.—Its nature and process.—The apostolic doctrine and its corruption.—Extreme materialistic and idealistic conceptions.—Elements of the biblical doctrine of the resurrection.—The continuity of the life of the individual.—Naturalness of the resurrection.— Its place in the constitution of the creation.—Contrast with Herbert Spencer's view of the end of evolution.—The supernatural evolution.—Dualism and unity of the creation.—Conclusion. 349-391

OLD FAITHS IN NEW LIGHT.

CHAPTER I.

THE IDEA OF DEVELOPMENT, AND THE NEW QUESTIONS ABOUT OLD FAITHS.

It is an open secret that there has been of late an increasing separation between many views of the Bible and religion gained by eminent Christian scholars, and opinions generally held to be the truth in the religious communions with which they still retain fellowship. Even thoroughly evangelical divines are sometimes made painfully aware of the distance to which they have been carried by the course of their studies, or have unconsciously drifted with the current of modern thought, from religious positions still firmly maintained by many among their people, or their ecclesiastical associates, with whom, nevertheless, in spirit and aim, they are agreed. As a result of this alienation between much of the best scholarship and much of the best life of the

Christian world, there is often to be found, on the one side, a half-concealed mistrust of the freer methods of modern biblical criticism, or a flurried opposition to the claims of science; while, on the other hand, there is sometimes manifested an over-confident and rude display of a little knowledge of the new learning; but more often a cautious reticence is observed on the part of sober-minded scholars, who are slow to disturb by their own questionings, or by their improved methods of faith, the long-settled beliefs of the people. They wisely prefer to hide many questions in their hearts, rather than to proclaim their doubts upon the housetops. In Cicero's treatise concerning the nature of the gods, Cotta, an orator and magistrate, is represented as saying that it would be allowable in a private conference to hold views which it would be difficult to advocate before a public assembly.* Some of our too eager disputants of received opinions might learn a useful lesson from the hesitancy of the Roman magistrate to shake the foundations of the popular faith. But the doubts of the philosophers could not always remain hidden, and when the soothsayers could hardly refrain from laughing in each other's faces, as they consulted the omens, there was little

---

* De Nat. Deorum, i. 22.

hope left for the popular religion of the Romans. In the nature of modern society, what is whispered in secret must soon be published abroad. Learning is no longer a cloistered virtue; and any wide or continued separation between the best thought and the received opinions of the Christian world would be full of hazard to religion. The mere suspicion that the advanced scholarship and the old faiths are to-day at variance, is itself a fruitful cause of popular indifference and unbelief. Indeed, the Christian faith suffers more from a certain vague mistrust, or undefined unbelief, among the people, than it does from any one positive and definite form of infidelity. This indefinite mistrust, moreover, arises partly from knowledge, and partly from ignorance. It emanates from the knowledge that there has been of late much destructive criticism of the old theologies, and from ignorance of the methods and the results of the best Christian scholarship. As a little warmth of the rising sun may call up the very mists which are to be dissipated by its more powerful shining, so this vague and chilling popular unbelief is to be dispelled, not by withholding knowledge, but by shedding abroad all possible light. Whatever may be known concerning the origin and comparative place of our sacred Scriptures; whatever changes in the methods of studying the Bible, or the theology of the Bible, have commended themselves to the judgment of the best-informed minds; and whatever new views of old faiths have been opened by the advances of science, must be brought forward cautiously, yet freely, in the teaching of any church that is to retain its hold upon the people. The history of doctrine shows that one work which is required, every generation or two, of Christian thought, is to rearrange its faiths in new lights; and many signs indicate a present and growing need of some resetting of the so-called Christian evidences. This work, also, needs to be popularized, as science nowadays is popularized. Our age comes speaking new tongues, which our fathers knew not of. We, who have inherited their faiths as our birthright, have tried, also, to learn these strange tongues, and we find to our joy that we can still prophesy in them; that in some of the very words which at first we feared were without God, and without hope in the world, we begin to discover the best words the human reason has ever found in which to declare the ways of the Spirit.

The one word, which more than all others has been a revolutionary call to modern thought, is the word Evolution. The term covers many opinions which, though united in a common opposition to former views of the creation, are far from being at one among themselves. It is the watchword of the most gross materialists, and also the guiding principle of others who are led by its clew through the mazes of visible phenomena out to the borders of the unseen, and into the presence of the living God. The laws and forces, the nature and extent, of evolution are still under discussion; and the most ardent believers in it differ widely among themselves. The late Mr. Lewes, for instance, was of the opinion that Mr. Darwin has mistaken the effect for the cause in his famous doctrine of Natural Selection;* and, in opposition to the Darwinian theory of descent from one far-off ancestor, he insisted upon the necessity of supposing innumerable starting-points to explain the vast variety of organisms.† And it was after Prof. Huxley had informed us that evolution is demonstrated knowledge, ‡ and after Haeckel had said that "to demand proofs in favor of the theory of descent . . . is to give evidence of a lack of knowledge and understanding," § that Prof. Virchow, himself an evolutionist, not destitute of either, declared: "We cannot

---

* The Physical Basis of Mind, p. 121.
† Ibid., pp. 125–126.
‡ See American Addresses.
§ Munich Address.

teach, we cannot designate as a revelation of science, the doctrine that man descends from the ape or from any other animal.*

But questionable, or incapable of proof, as may be particular scientific theories of descent, and whatever may be the final form of the philosophy of evolution,—it is already evident that all our modes of reasoning and our most settled faiths are to-day brought to judgment before the idea of development. It is not altogether a new idea, but it is an idea invested with new power. It admits of different definitions, but in some form it claims to preside over all scientific thought. It bids us beware of regarding existing things as though they were struck into being by successive blows of creative power. It maintains that, so far as things can be observed and events followed, they are continuous, and form one order. It directs us to trace everywhere processes of unfolding and growth. It declares that the world is the fruit of ages, and not the manufacture of a day. It accepts nothing as ready-made, but searches for the modes of production by which all thing have come to pass. Whether these great processes of formation be regarded as " a mechanical evolution," as Haeckel holds them to be—blind forces building better than

---

* The Liberty of Science in the Modern State.

they knew—or whether they be conceived as
the course or method of creative wisdom, intelligently pursued from the beginning, it is
beyond question that the idea of development,
in some form of it, is the dominant idea of
modern thought. To the test of that prevalent and powerful idea we are required to submit our most sacred spiritual and religious
faiths. The Bible, Christianity, the hope of
immortality, we shall bring under the light of
this modern principle. I need hardly add that
a theistic conception of evolution is the only
one to which, in the last appeal, I feel bound
to carry the argument for our old faiths.*

The complete execution of the author's plan
would involve a comprehensive treatise on
Christianity and development—an entire re-
working, in view of modern ideas of development, of the department of apologetics. In
this volume so great a task—almost too great
for any one mind to hope to accomplish—is
not attempted; but, as already indicated, I
shall endeavor to examine certain connected
and strategic points along the line of defence

---

* Having, in a former work (The Religious Feeling, New York, 1877), examined how our idea of God remains undissolved by the evolutionary philosophy, I take the liberty of referring to that work for any theistic assumptions of this. Incidentally, however, these will receive further justification, and the author's idea of development be further defined, in the course of the present discussion.

of the Christian faith. Before addressing ourselves, however, directly to the work proposed, something should be said concerning the temper of mind in which an essay like this should be both written and read.

The themes with which we shall be occupied must ever be of supreme concern to any who can appreciate the motives which led Bishop Butler to write, in a letter to a friend, before he left school, that he intended to make truth the business of his life. It is said that Jacobi, the faith-philosopher, as he was called, while still a student at the university, upon reading for the first time Kant's treatise on the proofs of the existence of God, was seized with a violent palpitation of the heart, so intense was his interest in the renewed discussion of man's oldest and greatest faith. True or false, these faiths are the supreme concern of our lives. It is above all things our business here to think of them, and to work them out in our lives. For those who are indifferent to the value of truth; for any persons like the traveller in that shrine of art, the Tribune of the Uffizi Gallery at Florence, who, after a moment's glance at the great paintings and statues, was overheard to express the desire to go and visit the king's stables, such themes may be too high and sacred;—a passing glance at the visions of prophets and seers, a moment's thought upon the greatest truths with which a human mind may be concerned, are all that can be expected of those who can be contented with visiting the king's stables; who are pleased with the mere trappings and externals of this royal realm through which our souls are travelling, while they might linger in the palace itself and rejoice in beholding the wonderful treasures of the kingdom of Truth.

Among those who are interested in such discussions, there is sometimes cherished a temper of mind, which, wherever found, is wholly alien to the spirit in which inquiries like these should be conducted. It may aptly, and not too harshly, be characterized as the temper of the religious, or the scientific, demagogue. For it is unfortunately true that there may be veritable demagogues in the republic of letters as well as in the State; and, as in politics, so in religion, they are to be found in the ranks of all parties, and their spirit is peculiar to no creed or sect. Liberalism and orthodoxism alike produce them. Popular infidelity, too, has its arrant demagogues—lecturers who carry on a notorious business of atheism on a small capital of philosophic or scientific thought, and usually borrowed capital besides. Thus a man of fluent wit will go up and down through the Bible, or ecclesiastical history, very much as a political stump-speaker will look through the Congressional records, or our national history, for the points of his partisan speech. He will begin with Genesis and find "mistakes of Moses" in abundance. He will expatiate upon the absurdities of the story of the ark. He will pause in dramatic horror before the cruel wars of the Jews. He will single out an imprecatory psalm or two; and when he comes to the New Testament, he will find in it discrepancies and misstatements enough to prove that all the Apostles were little better than literary thieves and robbers. Then he will run up and down through the Christian ages, beholding every rack and thumbscrew, but regardless of the many martyrs; putting his finger upon the dark stains, but not noticing the illuminated pages of ecclesiastical history; complaining of the gloom of the scholastic theology, but blind to the growing light. He will have at his tongue's end second-hand and unverified quotations from the Calvinists, and he will descant knowingly upon the "Conflict of Religion and Science," though, like Dr. Draper in his book, it never occurs to him to spoil his declamation by giving an exact definition of either—and so on to the end of the chapter. Now all this is pure and simple demagoguism, —the more wicked and mischievous, the more sacred and momentous the themes which it degrades.

But the demagogism of popular infidelity certainly does not justify, and cannot be put down by, the manifestation of a similar spirit on the part of the accredited defenders of the faith. The theological demagogue is unfortunately a historical and not altogether antiquated character. He passes through the Bible and history in the same blind, partisan way. He fits the Bible to his notion of what it should be. He casts his drag-net over the Scriptures, to gather—it matters not from what part—proof-texts for his favorite dogma. If a religious itinerant, he provides himself with no scrip or staff, save a Bagster's Bible and a Concordance; and upon these, and the enlightenment of the Holy Ghost, he relies for the removal of all difficulties. Not knowing what he does, nor always of what spirit he is of, he teaches the instructed, and often turns the Concordance itself into the worst enemy of a sound biblical theology. Or, if the theological demagogue be not a mere wandering exhorter, but a man of some training, or even one wearing some official title as a valiant defender of the faith, he will still be inclined to look upon all biblical learning which does not make for his traditional opinions, as essentially rationalistic and unsound; he will have a confident answer for every doubt, a definite knowledge of truths lying beyond experience on the very borders of revelation, and a ready method of harmonizing all discrepancies. He rarely, if ever, will arise in the morning, like Dr. Arnold, with the feeling that anything pertaining to his creed can be an open question; and if Christian thinkers to whom nature, also, is a revelation, and its laws as sacred as the commandments of Sinai, and to whom all history is holy ground, refuse to accept his favorite interpretation of God's Word, or his theory of its mechanical infallibility, he stands ready to read them out of the party which in his sincere, perhaps, but narrow, zeal he mistakes for the Orthodox Church. But nowhere, surely, is this spirit so hurtful as in the consideration of those august themes of which Jesus spake in parables, and before which the wisest are as little children. Not with such help are the threatening forms of unbelief to be laid! A faith that leans upon its own prejudices cannot stand long in the days when all things are shaken. There is only one state of mind which in such investigations is truly and profoundly reverent and religious, and that is, the desire to find the facts as they are. Whoever is afraid of science does not believe in God! Though the truths which the several sciences have discovered in the various fields of inquiry are, with difficulty, brought together and harmonized; though the facts of nature, history, and consciousness, lie before our reason often unconnected and broken, like those fragments of Assyrian records which have been thrown together in the British Museum; we should, nevertheless, regard every one of them as of value, and as having its own place and worth in the record of God's creative purpose which, some day, we may hope not merely to decipher by syllables and to know in part, but to comprehend in its length and its breadth, and to read as one grand, connected story.

Another caution should be observed in the discussion of these topics, and particularly in the consideration of those questions which belong partly to natural science and partly to moral and religious philosophy. It should not be forgotten that we have entered, or at least our most scientific science and most believing faith are now entering upon, what may be described as a third epoch of modern thought. For the great question between religion and science, like other important movements of human thought and life, seems destined to pass through three distinctive stages or epochs. First there came the age of violent attack upon the Bible from the scientific side, and defence as violent. This controversy was inevitable. It resembled the age of agitation on the question of slavery, or of intemperance. A great many things were written and said— in the order of history had to be written and said—which we do not care to read or remember now. We can profitably forget many books and articles in which writers whose eyes were opening to the truthfulness of the Creator down to the last atom and least fossil of the world, attacked the received biblical account of a creation in six literal days; and we can profitably commit also to the limbo of forgotten things the many sermons and treatises in which good men whose eyes, though not yet open to the new light of science, were not closed to the old glory of revelation, waxed valiant in their mistaken controversy with the prophets and priests of the God of nature.

Following this age of agitation and inevitable controversy, was the second epoch, marked by ingenious attempts at the reconciliation of religion and science. It resembled the age of compromise in our political history. Minds of great ability have been engaged in this work. Their writings are characterized by mutual concessions and a general air of candor. Theologians revise their interpretations of Scripture, and are fertile in theories of the harmony between Genesis and geology. Scientists on their part, their liberty of investigation being granted, grow somewhat less venturesome on religious grounds. Many eminent scientific men, at the present day, find for their own views satisfactory terms of truce with theology and the Bible, and even Prof. Huxley, when on the scientific war-path in this country, preferred to attack the Miltonic rather than the Mosaic hypothesis of a creation.*

The third epoch presses hard after the second. It is the age in which the question is hardly asked, Can religion and science be reconciled? but rather its question is, How are we to use the help of both—the light of science, and of the spirit—in a rational interpretation of the universe? It is, in short, the age of critical review and of judicial reconstruction. There are not wanting signs that we are already entering into this better era. At least there are leading minds, profoundly reverent of truth, in both camps, who entertain this better spirit, and who represent this more advanced movement. The popular mind, possi-

---

* To this age of attempted reconciliations and compromises belong many works still worth reading; like the writings of Hugh Miller, and Prof. Dana, and Prof. Hitchcock, and those papers of Agassiz which touch upon the questions of development and typical forms; and, on the part of the theologians, the essay, in "Aids to Faith," of Dr. McCaul; the "Six Days of Creation," by Tayler Lewis, the essay of Rorison, in "Replies to Essays and Reviews," and other articles of similar tenor.

bly, may be now in the thick of the controversy: religion and science still seem to be at war in the workshops, on lyceum platforms, and in the columns of the "Popular Science Monthly:" but there are not wanting on both sides leaders who realize that there is and can be no warfare between religion and science. It is simply an indication of human ignorance and error whenever the two are brought into collision. And it is a noticeable sign of this more catholic spirit of discussion—of this new and better era—that nowadays theologians are the first to rebuke theologians for any manifestations of an unscientific spirit, while there are scientists quick to condemn scientists for any over-confident triumph over man's religious faiths; that our schools of theological training are endowing chairs of instruction in the relations of science to religion; that clergymen are the ready purchasers of the latest scientific literature; and that, on the other hand, an eminent scientist like Prof. Tait replies to Mr. Froude's needless alarms. Even that stalwart positivist, Prof. Tyndall, seems ready to consider terms of truce with religion; Virchow is constrained to administer a needed chastisement to Haeckel; and our own Prof. Gray can preface a book of sympathetic criticism on Darwin with a confession of substantial faith in the Nicene Creed. Eminent authorities, it is true, may still be cited both for a science that removes all basis for belief in the spiritual and the supersensible, and also for a science which finds the only possible ground of explanation for the natural order of things in a spiritual omnipresence. If Herbert Spencer's "Physiological Metaphysics," as Pres. Porter has justly described it, represents the tendency of thought in the former direction, Hermann Lotze stands in eminent authority as the representative of the opposite tendency. But truth, as Lord Bacon long ago observed, is the daughter of time not of authority. It is well if we are emerging from the age of storm and bitterness into the season of calm, and broader vision. There is a classic story that a fire once ran over the Pyrenean mountains, destroying all the vineyards of the inhabitants. But, as the villagers mourned for their vines, they discovered that the fire, which had destroyed their grapes, had opened by its heat deep fissures in the rocks, through which gleamed rich veins of silver. I believe that the terribly destructive criticism of our day is to leave us richer than it found us. It may burn up many of our traditions, but it will disclose to us deeper and precious truths. Even the rationalistic critics of Germany, who have labored so hard to destroy the historical credibility of our Gospels, have left us greatly indebted to their work for our understanding of the Bible and religion. There was once an island, so runs a fable, as old as the times of Plato, in which it was reported there was buried much fine gold. Many came and upturned the stones, and, though they never found the gold for which they looked, yet their searching after it prepared a barren soil for the reception of the seeds which the winds and the birds brought, and at last the hidden treasure appeared in olive-boughs and clusters of grapes. In the history of human thought the Grecian fable has often been repeated. Wherever we see the investigators at work, even though they search sacred soil and undermine settled opinions, we may rest assured that the Spirit of Truth has its own ends to accomplish. The results which the workman would find may prove worthless, but their labors shall not be wholly lost. Other men shall enter in and partake of fruits of which they never thought. So the evangelical scholarship of to-day is reaping, and is destined still more richly to reap, the rewards of the labors of the rationalistic critics of Germany. Though the Tübingen school have not succeeded in finding the explanation of Christianity for which they sought, they have succeeded in making a great historical field fruitful. Historical faith is to-day greatly indebted to historical skepticism. The better era already partly come, and in part still to come, is the heir of the spoils of all these sciences.

Such considerations should remind us of one more needed caution in discussing these large subjects. They belong confessedly in part to the future. We stand only in the dawn of the coming day of the reconciliation of the sciences, and of mental peace,—that millennium of minds for which all sincere thinkers pray. Much even of our most positive and lusty science is still only in its infancy. Many theories which now belong to the scientific imagination may yet be brought within the limits of definite knowledge. Much also still remains doubtful concerning the results already won. We must be cautious not to mistake scientific speculations for certain revelations. We are to review old faiths in lights which are themselves, sometimes, shifting ; before sciences which are still, at many points, open and growing. We must of necessity therefore advance, at times, views which we regard simply as tentative, or which can be determined as yet only in their outlines and broader proportions. The details requisite to fill up some views, and to give to our conceptions that distinctness and vividness which make evident their agreement with the truth of things, are not always to be had from the assured results of present science. But, notwithstanding these confusions and limitations of our knowledge, it is already time that we should begin to reset our theology, and to determine the question, which every generation must ask for itself, whether what we have learned and do know, confirms, or not, what we have believed. With this purpose, and in recognition of the demands made upon any theological writer by what I have called the third and crowning era of modern thought, the following pages should be both written and read.

CHAPTER II.

THE HISTORICAL GROWTH OF THE BIBLE.

We are to bring, then, our inherited faiths for judgment before the idea of development, which, as we have just acknowledged, is a regnant principle of modern thought. We submit, first, to the new criticism our belief in the Bible. Will that be dissolved, or come forth purified, if we search it thoroughly by this scientific method of inquiry into the origin and growth of existing things,—a method which seems to be the powerful solvent of old beliefs? How was the Bible formed? Does it bear witness to, and is it the result of, a great historical process of revelation? It will be noticed that we do not bring to the front in this inquiry any question touching the nature or extent of inspiration. We do not regard the question of inspiration as the real hinge upon which modern controversy over the Bible turns. We do not meet the scepticism of the hour simply by proceeding to gather evidences from the Scriptures in favor of their inspiration. The doubt is larger and broader than that customary circle of reasoning. It questions the historical fact of revelation; and the first and chief inquiry for us, therefore, concerns the historical fact and progress of revelation; the second and subordinate question relates to the manner or ways in which men may have been trained, or inspired, to receive and to become the bearers of a revelation. Hence an affirmative and very positive answer may be given to the former question, Have we a series or order of events and teaching which constitute a revelation from God? while doubt or hesitancy may be felt in answering the other question, How was the Word of God made known, or what was the precise nature and degree of inspiration? "Every 'how,'" long ago said Aristotle, "rests upon a 'that;'" and we may have very different conceptions of the manner of a revelation which, nevertheless, we may be agreed in accepting as a fact.

Indeed, to require assent to a particular theory of inspiration may put in jeopardy belief in the very fact of revelation which that theory is intended to secure. We dwell upon this obvious, but too often overlooked, distinction because it is of great importance for us to remember that the real, decisive point in the modern attack and defence of the Bible is a question of the historical fact of revelation; and that question can be determined only by a large and many-sided view of the forces and processes which have made human history and the Bible. Ewald, in one of his suggestive passages,* reminds us that God stands alike over against all man's powers and capacities, though at times drawing nearer to one side of us than to another; and, therefore, man must turn his spirit, with all its powers and capacities, perfectly unto God in order not to be estranged from him. Thus, when we consider the manifoldness of God's relations to us, and the variety of our possible impressions of the Being who besets us behind and before and on every side, we should expect that a revelation from God would be a Divine manifestation " at sundry times, and in divers manners;" † we should expect to find it as a great diversified fact and manifold influence in human history, pressing in upon man from different sides of his complex being; moulding society, shaping events, forming history; not merely confirming itself at times by special signs and wonders, but permanently embodying itself in ordinances and institutions; and, if one may so speak, naturalizing its supernatural powers in the forces and laws of a

---

* Lehre der Bible von Gott., vol. ii., p. 101.
† Heb. i. 1.

theocracy, or a church. The Bible, certainly, was never dropped ready-made from heaven. Max Müller, indeed, goes so far as to declare that a revelation ready made and given to men, like a language formed in heaven, would have been a foreign religion that men could not understand.* Neither is the Bible a collection of sacred oracles. Prof. Beyschlag may overstate the frequency of this misuse of the Bible among theologians, but he hardly exaggerates the evil results of treating the Bible as a mere collection of oracular texts when he says: "So long as the majority of theologians treat the Word of God as a book of oracles, so long will it appear as a book of fables to the majority of the educated laity." It is equally certain that the Bible is not, either in its contents or form, a systematic text-book of divinity. On the contrary, if we wish to abstract a system of theology from the Bible, we fall into hopeless contradictions if we begin by regarding it as a text-book of divinity. It is rather a book of life; and we must discover its meanings as we would study the mysteries of nature, or interpret the changeful drama of life. Jesus regarded the truth of revelation as a word to be done. (John iii. 21.) Revelation is pre-eminently truth

---

* Contemporary Review, Nov. '78, p. 709.

which has been done in history. The Bible, certainly, presents a spectacle of the contests of embodied truths with falsehoods clothed in human forms; a spectacle in which we behold right and wrong coming and going in a prophet's mantle, or the armor of a king; where we see truth succeeding, and error dying, in the issues of human lives, and the rise and fall of kingdoms. The great doctrines of the Bible are vividly revealed through its characters, and their work, and in the progress of the whole history. In this book for all peoples and ages, the most abstract and impalpable truths seem taken, as it were, from the very air, from distant realms of the spirit, and clothed with flesh and blood; they are revealed walking with men, dwelling in their homes, made concrete and visible in the person of patriarch, prophet, or apostle; and they are summed up and declared, in the vernacular of every man's heart, in the Word made flesh.

If, then, we have any revelation from God at all, we have it at the heart of a great historical development; and if we are to find the evidence of it anywhere, we must seek for it as the cause and vital force of historical movements and events which otherwise would never have arisen, or, at least, would not have assumed their special shape and significance. Revelation is in deed as well as in word, " in its core historical"—a "Thus did the Lord" as well as a "Thus said the Lord."* We are to mark the footprints of a higher Power along the ways in which he has led his people. Revelation was an inspired course of history. The prophetic word accompanying the dealings of God with his people, the written Scripture, is only one element, and sometimes the least important part, of the broad historical process of revelation. In this larger and more satisfactory view of revelation, to which fortunately modern biblical criticism has compelled us to advance, two distinct conceptions of the Bible and the religion of the Bible are involved. It will be necessary for us to linger with the first of these only long enough to enable us to secure a firm foothold from which we may spring to the second and higher conclusion which many of our best guides in these matters have already safely reached.

The first and lower truth, then, is the evident fact that our Bible is a historical growth—that is to say, it is a book, or literature rather, which grew up out of the life of a people; which in its growth was intimately connected with, and dependent upon, the development of that national life; and which consequently bears in its very structure the

---

* See Fisher, Beginnings of Christianity, Ch. i.

marks of the times amid the ideas and exigencies of which it grew to be at last the world's Bible. The evidences of this historical formation of the Bible lie upon its very surface, and they are confirmed by the more critical study of its contents. Very much as the wood-cutter can judge, from the successive layers of wood laid bare by his axe, how many seasons the tree has been growing; so a close scrutiny of the Bible shows unmistakable signs of the different ages and conditions of its growth. The very first book in the Bible, for example, the book of Genesis, discloses to the critical eye the marks of a composite structure—of different layers, if I may so speak, in its formation. It evidently has passed through several periods of growth, and was not the pure creation of Moses' mind evoked in a day. In the "Chaldean Account of Genesis," Prof. Smith, the successful Assyrian scholar whose early death is a positive loss to human knowledge, has deciphered fragments of a tradition of the creation which seems to have floated down from beyond the beginnings of history, and with some versions of which Abraham, in his childhood, may have been familiar, and which in some Hebrew song Moses may have been taught from his mother's lips. In our book of Genesis, it is now generally admitted, two streams of narrative, at least, may be distinguished; and some Hebraists think they discern indications of still other sources of the history, which were combined in one account by the final editor of the whole. Without adopting to the full extent the often too ingenious opinions of these critics, we do not leave firm ground when we say that, however God may have inspired Moses, he probably did give to the writer of the book of Genesis earlier narratives, and considerable historical material for the composition of that book in its present form. The results of biblical criticism do not warrant us in representing God as the hard taskmaster that some of our mechanical theories of inspiration—unwittingly, perhaps—cause him to appear to be; for he never set sacred historian or prophet at work to make bricks without straw. The historical materials, and all the necessary conditions, we may be confident, were present whenever the workmen were called by the Lord to do his work.

In general, it may be said, that three sources and three great currents of Hebrew life are to be discovered in the Old Testament—the prophetic teaching, the priestly lore, and the reflective wisdom of the wise among the people;* and these three influences are

---

* Smith: Art. Bible, Encyclopedia Brit.

sometimes blended, and indistinguishable; at others, separate and distinct; and, sometimes, while flowing side by side, in the same narrative, they retain each its own peculiar coloring. Some Hebraists go much farther than this in their analysis of the component parts of the Pentateuch, but it is enough for our purpose, and safer, to keep here well within the limits of the facts generally admitted by those biblical scholars whose opinions are of weight. Striking evidences of the growth of the Bible, of the prolonged historical process through which the Word of God came to man, might easily be gathered from the writings of the prophets. Even in their visions, and most glowing inspirations, the prophets are not independent of the past. The history of the chosen people appears reclothed in the drapery of their visions; and the experience of former days is echoed, again and again, in their speech of coming blessings or retributions. Every successive book of the Old Testament represents more inspired thought, more religious experience, more Divine influences, than were granted directly to the prophet who wrote it as his own personal gift. We have, in short, in the Old Testament, the growing life, the maturing thought, the ripened fruit, of the Hebrew mind, and the Hebrew history. Accordingly the Old Testament shows throughout the stamp of the genius of the people out of whose history it grew. Its structure reveals peculiarities of the Semitic genius. What the architecture of the Temple at Jerusalem was to the architecture of the Acropolis at Athens, that the style of the Hebrew Bible is to the literature of the Aryan world. The literature of Greece is not more thoroughly Grecian; the literature of the age of Elizabeth is not more genuinely English; than the Old Testament is thoroughly and genuinely the literature of the peculiar people, bearing upon it the unmistakable stamp of the Semitic genius. Under this broad seal of the national genius of the Hebrew race, there appears often the mark and superscription of individual minds in these Scriptures. Whatever may have been the nature of the inspiration of the prophets, we have no evidence of the miraculous conversion of any mind into a different order of genius by the spirit of the Lord. Ezra, the priestly scribe, who collected and edited the book of the law, might have been made a better and more accurate scribe by the grace of God; but he was never born a poet, and we cannot, without violence, conceive of him as so inspired as to have been the author of those vivid descriptions of scenery, those little side-pictures of human life, those fine touches of feeling in view of natural objects, which abound in some of the Psalms of the royal shepherd, or in the imagery of the later prophets. However, then, the Spirit of God may have used for his higher purposes the minds of men, we can be assured that he did not overpower their natural habits of expression, or hold individual genius, as one might catch a songbird, passive and palpitating, in the grasp of his Almighty hand.

While endeavoring to fix in our minds a true historical conception of revelation, one other fact should not be forgotten. The object for which each Scripture was written, was first an immediate and local one. The lawgiver was sent with the tables of the commandments in his hands to Israel, and the prophets were the preachers of righteousness in their day and generation. The successive sparks of Divine illumination were struck, all of them, out of the necessities of the times. The different Scriptures had first, an immediate, national, or even local, work to do, before they had, or could have, a remote, universal work for all nations and times. If we are not to do despite, therefore, to the Spirit's chosen historical method of revelation, we must read every Scripture in its own light, and interpret it in view of its own surroundings, and in its place in the gradual development of the Bible.

The historical process of revelation must be brought to the forefront, if we would see justice done to-day to the Bible.

We have now cleared the ground for the second and more important work before us. Granting that the Bible is a historical growth, and that it shows on every page the signs of the national life in connection with which it was developed, how are we to explain its growth, or to conceive of its development? What was its origin and course? of what forces was it the product, or, if you please, the evolution? Renan seeks for the sources of this wonderful literature, in the naturally monotheistic temperament of the Semitic people. But the great rationalistic authority, Kuenen, taking his stand for the survey of the history of Israel amid the prophetic literature of the eighth century B.C., seeks, by means of "Israel's peculiar fortunes," to account for the rise of the pure worship of Jehovah, from the originally polytheistic religion of a rude people, once living in Goshen, whose tribal God was Jahveh. So the critics who seek for some purely natural explanation of the altogether peculiar religious history of Israel fall out among themselves by the way. The negative criticism of the Bible, as it is called, because it begins its inquiry with a denial of anything supernatural, has displayed great skill in detecting any cross purposes in the biblical narratives which may be construed as historical signs pointing in the direction of a naturalistic development of the Hebrew worship; but the plain, broad landmarks of the course of revelation from Moses to Christ, the generality of men cannot so easily pass by.*

But can we who have felt ourselves constrained to go a certain length with the rationalistic critics, stop short of their extreme conclusions? If we go with them one mile, will they not compel us to go with them twain? Is it not safer, it will be asked, not to yield an inch to this destructive German criticism—to stand firmly in the old ways? But we cannot, without covering our own eyes, and deafening our own ears, refuse to confess that we have received from modern biblical scholarship some new light, and that voices which we may not mistrust

---

* Kuenen's "Course of Israel's Religious Development," seems to me to be decidedly *top-heavy* ;—the overgrowth of prophecy in the eighth century B.C., is too great for the historical stem which he supposes in the ninth and tenth centuries, and for the root which he would place beneath it all in the Mosaic age. I should think a critical reply of great force, to Kuenen, and the rationalistic interpreters, might be made by taking simply those parts of the Old Testament which they admit to be of historical worth, and by showing, on their own ground, how these Scriptures have more in them, and require more before them, than the theories of those writers allow. Besides this, are the evidences of the genuineness and worth of historical writings ; and the positions of scholars like Delitzsch and Keil show, at least, that the negative criticism cannot claim undisputed possession of that field.

call us to advance to some fresh views of the providence of God in revelation. The facts, which up to a certain point all look one way, have led us to follow the modern biblical criticism so far, at least, as to acknowledge the historical development of the Bible. But we find no road further in the direction pursued by the most advanced negative criticism. We hesitate to take our direction from our imagination, and to plunge into the thicket. We look around, sceptical of our own impressions, and sceptical of our new and over-confident guides, and we notice signs still discoverable in this ancient history, and still to be read broadly marked upon this literature, which, if we follow them carefully and without a predetermination to take the short cut of some favorite philosophy, may possibly lead us out to a clear and safe conclusion. We who entertain no invincible prejudice against evidences of God's special action in human affairs (though that Divine action may seem at times to our partial knowledge of the universe to work contrary to nature, or miraculously) are ready to see the signs of natural forces and conditions which others point out in the course of the religion of Israel—to go the first mile with the critics; but we are prevented by many signs, which we also observe, of God's special method in training Israel and forming a Bible for the world, from going a second mile with the rationalists, and losing ourselves in their maze of uncertainties and conjectures. We cannot stand still, indeed, with the older supernaturalists to whom the laws and courses of nature are as though they were not; but neither can we run to the extreme of that philosophy in whose view spiritual powers count for nothing in this world. Believing in both God and nature, we have in these studies of the Bible, and the religion of the Bible, to keep, if possible, open eyes for all the facts. And we have, at this point, to deal with this question of fact: Could the Semitic genius of itself, in its actual historical environment, have produced the world's Bible? Or are this history and this literature, which is its fruit, in a peculiar manner a sacred history and a sacred fruit? Can we account for Israel, and his Scriptures, without some special activity of God? When we have admitted all that we must admit concerning the natural forces at work in the gradual formation of the Bible; when we have learned all that can be known of the soil, the climate, the seasons, the whole conceivable effect of natural forces in producing and shaping the Hebrew life and literature; then, are we prepared to say that these causes are sufficient to explain this historical growth of which we ought to give some reasonable account? or must we admit that the light of Heaven, as well as the chemistry of the earth, had something to do with the growth of this tree of life whose leaves are for the healing of the nations? Our final answer to this great question between naturalism and faith in a Divine revelation, can be reached only as the result of several convergent lines of reasoning. Whatever it may be, it should not be the conclusion, as it too often is made to be, of some single course of inquiry, or special study; but it should be the conclusion of all our reasonings—a wisdom which is the sum of the whole matter.*

In entering upon this broad inquiry concerning the supernatural development of Revelation we begin with certain significant facts which the progress of our questioning thus far has brought close at hand. One circumstance, which at once arrests our attention, is the singular fact that Israel by some means gained an exalted religion, while those tribes to which it was nearest of kin remained on the lowest levels of idolatrous corruption. But this contrast between Israel and his brethren, remarkable in itself, appears the more significant

---

* So Henry Rogers, in his "Superhuman Origin of the Bible," supports, by a great variety of considerations, this thesis: "That the Bible is not such a book as man would have made, if he could; or could have made, if he would."

when we detect in Israel the same disposition to evil which ran riot in the idolatries of kindred and surrounding tribes. We find it difficult upon any known law of heredity to conceive of the pure worship of the prophets as the outgrowth of "the natural religious geniality of Israel," when we remember that the Israelites were naturally a stiff-necked people, and that their religion seems to have gained its authority over them only by a prolonged struggle against their nature. Here is an evolution not in accordance with the natural tendency to variation, and contrary to the immediate historical environment. The development of the Bible, and the religion of the Bible, makes head seemingly against the natural gravitation of the Israelitish history. A people are pressed forward who are always turning back. A religion is lifted up into the light when the external forces tend to carry it down into the darkness. The prophets, whom Kuenen himself admits as trustworthy witnesses, give unequivocal testimony to this prolonged resistance of Israel against the stream which, nevertheless, carried it along as by a resistless power. The children of Israel are not willing pupils under this higher education. Isaiah represents their God as saying, "Thou hast made me to *serve* with thy sins, thou hast *wearied* me with thine iniquities." (Isaiah xliii. 24; Jer. ii. 10, seq.) This opposition of the nature of Israel to a religion supposed to be derived from its nature presents a strange anomaly. We find a dualism between the heart of the people and the formative principle of their religion, which suggests the influence of a higher Power. Oehler seizes upon the divine significance of this fact when he says: "The whole Old Testament remains a sealed book, if one shuts himself against the perception of how the overcoming the natural being of the people of Israel is the goal of the whole divine education, and therefore the entire leading of the people moves in a dualism." *

The historical growth of the Bible presents to our notice another peculiar fact which we should consider at this point. We have to render a reasonable account of the formation of the canon of the Scripture. What, we ask, was the principle or law of selection in the formation of the canon? Israel was evidently a selected race—the chosen people. Its career from generation to generation thrusts upon our notice, at a thousand points, the signs of its selection. The working of the same power or law of selection, by which Israel was chosen, appears also in the formation of the

---

* Theologie des A. T., i., s. 21.

Bible. It is a *selection* from the literature of Israel, which betrays some principle or method of selection. That principle governs also the formation of the New Testament as well as the Old. The canon apparently formed itself. By virtue of some peculiar selective principle of its own, the Bible grew into its present canonical form. We cannot trace the determination of the Scriptures of the Old and New Testaments back to the will of any one man, or the decree of any body of men. It will hardly be argued that Nehemiah, or the synagogue, or the authority of any great scribe, fixed the bounds of the Old Testament; and Ezra's work in gathering together the books of the law could not have been an arbitrary selection of a portion of the existing Hebrew literature. The work of the scribe followed the indications of some principle of selection contained in the sacred writings themselves which were delivered to him. Still less was the New Testament canon formed by the will of man. The Church did not create it by the decree of any council, though afterward the Church by its councils recognized the fact that a certain body of writings had grown into canonical authority. The canon of Scripture cannot be made to rest upon the Church; for the Bible and the Church were both the simultaneous outgrowths of something which was in the world before them both—they were the twin-fruits of a life which was before them both. Ewald has put, as a running caption over one of the chapters of his last work, the words: "The sacredness of the Bible is neither arbitrarily willed nor arbitrarily to be determined." * The will of man did not fix the canon of Scripture, and it is not to be determined by the will of man. It is not, it never was, the creation of any human act. But neither can we refer to any miracle for its origin. We certainly have no supplementary revelation to determine the metes and bounds of revelation. Nothing, moreover, is gained by saying the canon of Scripture was formed by the general consent of men, for that is an explanation which is no explanation; it is simply another form of stating the same fact that we have a body of writings which are universally recognized as authoritative Scripture, that is, as canonical. The general consent, or uniform tradition, by which the Scriptures are accepted, is itself the effect whose cause we wish to know. What power has formed, and bound together in one cluster, and preserved, these fruits of the life of Israel, and suffered others to fall to the ground? What is the law of survival here? What is the real forma-

---

* Lehre der Bible von Gott, i. 3, 8.

tive principle of the biblical canon? The person who can recognize no influence of God anywhere in the world, or in his own heart, must of course seek to explain the formation of the Bible on some principle of merely natural selection. He can allow nothing but the ordinary forces and laws of the human mind to have been at work in the production of this unique historical phenomenon—the Bible of the world—however he may endeavor to help himself by emphasizing the peculiar circumstances or conditions of earlier ages. The person, on the other hand, to whom a slow historical process without miraculous signs can afford little proof of the work of God, will seek to find in the inspired act of some prophet or apostle, or, if that is not to be thought of, at least in some divinely imparted authority of the Church, a special, supernatural basis for the present canon of the Scripture. But to the mind that has learned to recognize the divine action in the whole movement of human history, this seemingly natural selection of the Bible—this growth of the Bible, as it were of itself, without observation—may be a very impressive sign that it was God's work; that its development to its perfect and final form was after a divine method and power. And this conviction is deepened by the fact that this quiet, unobserved, most natural process of selecting the Bible from all surrounding literature shows, if we mark closely its progress, and survey the whole result of it, unmistakable indications of intelligence and design. The very naturalness and ease, if one may so speak, of the manner in which the Bible was formed, evinces the work of a Power which had perfect mastery over the springs of human history. It is difficult to explain the progress, order, and unity of purpose in the Bible, unless we take into the account something more than individual genius, national temperament, or peculiar historical conditions. There seems to be some power behind all these, co-ordinating them, arranging and guiding them, for the production of this organic whole of the Scriptures. There seems to be here the manifestation of some one directing and unifying vital force. There are peculiar and distinctive features of the Bible which cannot be pressed without violence into a merely naturalistic conception of its growth. One is the progress of revelation, or the orderly development of doctrine, which, now that the canon is completed, can be seen to run through it from beginning to end. This altogether peculiar and wonderful feature of the Bible appears at a glance when we bring it into contrast with other literatures. Our English literature, for example, is the product of English history, and it reflects, in each successive age, the life of the English people. But, gather in one volume, and in historical order, the best poetry and prose of England, and, though we should have a truthful representation of the changes of the national life, and the development of the national genius, from the first spring-time of Chaucer, nevertheless, we should not have in a collection of that kind any appearance of a definitely ordered and patiently followed progress of doctrine, of one deep plan and plot running through it all. The collection would be an anthology, not one organic whole. It might illustrate the development of the English mind, but it would not be itself one progressive manifestation of truth. Or, we may contrast in this respect the Bible with the Vedas. They, too, were products of one national genius. They likewise appeared at different times, and are the work of many generations of poets. They constitute also a religious or sacred literature. But, of orderly development, of a progressive self-manifestation of one deity, there is not in them any trace. On the contrary they run into confusions. We are not led by them out into the clear; we do not gain, when the last poet has seen his vision, any one exalted conception from which we can survey the whole course of their revelations. They lead up to no height from which all becomes clear. The sacred literature of the East reminds us rather of an Indian jungle. It is luxuriant—it abounds in tropical fruits—but it is a pathless confusion. We look into our Bible, and it is a highway of the Lord. The Vedas present a shifting play of lights and shadows; sometimes the light seems to grow brighter, but the day never comes. We are left still to dream. In the revelations of the Bible the promise grows in the darkness until the shining of the perfect day. Or, to take one other example, and that, too, from the same historic soil upon which the Bible grew, compare it with the Talmud. There is not in the latter anything like the organic unity of the former. It is a collection of wise sayings, not a growth of truth; a tedious commentary, not an advancing revelation; many books of many scribes, not one book of one mind. We have, then, in the progress of doctrine in the Bible a most striking peculiarity of it, which we cannot quietly overlook. Here is an order or evolution of truth which requires as its sufficient cause some one power or law of revelation. What was that guiding principle, that co-ordinating power of the Bible? Such questions press significantly for an answer when we observe the evidences of a higher design in the completed Bible. Like nature itself, amid all its diversities, the Bible is one continuous whole, and one grand design. But that design was not in the minds of the successive workmen. They knew not the perfect whole into which their lives and work, as we now can see, are fitted. Prophets and apostles, called by the Lord to speak to their own age, little knew what a Bible they were making for mankind. That work was beyond their ken; that design was larger than the knowledge of the very men who were providentially called to execute it. Our Bible in its completeness and its unity might be a vast surprise to Moses or Isaiah; and Paul, and the last of the disciples, St. John, hardly could have stood far enough away from their own work to see how perfectly it completed the whole. This great design of the religion of Israel is an ultimate fact to be accounted for—a design which was ages in execution; which was carried on by men separated by hundreds of years; which began in a word of promise, and ended in a fact of redemption in the fulness of time.

The following chapters will lead us to consider more definitely these remarkable features of Revelation as one great, progressive, historical work. But the law of selection in all this marvellous development of the Bible seems at first sight to be a higher law. The Bible and the religion of the Bible, we should infer from this general preliminary survey of their historical growth, are the evolution of higher than earthly forces. Those, at least, who have eyes to see the presence of God in history, will need nothing more than these significant facts to commend to their reason Bunsen's description of the Bible as " a book full of thousands of years ; full of apparent contradictions, as nature and man, and the history of our race ; but always young and in itself one through the unity of the spirit out of which it proceeded, even as the creation is itself one, with all its oppositions, yes, even through all its oppositions."* We reach beneath the surface, and touch the real cause of these remarkable phenomena which the historical growth of the Bible presents to us, when we lay hold of the fact of a Divine course or process of human education and redemption. Its law and progress and unity lie in the one purpose of a self-revealing God. Here, through transactions, institutions, customs, laws; in short, through the whole manifold development of a Divinely selected national life, as well as through the sacred literature which flows out of that life, or carries it on, we find the special presence and power of the self-revealing God of history.

But, not to anticipate too much our conclu-

---

* Gott in der Geschichte, i. p. 94.

sion, it will at least be acknowledged that we have already gained one vantage-ground in the course of our questioning. If we should be compelled to lose faith in revelation, we must reject it on broader and better grounds than those familiar to the common infidel. We must be robbed of faith in the divineness of the whole history of Israel, before our Bibles can cease to be sacred to us. He who has once gained this broader view of the Bible as the development of a course of history itself guided and inspired by Jehovah, will not be disconcerted by the confused noise of the critics. His faith in the Word of God lies deeper than any difficulties or flaws upon the surface of the Bible. He will not be disturbed by seeing any theory of its mechanical formation, or school-book infallibility, broken to fragments under the repeated blows of modern investigation;—the water of life will flow from the rock which the scholar strikes with his rod. He can wait, without fear, for a candid and thorough study of these sacred writings to determine, if possible, what parts are genuine, and what narratives, if any, are unhistorical. His belief in the Word of God from generation to generation does not depend upon the minor incidents of the biblical stories; it would not be destroyed or weakened, even though human traditions could be shown to have overgrown some parts of the sacred history—as the ivy, creeping up the wall of the church, does not loosen its ancient stones. He can listen with incurious complacency while small disputants discuss vehemently the story of the ark, or Jonah's strange adventure; and he can look on with an indifferent smile while learned magicians attempt to dissolve the accounts of Samson's famous exploits into a sun myth;—for is not Samson, they ask, a proper name derived from a Hebrew word signifying the sun? and in what is the strength of the sun but in its beams? and is not Delilah a Hebrew word for the night, who receives the sun into her lap and shears him of his beams? and, presto! the change is wrought, and the Samson of the Bible, with all his human nature and mighty deeds, is transformed, to the credulous satisfaction of the new masters of critical legerdemain, into a primitive myth of the sun! But he who has once gained the broader view and larger faith, is above the din of the critic's hammers, and he is not to be troubled henceforth by the small dust of biblical criticism. If he ever loses faith in God's Word, it must be for reasons that shall blot the glory of God from the heavens, and make the light which is within man darkness. The person who throws in our faces what we have just characterized as the small dust of biblical criticism, and asks us, what has become of the Word of God? resembles the man who should toss a spadeful of sand, scraped from the surface of the rock, into the air, and ask, as we rub our eyes, what has become of the world? It is still beneath us as of old, though our eyes may be too full of dust to see where we stand. After all the work of the critics, the Bible still remains, the great, sublime, enduring work of the Eternal who loves righteousness and hates iniquity. If only, however, we are allowed to plant our feet quietly on the everlasting rock, and are not compelled by a mistaken zeal to keep every grain of sand—to hold fast to any traditions of men which may have accumulated upon the surface of revelation, and which, possibly, the rising winds of controversy may blow away!

CHAPTER III.

THE COURSE OF MORAL EDUCATION AND PROGRESS OF REVELATION.

In pursuing this broader inquiry, in which revelation is sought for through great historical processes, and in which our Bible is regarded as a growth slowly matured under the influence of both natural and supernatural forces and laws, we have next to ask how the Bible stands in relation to the educational method and work of God in human history. Let us first, however, make clear this view of history with which we intend to bring the Bible into comparison. This is all the more necessary since there have been almost as many philosophies of history as there have been philosophers. But their conceptions of many hues, and almost endless combinations, may be reduced to three primary colors; and to distinguish between these will be sufficient for our present purpose. According to the first of these views nothing is to be seen in history but the operation of physical laws; and the philosophy of history is reduced to a science of social statistics. Buckle, with his impatience of metaphysics, and his fondness for statistics, was the readable and superficial advocate of this so-called positive science of history. But Herbert Spencer is its profound student and great master. The new science of "Sociology" seems to be an application of arithmetic to history. It treats motives, and beliefs, and volitions, as though they were so many quantities, the laws of whose combinations, in working out the problems of human society, our philosopher is to discover, if he can. All goes very well with our statisticians and social arithmeticians, with their "tables" and "multiplication of effects," and "differentiations" and "integrations," until it occurs to us to ask the inconvenient questions, "What do these formulas represent? What are these numbers worth? What do the unknown quantities, the symbols of their equations, mean?" and then we must be put off with the answer, "Oh, science simply has to do with the succession and combinations of things, and has nothing more than algebra to say about what things stand for, or are worth." But as men and women—feeling, thinking, living, dying— we do have a great deal of concern with the meaning of things; and in our own personal consciousness we have a sense of being and of moral worth which, to the generality of men, will always be more intelligible and important than the formal principles of Mr. Spencer's complete philosophical multiplication-table. In short, this positive science of history seems to us to gain the whole world and to lose its own soul, and so to profit us little. It seizes the form, and misses the spirit of history. It observes the uniformity of the waves, and the regularity in their rise and fall; but it does not measure the tides, and their higher law. It may be an accurate science of the relation and succession of social phenomena; but it is not a philosophy of history, for it holds no plummet by which to fathom the deeper currents, and has no means of determining the destiny toward which the life of man is swept on.

The opposite extreme of the purely idealistic philosophy of history we may dismiss with a few words. Since Kant, idealism has had free course in Germany, and been glorified. Hegel expanded idealism to the utmost limits of the power of language to contain thought; and, since his death, it has exploded into we know not how many rarefied philosophies, each of which is claimed by its possessor to be the very idea of the master. Since the general breaking up of Hegelianism in Germany, it would be a work of supererogation for us to venture to condense it into any one intelligible English phrase, or to burden our pages with an extended notice of the great truths, and greater assumptions, which have marked the modern attempt to make the history of man turn itself into a process of thought, and behave like a proper Hegelian. We may gladly avail ourselves, however, of the evidence in behalf of the truth that there is reason in all things, and that Spirit is everywhere present and active, which is presented by the persistent vitality of idealism in modern philosophy; though we may refuse to entangle our understandings in the mazes of this infinite speculation. The German idealism has been a worthy witness of the Spirit against a short-sighted materialism; but, in turn, it has become a blind leader of the blind when it has presumed to find its way through nature and history by the inner light of its own thought. If Hegelianism manifests something of the faith which can never be confounded when it regards "history as the development of Spirit in time, as Nature is the development of the Idea in space;"* it has, also, been put to shame by its forgetfulness that the thoughts of the Eternal Spirit are not as our thoughts, nor his ways as our ways. If idealism has seized upon the truth, too often neglected in Christian theology, that God has been, and now is, in the world, manifesting his

---

* Hegel: Phil. of Hist. (Bohn's Trans.), p. 75.

glory, and reconciling it unto himself; it has too often lost the other truth, that he is also God over all blessed forever. This absolute idealism ought, it has been said,* to be able to reveal the future; but it has not been able even to interpret the past with historical truthfulness by its logic. Hegel's "Philosophy of History" contains far more Hegelian philosophy than human history. If the world is "a crystallized syllogism," unfortunately for our philosophers it has not crystallized always according to their laws of thinking.† Judaism is said to have been a dark riddle which tormented Hegel all his life,‡ and his disciples

---

* Bowen: Modern Phil., p. 362.

† For the unhistorical distinctions of Hegel with reference to the ancient religions, see Oehler, Tho. d. A. Test., i. s. 57. For his failure to apprehend the idea of Christianity, see Dorner, History of Doctrine of Person of Christ. Absurd instances of the application of Idealism to natural science abound in Hegel's writings; as for example, the following:—"Caustic potash makes carbonic acid out of the air, in order to become mild." Natur-Philosophie, § 332. "Warmth is the self-restoration of matter in its formlessness, its fluidity, the triumph of its homogeneity, etc.," Ency., § 303. "There is a darkness existing for itself, and a light existing for itself, and by mediation of transparency in its . . . unity is the appearance of color." Ibid., p. 280. Hegel calls the Newtonic theory, that white light consists of the union of seven colors, "a barbarism over which one cannot express himself too strongly, . . as though," he says, "a pure stream of water could originate from seven kinds of earth." Ibid., p. 285. The immanent dialectic of light passing back and forth, through the colors of the rainbow, in and out of its opposite, darkness, is prodigious! But let these few examples of idealistic science suffice for many.

‡ Rosenkranz: Biog. Hegel's, s. 40.

of the Tübingen school have mistaken a mirage for the reality of primitive Christianity. They point to an airy inversion of the substantial facts with which a sober criticism is acquainted.

With this passing notice of these two extreme conceptions of history, the positive and the idealistic, we hasten to the statement of the third view with which our reasoning in regard to Revelation is concerned, and which we may describe as the conception of a providential development of history.* Its law of progress is a divine purpose, and its goal is the greatest possible moral good. Its development is not that of an abstract Idea, or a World-spirit, or the blind working of impersonal laws; but man is taken up in the purpose of a higher Being, and human history, with all its lights and shadows, with all its eddies and retrogressions, is the progress of a divine purpose, whose end is the greatest possible good. This view recognizes a power in human affairs that "makes for righteousness," and makes for it likewise with apparent forethought, and intelligently.

This conception may be thought out in

---

* That development does not exclude providence, but is a complex adjustment of forces which requires purpose, M. Janet has maintained conclusively in his recent book on "Final Causes," against a prevalent unphilosophical tendency to dismiss superciliously the old argument from design.

several different ways, but it implies belief in a moral order in history, and in One whose orderings are everywhere to be sought for and followed. It is, in its best statement, that Christian philosophy of history as the coming of the kingdom of God to which, alike from the abstractions of thought and the necessities of daily life, the hearts of men are always returning. It is, in short, a theology of history as well as a philosophy of history.

Lessing first threw into modern theology the fruitful idea that revelation itself may be conceived of as a divine education of the race. Lessing's conception, when taken up by theology, and set in the light of a clearer faith than Lessing found in the Orthodoxism of his day, gives us a view of history which seems to be both simple and comprehensive, both true to the facts and to the spirit which is in man. The Christian philosophy of history as the carrying on and out of a great divine work of human education and redemption unites in its comprehension the statistics and the ideas; the necessary laws of human development, and the freedom of the spirit; the order of nature and the operation of supersensible powers. There is no need, however, for us to pause in order to array at this point arguments and facts in support of this conception of the moral ordering of history, as the evidences of it will be involved in our whole reasoning—the light of it plays in and out through all our thinking; and if our subsequent positions be admitted, the correctness of the moral and theistic beginnings of our argument will need no other proof.

We proceed, then, to examine our Bible further under this conception of the moral development of human history, and the Divine education of man. If a revelation really comes from the moral Orderer of the world, it must flow with his purpose. It must be a part of his order, it must carry out his method and work. The supreme moral test of the Bible therefore, is, Does it flow with and increase this diviner current of history? Did it, as it first welled up and began to flow in Israel, does it now, in the fulness of its power, run into and sweep on with the deepening righteousness, the enlarging truth of history? We have, in short, to do with a question of the whole moral tendency and educational work of the Bible.

In putting the Bible to this moral test no artifices of interpretation, or trifling with the moral sentiments should be tolerated. Man's conscience and its education through centuries of history are the work of God, or nothing is. Man's moral sentiments, and their growth, come from the Father of lights, or all is darkness. If the light which is within us be darkness, no revelation would be of any avail to us. When Jesus said, Every one that is of the truth heareth my voice, he declared unequivocally that the sense of moral truth within man is the final test of revelation. But, admitting this, how does the matter stand between the Scriptures of Israel, and the conscience of to-day?

The case seems, certainly, to stand very poorly for the Bible, if the Bible is to be defended as an infallible treatise of morals and divinity, of equal inspiration and authority throughout, finished and accurate in every sentence and part. There are passages of Scripture which an enlightened Christian conscience is far beyond. There are rules which it would be bondage for us to observe. A man who should attempt to regulate his social life by the laws of Moses would be sent to the penitentiary. A person who should adopt, as the professed creed of his life, the wisdom of Solomon, might knock in vain for admission at the doors of an Evangelical church. But the Bible is not the Koran, and we are not called upon to tear revelation from its historical surroundings, and to treat it as a creation of God independent of all the other works of God from age to age. As the sun and the solar system are supposed to have come forth together out of the original nebula—the same primal force evolving both simultaneously and harmoniously, the consolidation of the earth proceeding as the cloud-light of space was condensed into the orb of day, all things in the creation keeping perfect time in the great march onward, so that, at length, when a world ready for the life of man was gained, there rose above it, in its clear sky, a sun to rule the day,—so was it with the progress of revelation and history. They were developed together, and in harmony, and by the same Divine Providence. The advance of the one keeps time with the progress of the other. The light brightens as the world is prepared for its shining. The sun of to-day might not have done for the atmosphere of the carboniferous age. Our light would have been out of season in patriarchal times. The sun was once hardly distinguished from the earth, and it wrapt the whole orbit of our planet in its strange, diffused light before ever the two were divided, and the sun rose clear above the earth's horizon as the one dazzling orb. Revelation and human life seem, in the dim dawn of history, to have been strangely blended, and it is hard to separate the awakening human soul from the Divine manifestation in which man first came to himself, and which threw ever around the childhood of humanity a strange glamour, and to us unnatural light: not until centuries had passed did the growing revelation clear itself of the earthly, and, in the fulness of time, concentrating its beams in one perfect manifestation of God, become henceforth, in the firmament of the world's faith, the true Light which lighteth every man that cometh into the world.

The case, then, stands very differently with our Bible the moment we place before our minds this conception of the intelligent coordination and simultaneous development of the world's Bible, and the world's history, the final result of which is a finished revelation and a Christian era. Before we can bring any part or precept of the Bible under the condemnation of conscience, we shall have to settle this larger question—whether there has been a course of human education and progress of doctrine in the Bible wisely arranged and patiently carried out; whether, indeed, our Bible bears witness to a special education of man according to a good purpose by the Spirit of God.

We shall notice, first, some general indications of this educational character of revelation, and then call attention to some particular illustrations and confirmations of it.

First, the general formative truths of the Old Testament were progressive forces in early history. They were necessary to progress, and they pressed man on. Revelation forbade man to look back, by its threatenings, and led man on, going before him as the angel of the Lord, with its promise. The Old Testament repeatedly threw into human affairs just those truths which man needed to make him move on—to keep him from falling hopelessly back. Consider, for example, the moral effect in early ages of that account of the creation preserved, and evidently arranged in a form convenient to be committed to memory, in the first chapter of the book of Genesis. Whatever may be its present scientific value—and we shall seek to estimate further on its worth as a contribution to scientific progress—no student of the history of nations can entertain any doubt of its moral value, its inestimable service, that is, to the moral progress of mankind. We could more easily, indeed, compute how much a pure spring welling up at the source of a brook that widens into a river, has done for meadow, and grass, and flowers, and overhanging trees, for thousands of years, than estimate the influence of that purest of all ancient traditions of the creation, as it has entered into the lives and revived the consciences of men; as it has purified countries of idolatries, and swept away superstitions; as it has flowed on and on with the increasing truth of history, and kept fresh and fruitful, from generation to generation, faith in the One God and the common parentage of man. A primitive and pure Hebrew tradition of the creation was probably one of the impulses of the first great religious reformation in the patriarchal age. The truth witnessed by it was enough to make Abraham a reformer. With some spiritual song of the creation in his heart he could not join in the idolatries of his neighbors, and he seeks another country. The Chaldean Genesis, which has been partially deciphered from the broken tablets of the royal library at Nineveh, though corresponding in some interesting particulars with the biblical narrative, lacked precisely this moral worth, and reformatory power. These traditions of the creation never became powers of a growing religious history. They are like stagnant pools of water, themselves choked with corruptions—not flowing fountains of life. They did not stir and cleanse the moral stagnation of Babylon. The vital power of truth to create a purer and growing life is the characteristic virtue of the very first words of inspiration. A thoughtful man, with the biblical truth of the Creator working as a moral force in his soul, became the father of a nation whose end is not yet. It is not an unreasonable, but a very probable, conjecture that the children of Israel, during their bondage in

Egypt, preserved their ancestral tradition of the creation, and had in it a bond of religious faith, never wholly broken, to keep them as one people for the time of their exodus. The truth with which our Bible begins may have been one of the truths which prepared Moses, during his exile with the priest of Midian, to come forth as the deliverer and lawgiver of his people; the grand faith that God made the heavens and the earth becoming thus a second time a source and impulse of a great religious and national movement. But how shall we trace through the history of Israel the inestimable influence of that primeval revelation? On and on through the Hebrew life and literature those pure truths of the creation flow, and mingle with the deepest and best currents of the national life and thought; and if we, to-day, would follow the lifegiving stream of Divine influence backward and upward through history to its earliest sources, we shall pass beyond the broad and fruitful teachings of Christianity, beyond the grand reaches of prophecy, up through the stern commandments of the law, to this first clear spring and earliest fountain of revelation—In the beginning God created the heaven and the earth.

Thus it may be shown that other leading ideas, or great formative truths, of the Old Testament, move on always in accordance with the moral order, along the deeper moral grooves of history. The moral tendency of the Bible, in general, works together with the moral gravitation of things, for righteousness and against iniquity.

Secondly, these Scriptures, one after another, seem to have been thrown into the course of the moral education of the world when they were needed. They came not too soon or too late. When the age needed the lesson, the schoolmaster stood before it, sent from God to teach it. Revelation in this manner led step by step, and age after age, the moral progress of man. The Bible kept ever just ahead of the times, and so was fitted to bear the part of moral leadership in history. At no one time was its word of prophecy too far advanced for the people to follow it, if they would; at all times its message pressed events on toward the better day. The messengers of revelation were of the people, limited by their conditions, and bound under the burdens of their own generation; each was called to wrestle with the questions of his own times. But truths from God, stirring in the heart of their age, broke forth in their inspired speech, and visions of the glory of the Lord made them leaders and reformers. This continuous and unmistakable moral leadership of the Bible, so singularly perpetuated from prophet to prophet, and running, like one inspiration, through many generations, is itself a sign of God's work, and an indication that we are following here the course of a revelation. Observe how orderly and progressive this moral leadership of history by the God of the Bible is. We seem to be following along this history a sagacious and indomitable work of moral engineering,—over mountains and across valleys, to use again the vivid prophetic description of its progress, there is made straight a highway for the Lord. Fix in mind the great epochs—the Reformation of the patriarchal age, the Exodus, the Monarchy, the Exile, the Return, the Interval—and around these periods gather in their order the literary products of the life of Israel—prophecy, and history, and proverb, and psalm,—and the moral purpose and progress, the providential design and leadership through it all will become at once self-revealed and obvious, as the meaning of some great picture, with its lights and shades, and convergence of lines in one perspective and toward one point of sight. Read the Bible as our modern discoverers of the mistakes of Moses read it, without taking in its historical perspective; look upon the biblical revelation as a plain surface without depth and distance,—and you cannot possibly gain a much truer conception of the divine wisdom in it, than you could of the glory of God in the heavens, if you should regard the sky as a flat surface in which the stars are fixed, forgetting the vast astronomical distances, and the groupings of worlds, and the harmony of all. The unhistorical interpretation of Scripture is as childish as an unastronomical view of the sky. We must endeavor to see things as they are, not as they appear, if we would discover the higher thought, the divine law, in their arrangement. Follow, then, through the Bible the continuous adjustment of the revelation of truth to the conditions of the life of Israel—and in this adaptation of the environment of revealed truth to the struggle of the higher life in Israel, there lie the evidences of a more than natural evolution. The Bible, when interpreted with any adequate historical sense, shows throughout unbroken moral leadership. Its truths meet the exigencies of its epochs, and lead on into new eras, toward the one far-off Messianic goal. Thus (for we can now only glance down the course of development) Abraham receives the word of the Lord which enables him to open the way of reform, and to become the father of a monotheistic nation. Moses, with the commandments of the Lord, leads a chosen people one great step onward toward the land of promise. Samuel receives the truth by whose power he leads the twelve tribes out of political chaos. David leads the kingdom to a throne established in righteousness; and the older prophets come with the word of the Lord which kings must hear. Isaiah, and the younger prophets, lead religion through the deadly tangle of Canaanitish idolatries, over the arid wastes of formalism, beyond the rocky fastnesses of Judaism, to the living fountains of a spiritual worship, and into the illimitable prospect of the Messianic glory. The nation, in order to learn its truths by heart, is sent into exile, "goes into retreat to do penance for its sins." It is called back, sobered and purified from idolatry, to enter upon the Puritanism of the Jewish Church, which also must precede the victory of faith, and its final Christian liberty. Again revelation proves true to its mission, and leads the history. In the later Hebrew writings, which have found a place in our Bibles, the truth of the individual, and his responsibility, sounds forth. Jeremiah struck this new note; it rings through Ezekiel; it calls, like a trumpet, to courage and conscience, and the hope of immortality, in the book of Daniel. There follows an age when the voice of the prophet ceases. The drill of the schoolmaster has its appointed time. The hedge is built around the law. The heroic warrior recovers the sacred rolls which the "Madman of Syria" had left unburned. The scribe sits in Moses' seat. Already the soil is prepared by the Roman ploughshares for the seeds of a better faith. But the life of the true religion must first, it would seem, return into itself, become dry in the hard kernel of Judaism, be buried in the ground, and die, before it can rise again in the new vigor of Christianity, and bear the ripe fruit of the Gospel for the world. At last the greatest of the prophets points to One greater than he, in whom all is fulfilled, and in his disciples the true Israel is sent at last as a "nation of teachers" through the world.

Thus, moral leadership, kept up through a succession of centuries, and toward a Messianic goal, is the peculiar divinity of the Bible and the religion of the Bible. Rightly to appreciate what divine Power, standing as it were behind history, ever pressed Israel on, and often against its own stubborn will, to the moral leadership of the world—what higher forces were ever at work in and through the Bible, we need to leave our own position amid the worked-out results of revelation, and we should divest ourselves of our Christian associations, which are the results of the whole educational work of God in history; we must enter into the moral ignorance, the superstitions, the cruelties, the thick darkness and sin, from out which revelation emerged; we must take our stand before the might of evil, and hear the noise of the battle, and behold the powers of darkness rising up everywhere against this great march forward. Whence, then, we may well ask, came that Spirit which wrestled with Israel and prevailed? What earthly science shall name this unknown Power which conquers and reigns? Keen observers have noticed the existence of what they call an anti-Darwinian conscience in man. There is an invisible something in man which often sets at defiance, and prevails over, the inherited tendencies of human nature, and which does not always give the battle to the strong. Whence came, and of what manner of spirit is, this *anti-historic* power in Israel and the Bible? Some inner principle of development struggles against the outward historical environment, and will not rest until it prevails. What was it which selected Israel, and in one narrow land, while all the surrounding country was sinking, lifted man up in spite of himself? which along the course of one national history carried on a progressive development of religious life and truth, while other people, though taught by many wise men and seers, and not without their truths, still can show no one connected and progressive revelation like this? At all events, here are phenomena to be taken carefully into the account in any fair estimate of the moral nature of the Bible. But let us consider these general phenomena more in detail. Certain special characteristics which indicate one educational plan, and which suggest the superintendence of one mind throughout the whole course, remain to be noticed.

1. There is a plain progress of doctrine in the Bible from without inward, from external restraints to inward principles, from law to love. The object-lesson is given first, the truth of the spirit afterward. The discipline of conduct precedes the renewal of the heart. The sign and symbol prepare for the essential and the real. God's method in the Bible is like the mother's method with her child. The best truths of the home are the last learned. Those things which are outward, temporary, and of least worth, are the first gifts and earliest lessons of the home. Its higher spiritual blessings, its real wealth of love, lying from the beginning in all the care of the home, cannot be opened to the child until after many days; they are the memories of the home which men cherish by the graves of those who bore them. God's method of revelation, like the course of human education, begins, of necessity, with outward regulations, and provi-

sions for the day; it proceeds by the lessons of tutors and governors, and ends with the freedom and love of the new heart. This progressive method is to be observed in the manner of revelation, or in the means employed by God for the purpose of manifesting himself. The earlier means of divine manifestation were the appearances of angels, the voice, and vision of the night, the Shekinah of the sanctuary, and, in general, supernatural signs and works. The conception of the presence and power in Israel of the Holy Spirit grew up slowly, and required times of trouble and exile for its development.* Even the word "conscience," without which we can hardly conceive of any religion, and through which revelation shines upon our hearts, is not to be met with in the earlier books of the Bible. A trace of it is to be found in Ecclesiastes,† but not until the deep religious experience of the apostle Paul did it become a customary Scriptural expression. Its use marks a late, developed, Christian idea of individual responsibility, and the indwelling law of the Spirit.

The educational work of the Mosaic ritual, the plain pedagogical intent of the law, will at once occur as an example of this method of revelation. Working from within outward, its

---
* Compare Ewald, Lehre d. Bible von Gott., i. 293.
† Chap. x. 20; Ewald: Ibid., i. 35.

object and intent, as has often enough been pointed out, was "to prepare and awaken the inward spiritual life, the inner consciousness of God."* It will be only necessary for us, therefore, to call attention to some illustrations of this work of the schoolmaster performed by the law which are not so familiar, or which need nowadays to be emphasized.

From this educational point of view we are to judge rightly the vows enjoined or permitted by the Old Testament. Vows mark a lower and more external stage of religious progress, and they were permitted by the God of the Bible as useful in the earlier periods of religious growth. We feel that the great apostle acted in a spirit of accommodation to an outgrown Jewish scruple when he took upon himself a vow in the temple. Vows disappear with other "beggarly elements" of this world from the later revelations of the Spirit. Religious and moral vows, as total abstinence pledges, are pre-Christian morals. They may still be necessary for persons who in their moral development belong to the ages before Christ, and who cannot be constrained by the law of the spirit. They may still be useful, at times, in view of the necessities of the weaker brethren. But they possess no virtue

---

* Oehler: The. des A. T., i., s. 460.

or sanctity in themselves; as even in Deuteronomy we read: "But if thou shalt forbear to vow, it shall be no sin in thee" (Deut. xxiii. 22), and they have no proper place in the covenant of the Christian Church.

The same pedagogical intent of the law, in leading men from the negative and outward morality to the inward and positive virtue, is very marked in the successive precepts concerning an institution which, because it is often so misunderstood, deserves, in this connection, special notice. We cannot maintain the perpetual obligation of the Sabbath unless we observe carefully the preparatory and educational intent of the fourth commandment. The original commandment is mainly negative. "Thou shalt not do any work." The first object of the commandment is to gain control of the conduct, the work of the hands. It introduces a restraint rather than a privilege. The privilege, however, lies at the core of the restraint, waiting to be brought out. The Sabbath precepts, and indeed the whole ritual of the prophets, look forward to a more spiritual worship, and the better consecration of the seventh day; and the Sabbath waits for its Lord. His word—"The Sabbath was made for man"—finally makes the glorious Christian privilege break loose from the restraints of the law. The Jewish traditions had checked this blossoming forth of the law. The precepts of the synagogues, which had been formed between the times of Ezra and Christ, were so many attempts of mistaken zeal to bind up and stay the development of the blessing intended for man in the Sabbath day; and Christ took them all away. So the Jewish Sabbath passes naturally, and in accordance with the divine law of the development of revelation, into the Lord's day; and the end is better than the beginning. We may not, as Christians, confine the sacred blessing and joy of the Lord's day within the earlier and narrow Sabbath of the commandment. That would be a Judaizing which gendereth bondage. In the joyous worship of the first Christians the Sabbath idea began to be fulfilled. No longer a day of burdensome restraint, and more than a day of rest, the Sabbath, in the Christian observance of the Lord's day, became indeed a day made for man, a day sacred to the highest and best communion with God, a blessing of the Spirit for mankind. The older Sabbath, lingering for a season in Christian usage beside the Lord's day, like a shadow by the substance, at last, in the more perfect day, disappeared, while that which, as the apostle said, is more glorious, remains. Not by returning, therefore, to the law of ordinances, as we are sometimes ill-advisedly urged to do, but rather by following up the advancing purpose and process of revelation, until it gives man a Sabbath in its full idea and perfection, are we to justify, without artifice of interpretation, the present and perpetual obligation of the Christian Sabbath. The divine principle of the development of revelation is our only and our sufficient reason for the change to the first day of the week. The divine sanctions of a finished revelation invest the Christian Sabbath. Not to avail ourselves of its blessing is worse than to break a commandment. It is to neglect the Christian conclusion of the whole educational course of the law, and to profane a perfect gift of God to man.*

2. The educational progress, or pedagogical intent of the Bible, may also be characterized as an advance from the general to the specific; from the indefinite to the more definite. The lessons in coarse print come first; the fine print is learned afterwards. The general principle or rule is given first; the teaching

---

* The second commandment, also, has passed through a notable change. Mozley (Ruling Ideas, Lecture III.) shows that the idea natural to the Jewish mind in the times of Moses, of a judicial visitation of the sins of the fathers upon the children, began to be superseded by a different view as early even as the age of Ezekiel, and in Christian theology has passed into the conception of a law of natural providence. We have here another instance of the principle of development of revelation, by which that which is imperfect is gradually done away.

of subsequent experience brings out its more spiritual meanings, or its more difficult applications. The progress of the revelation of the nature and perfection of the Godhead is a signal illustration of this feature of the historical course of revelation. This advance in the self-manifestation of the God of Israel may easily be traced in the succession of the names for God which occur in the Old Testament. These names are, if one may so speak, the high-water marks of successive revelations. They mark the limits reached by great historic movements and tides in Israel's enlarging knowledge of God. The name of God is that by which he is known, that by which he makes himself known in his relation to man, and hence, when Christians pray, often so thoughtlessly, "For thy name's sake," they pray for the sake of all that God in the past ages has manifested himself to be, for the sake of the whole revelation of God in which they and their fathers have believed. And the name of God grew more definite, more positive, more manifold with the advancing history.

Mr. Matthew Arnold, in his "Literature and Dogma," seems strangely to have overlooked the significance of this growth of Israel in the knowledge of God, which we can trace through successive periods by means of the names given to the Divine Being, at different times, in the biblical history. His failure to follow this clue to a right understanding of the religion of the Bible, is an instructive lesson of the need of something more than literary criticism—of the need, also, of the historic sense—in the study of the Bible.

We may sketch, in the following manner, the rise and growth of the names of God in the Old Testament.* There was one name in use among the Semitic people before all others, antedating the call of Abraham, and continuing, also, down the whole course of revelation. It seems to furnish the distant and vague background of revelation—like a receding and infinite sky—upon which, one after another, many distinct names and special manifestations of the divine glory are brought out, and into whose depths they disappear again.

From this older and undefined Semitic conception of God as the Lord (El, Eloah), we are introduced into the course of revelation by a name which became prevalent in the patriarchal age, and which expresses a somewhat more definite sense of Deity, "The Almighty" (El Schaddai, Ex. vi. 3). This patriarchal designation of the Almighty God is still,

---

* Compare Ewald: Lehre d. Bible von Gott., ii., pp. 327-348; and Oehler: The. d. A. Test., i., p. 131 ff., and Articles, in loco, in Herzog's Real Enc., for the detailed critical discussion of the views summarized above.

however, quite general and primitive; it introduces the conception of a power above nature, and thus is an advance upon the deification of the vast power *in* nature; but it is not a word of distinct moral significance, and it marks, therefore, as a name for God, the beginning rather than the middle or the end of revelation. The sense of dependence upon the infinite Power which is above all finite existence, is the beginning of the knowledge of God. The book of Genesis lacks, however, the more specific and richer names for God which can be learned, if at all, only from a prolonged moral experience. With the deliverance of Israel from Egypt, at the beginning of its career as the chosen people, is given that divine name which we might almost call Israel's proper name of God—Jehovah; a name by which was signified not only the unchangeableness of the God of the covenant, but also the appearance, or coming forth, of God in self-revelation. Jehovah is the self-manifesting God, God in the course of self-revelation, the historically appearing God.* The exodus and the founding of the theocracy give, also, the historical occasion for the revelation of God as the Holy One. The rise of this divine name in Israel is of peculiar in-

---

* Oehler : Ibid., i., s. 144, 150-1.

terest. We do not find it in the book of Genesis. The antediluvians and the patriarchs had not been overpowered by the awful holiness of Jehovah, as was the lawgiver upon the mount. The very name, the Holy One of Israel, marks a new epoch of the history. It is taught through a marvellous experience of the Lord who shone from the burning bush, and who led the people through the sea in whose mighty waters their pursuers sank as lead. (Ex. xv. 10–11.) And through a prolonged course of moral history, by calamities, and judgments, and blessings, the full significance of that divine name, the God of Holiness, shall be disclosed to the prophets. After the covenant was first broken there appear, for the first time, the further designations of God as the gracious, merciful, long-suffering God—divine names to whose refuge ever since the penitent have fled for a hiding-place from their sin.

There is another name for the Lord, not occurring in the earlier Scriptures, which evidently has a history. The exiled king offers his prayer for his return to the sanctuary in the name of the Lord of hosts. (Ps. lxxxiv. 1, 8.) To the covenant name, Jehovah, he adds in his appeal the words, Jehovah of Hosts. The Pentateuch and the books of Joshua and Judges lack this name which the Psalmist confidently utters. It came into general use during the times of Samuel and David, and is associated with the early fortunes of the monarchy. (1 Sam. i. 3, xvii. 45.) It is a triumphant, royal name for the God of Israel. It was a name, then, which had been historically given. Ewald thinks it first was heard on some great day of battle, and was hallowed in the song and jubilee of some signal victory. What unforeseen deliverances, and help of invisible allies, as the appearance over the battle-field of chariots of the Lord, and the heavenly host, may be commemorated in that new name of Israel's triumphant trust — Jehovah of Hosts! It was a name full of meaning and full of faith, because it was a historical name — a name of great memories and triumphs, of royal thanksgivings and national jubilee. It became the favorite expression of the later prophets when they would declare their invincible faith in the majesty of Jehovah, and his sovereignty over all powers and dominions, on earth and in heaven. They seal, as it were, the words of their prophecy with this exalted name, Jehovah of Hosts.

But these successive names for God, which were historically given and are full of historic meaning, all pass away before the rising of the Name in which the whole historical revelation was fulfilled. While the Mohammedan exults because the Koran gives him a "hundred names of God which he can weave in one wreath of prayer," the Christian rejoices that he can make known his request to the Father in the One Name, by which God has manifested his very nature, and finished the revelation of his glory, for in him dwelleth all the fulness of the Godhead bodily.* (Col. ii. 9.)

The didactic purpose of revelation, and the progressive work of the Bible in the moral education of mankind, may be further illustrated and confirmed by certain results which have been accomplished by it. The fruits which remain show the success of this divine policy of revelation. By this wisely-arranged and patiently pursued biblical course of human education, man has been taught certain great moral lessons, and taught them so effectually that he will never forget them. The lesson of the worth of the *family* is a case in point. In the blessing of the Christian home we have one of the worked-out results, one of the

---

* Ewald: Lehre von Gott., ii., s. 333, distinguishes five names for God, corresponding with the five great periods of the history of Israel. God is the " Almighty " of the patriarchs; " Jehovah " of the covenant; the " God of hosts " of the monarchy, the " Holy One" of the Deuteronomist and later prophetic age; "Our Lord" of Judaism—and Christianity brings no new name, but fulfils all. Though we may hesitate to mark with such definiteness the changes in the prevalent names for God in Israel, we can hardly fail to see in their succession an evidence of one gradually developing revelation of the true God.

thoroughly-taught lessons of a progressive revelation. If it required ages to school man in that truth, nevertheless, when the divine instruction was over, the lesson never needed to be taught again. The manner and progress of this teaching were as follows. The Old Testament begins in an age of the world wholly destitute of any just conception of the individual and his rights, and sets up, as a first lesson, or example, the Hebrew family—Abraham and Sarah, Isaac and Rebecca. Judged by our standard, these were by no means model families. They were, however, good examples for their own times. In the Hebrew family, imperfect and even polygamous as it was, one great blessing for the household was secured—the Hebrew love for a family-name and inheritance. Revelation is content first to teach a truth which the Hebrew mind can comprehend, and which Israel does thoroughly learn. Revelation lays hold first of a great natural instinct, and hallows it. The God of the Bible singles out the family-line as the means of conveyance of his promised blessing. Already, by this first lesson, the Hebrew family, in the patriarchal age, gains a sanctity which it possessed nowhere else in the East. Then, the germ of a better family-life being thus given, the laws of Moses close around it, and protect it. The teaching of the prophets purify and hallow it. But the law of divorce, given on account of the hardness of men's hearts, has not yet dropped away. The commandment is not yet perfect. At last a daughter of the house of David brings to womanhood the blessing of the Highest. In the teaching of Christ the scaffolding of the law, once needed, is taken away; the temporary expedients are cleared off; the imperfect is made complete; and, at last, grounded in the essential morality of the law, and built up and cemented by the experience and historic sentiments of a race, arises the institution of the Christian family. Look to the end, toward which the law of Moses was a great step forward for his day. God did not make the family, as he did not create the world, in a week. It was a slow but successful process, by which, under his guiding hand, so divine a creation was formed and perfected. The God of the Bible only began the lesson of the true nature and law of the family with Abraham; he continued it and improved it with Moses; he taught its inviolable sanctity in the penitential Psalms of David. It was a hard lesson to make a corrupt, passionate world learn by heart. But when the Bible is finished, behold! this divine institution is also finished. When the Bible is done, the family is secured forever. The family is itself a word of God—a word spoken in part by the prophets, but at last perfectly declared by the Son of Man, whose words shall never pass away—a final and authoritative word of the Eternal; and the gates of the Hell of our nineteenth century infamy of free love shall not prevail against it!

In connection with this course of revelation by means of which the Christian home was secured, two other results of the development of the Bible should be taken into consideration —the abolition of human sacrifice, and the abolition of slavery. Both of these customs were fatal foes of the family, and the same wise and patient course of divine dealing which established the institution of the family, swept away, likewise, these enemies of its peace. The trial of Abraham's faith, and its far-reaching consequences, introduces to us the biblical method of checking, and in time removing, the very source of that evil which made many a land in antiquity run red with the blood of sacrifices.

Herbert Spencer, and other statistical philosophers, are accustomed to regard the offering of Isaac as only one among many illustrations of a cruel superstition prevalent throughout the whole low level of a primitive culture. But that which distinguishes this transaction from all other ancient sacrifices, that which is altogether peculiar and influential in the trial of Abraham's faith, is quietly overlooked in the rapid generalizations of these writers. Its place and work in the development of a pure religious faith are the chief questions to be determined; and, when we have clearly grasped that, we shall find ourselves free from the moral embarrassment in which even Christian readers of the Bible have sometimes left this narrative. A common method of justifying the morality of the divine command to Abraham asserts the absolute right of the Creator over life, and the obligation of obedience to a divine injunction as the supreme duty of man.* But this apology for Abraham's action rests upon the untenable assumption that morality is based upon the will of God, and not upon the essential character of God; and it ignores the consideration urged by Canon Mozley that no miracle could be to us an evidence of a divine command, if it required a contradiction of our standard of morality; and one of the facts of the narrative to be explained is, how Abraham—moral reformer as he was—could conscientiously have believed that he was called by the Lord to offer up his only son. The reproach cast upon the morality of the Old Testament by unbelievers in its inspiration

---

* So Rogers: Superhuman Origin of the Bible, Appendix.

is partly justified by the arbitrary justifications of its imperfect or incomplete examples and precepts, still too prevalent among believers in its divine authority. Dean Stanley, with his usual genial historic sense, hints at the simple and true explanation of the difficulties which the conscience of to-day may raise concerning the offering of Isaac when he says, * "There are few, if any, which will not vanish away before the simple pathos, and lofty spirit of the narrative itself, provided that we take it, as in fairness it must be taken, as a whole; its close not parted from its commencement, nor its commencement from its close—the subordinate parts of the transaction not raised above its essential primary intention." Dr. Mozley leads his readers on the right ground, when he estimates the whole morality of the Old Testament dispensation by the moral standard of its own times, and by the intention or design of it, which appears when the end of the dispensation is reached. In his discussion, however, of the divine morality in the command given to Abraham to offer up Isaac, the historical effect of that divine policy needs to be brought more prominently to the foreground. The simple and satisfactory explanation of this vexed passage

---

* Lectures on the Jewish Church, First Series, p. 54.

of Scripture seems to us to be as follows:—A progressive revelation has a twofold object, a remote and a present work. Everything in it must be ordered in view of the ulterior design, and in accordance also with the conditions of society at each particular step of its course. Divine accommodation to a lower level of human ideas, or imperfect condition of man's knowledge of good and evil, is perfectly moral, in so far as it tends to overcome the imperfect and to help on the development of conscience to that which is perfect; in so far, that is, as it is the accommodation of the teacher to the pupil in carrying out, and solely for the sake of carrying out, the design of the whole course of instruction. Any accommodation to error or imperfection which gives the error new vitality, or makes the imperfection last longer, would not be a justifiable act on the part of the teacher, but rather a participation in the fault of the pupil. Here, then, was Abraham with a new truth of God growing in his mind, and ready to take his stand as a moral reformer in a corrupt world; with the promise of a future in which all nations of the earth should be blessed, glowing before him; yet with the memories, and instincts, and habits of the people, and the land, from which he was called to go forth, still dimming his moral vision, confusing his ideas, and binding him, the heir of the future, to the past. He needed to be taught, in the most impressive manner possible, the elementary lessons of the new faith which, eventually, was to bless mankind. He needed a special providential schooling adapted to his mental and moral state and capacity; a divine teaching which should take him up where his previous education had left him, and send him on beyond his age. He needed, in this special manner, to be taught of God, not only for himself, but also for the sake of the promised race. The whole design of revelation made necessary some effectual teaching and trial of Abraham's faith. Now, in judging fairly the method of God in trying Abraham's faith for his own ulterior purposes of good, we have to do with the actual historical influence, and result, of the method providentially chosen. What was the effect of the command to offer up Isaac on the superstitions which made idolatrous lands abound in human sacrifices? What, as matter of fact and history, did the divine teacher accomplish by his way of instructing Abraham? Surround yourself with the actual historical conditions of Abraham's time. It is no easy task to lift a man, to raise a race, out of the ideas and customs of their age. Yet Abraham must be lifted above his age, and Israel is called to be a peculiar people. But how? The difficulty is increased by the fact that many of the worst idolatries and superstitions, which a progressive revelation must utterly destroy, have truths at the root of them—and a divine wisdom of reform cannot move, like human fanaticism, with the besom of destruction in its hand. In that most cruel heathen rite of human sacrifice there is a truth providentially to be cared for, as well as a fearful evil to be abolished. There is a pure truth at the heart of sacrifice. Now, suppose that, as the moral teacher of an uninstructed age, in which the very truths needed for all human progress were overgrown with deadly superstitions, you wished to disentangle the true from the false; suppose that, as the instructor of the man chosen to be the reformer of that age, you wished to separate the true from the false in the doctrine of sacrifice. Suppose, moreover, you wished to prevent the fearful abuse, and to show the right use, of sacrifice, in a manner which should never be misunderstood or forgotten. Suppose you wished to teach the right idea of the offering acceptable unto God, in a manner so vivid and effectual, that the race whose moral education you had in hand, should ever afterward count it a sin to offer human sacrifice; and suppose, besides this, you wished to make your teaching, also, a trial of faith, which should develop and confirm the very spirit which you knew to be essential to the whole subsequent advancement of your pupil; and that you had, moreover, a still ulterior design whose meaning could become known only when the whole course of instruction should be completed, and all suggestions and types of the earlier discipline be read in the light of their perfect fulfilment. Now, can you imagine a better way to teach that lesson, a more effectual way of accomplishing those beneficent intentions, than that pursued by the divine wisdom in teaching Abraham, and fitting him to be the father of a chosen people? The lesson began with the truth at the heart of sacrifice. It continued by testing and confirming Abraham's faith in that truth, which it was most necessary Israel should preserve as his race grew up out of idolatry. The divine lesson ended by casting out completely and effectually the erroneous heathen ideas of sacrifice in which Abraham had grown up. God seems, at first, to acquiesce in the prevailing low theology of sacrifice;—the hard commandment comes according to the ideas of the age; and Abraham, not deterred by anything in the spirit of his times, obeys. Though it was a seeming contradiction to God's previous word of promise to him, and a fearful trial to his new-found faith, still he has not as yet a conscience advanced enough to make him doubt the divine command, and, though it all seems very strange, he believes and obeys. Thus the first truth, the truth needed for the whole future glory of Israel, is secured. God sanctions, by his commandment, the truth at the heart of sacrifice, that all that we have is his, and with entire faith in his goodness should be devoted to him. Man can take not a single step forward until he learns by heart this first truth of self-surrender. Abraham, under the hard commandment, learns it, and is counted the father of the faithful. But he prepares ignorantly to follow that truth. Then the divine word comes which prevents the fearful abuse of the truth which was sanctioned by the morality of his age. The divine interposition—not a moment too soon, not a moment too late—frees the truth of sacrifice from a fatal error, and sends the Hebrew race a great step onward toward the Gospel of mercy. The whole transaction, in short, is a divine object-lesson, adapted to the times in which it was given, and successful in its results. It is noticeable, in confirmation of this didactic view, or pedagogical interpretation of this scene, that in the Hebrew text the name of God in the first commandment to Abraham is the more general name for the Deity—the unrevealed God of the creation,—

while it is Jehovah, the self-revealing God, who speaks the word which prevents the shedding of blood; and the meaning of that sadly mistranslated word, God tempted Abraham, is, God tried Abraham, or, as we might say, God taught Abraham a lesson. Now mark the subsequent historical effect of that lesson so painfully taught the father of the faithful. Abraham never needed, himself, to be taught a second time that God does not wish the offering of blood. No Hebrew parent, reading that story in after years, and teaching it to his children, would ever think of pleasing the God of Abraham by offering to him his firstborn son; it became an abomination in Israel to cause children to pass through the fire of Moloch, and the later prophets knew that God loves mercy rather than sacrifice. Though the influence of surrounding idolatries may on rare occasions have led Israel into the tragic sin of offering human sacrifices, the Hebrew law and custom, and the whole providential leading of the people from Abraham's day on, were against it; and they who would sit in judgment upon this divine procedure should not be suffered to ignore the decisive fact that the God of Abraham is the God whose course of moral education succeeded in destroying the fatal errors, and saving the vital truth, of sacrifice; and that the beginning of this great, beneficent, providential instruction in the true meaning of sacrifice was the vivid historical object-lesson which God taught Abraham of old, and which Israel has not forgotten to this day.

Having dwelt at some length upon the method of divine education illustrated by God's dealing with Abraham, we may dismiss, with few words, the course taken by revelation in abolishing finally that other foe of domestic purity, and the welfare of society,—human slavery. The fact that arguments in defence of slavery used to be drawn from the Bible, shows the need of popular instruction with regard to the development of revelation, and the guiding spirit of the Bible. We may not stand holding fast to the letter, while the whole current of revelation sweeps on. Revelation in the end has succeeded in developing the idea of the individual and his rights, which was wanting in an early day, and which could be firmly secured only by a patient work of God in human history. That idea never would have been developed and made a fundamental truth of modern society, had it not been for the Bible, and the progressive revelation of the Bible. The fountain-head of this now universal truth is in the original Hebrew account of the creation. Man came to a knowledge of himself as an individual possessed of certain in-

5*

alienable rights, when God became to his thought a perfect and glorious Person, with whom he was created to live in a holy communion. The idea of the human soul, and its sacredness before God, springing out of the very fact of the creation, was deepened and increased with the enlarging revelation of God's glory in Israel. Human slavery was not suddenly abolished by any commandment from Sinai. But revelation threw the truths into history, and let them grow there, which made the abolition of slavery all over the world only a question of time. Rightly viewed, and fairly judged, the successive positions and whole historic influence of the Bible with regard to slavery are a signal illustration of the large and wise and successful policy of revelation in the work of man's moral education and social reform. A too early prohibition might have been a dead law. A living, growing principle of opposition to evil is what the world needs. A long course of constitutional treatment is requisite for the cure of humanity from sin—a patient history of redemption—not heroic surgery, not the fanaticism of a wild justice. In Moses's day the age of the individual was not yet fully come. The ages of the patriarchal family, of the tribe, of the kingdom, of the nation, are first in order before the age of fully-developed and well-adjusted individual rights. Revelation constantly presses forward the truth of individual right, and presses it on as far, and as fast, as man is fitted to receive and to keep it. The germ of the truth which shall overthrow at last every form of human bondage is contained in the inspired teaching of man's creation—all men have one origin, all men breathe the breath of the living God. The rite of circumcision, marking, as it does, the exemption of the children of Abraham from the hard necessity of being offered in sacrifice to appease God, was subsequently extended to the servants of the household, so that the patriarchal law threw the protection of its sacred covenant not only over the humblest and poorest child of Abraham, but also over those who had been purchased from a strange land.* The law, which rested on these fundamental truths of Genesis, proceeded to ordain regulations which should prevent the absolute power of masters; † which protected female slaves, especially, from gross cruelty; ‡ and which should make possible a day of emancipation. And over the humane regulations of the law was thrown the force of a sentiment which should still farther

---

* Gen. xvii. 12–13.
† Ex. xxi. 20.
‡ Deut. xxi. 10 seq.

mollify the condition of slaves in Israel—a sentiment of humanity ever kept alive in Israel by the memory that once their fathers had been strangers in the land of bondage. The precepts of the apostles with regard to servants are the Christian continuation of the truths and emotions which, from the beginning, along the whole course of revelation, had been quietly yet effectually at work against all cruelty, oppression, and bondage, and which have reached at last their most successful issue in the freedom of all Christian lands. We must judge the tree by the fruit; and freedom is the fruit of that revelation which was planted, a growing truth, in the soul of Abraham of old. Historically, the abolition of slavery is due to the Bible, and the religion of the Bible. The progress of truth in the historical course of revelation was all in that direction; and the influence of the finished Bible, of the whole Bible, has been, throughout modern history, a felt power on the side of the weak and the oppressed, and in defence of liberty of conscience and the divine sacredness of every human soul. Men must hide the Bible from the people, if they would steal now the liberties of man.

One other illustration of the progress of revelation according to the wise methods of the schoolmaster, we will select from the many that might be adduced, because we wish to group together examples enough, around our central idea of a divine development of the Bible, to make it definite and clear ; and because it is in itself a truth often discussed and of much interest. The question has been raised whether the truth of personal immortality is taught in the Old Testament. Here, also, besides the letter of Scripture, the documentary revelation which remains, let us mark the flow of the current upon which the religion of Israel was borne on. Personal immortality was evidently not the first word of life taught to man by the Divine Educator. On the contrary, the earliest promise is the vague expectation of some blessing to come to mankind in the dim future. One searches in vain throughout the earlier books of the Bible for any pronounced teaching with regard to personal immortality. It is a truth held, as it were, in reserve by the God of the Bible. One finds, however, laid in the first courses of revelation, a broad fundamental truth, which shall afterward be used as the substantial basis upon which the higher hope may rise. The permanence of human society, the worth of natural affections, and especially the sacredness of the parental relation, are the lower truths which are first providentially secured, and which form the firm foundation for faith in the higher relationships of a divine society,—for that belief in the fatherhood of God, and the sonship of man, without which there can be no real, abiding faith in immortality in our hearts. The lower, but most necessary, hope is first born in Israel. The expectation of a perpetual name in Israel is the germinant hope of immortality in the earlier ages. It was Abraham's all absorbing desire. This primitive hope of a family-name and inheritance became afterward enriched, and one might almost say, spiritualized, by its blending with the Messianic hope of Israel. The Messianic age was to the devout Hebrew in the prophetic times almost what Heaven is to us. And it is noticeable that the day when the Sadducees flourished most, with their denial of the resurrection, was the very day when the Messianic hope was well nigh given up in the despairing cry of the priests: "We have no king but Cæsar." The whole development of the doctrine of immortality through the Bible follows the divine law so clearly apprehended by an apostle, who lived far enough down in the history of Israel to have a philosophy of that history : " Howbeit, that was not first which is spiritual, but that which is natural, and afterward that which is spiritual." Through the family, and the hope of the preservation of a name in one's descendants, was formed an outward, natural sheath for the finer spiritual belief in immortality. We can observe with some distinctness the gradual unfolding of this better hope. It appears in some of the Psalms. The Hebrew poetry early felt the stirrings of the instinct of immortality ;—the shock of calamity strikes out, as it were, sparks of that divine light which ever lies latent in the soul of man. These moments of poetic illumination, however, were too evanescent,—but foregleams of the coming revelation. The loftiest minds glow with the dawn, but the common mind in lowly life seems hardly to have been illumined by it. The continual disappointment of their history, and the vision of the judgments impending upon Israel, drove the later prophets to more spiritual interpretations of God's great providential purposes, and hence they gained more elevated conceptions of the future kingdom of God, in which the dead shall live again, and righteousness receive its fitting rewards. The truth involved in the teaching of the Pentateuch, that after death the soul has still some relation to the living God, is developed more clearly and consciously by the prophets ; but still the thought of the overcoming of death for the individual is wrapt up in the more general conception of the final triumph, and everlasting inheritance, of the sacred community, the true Israel.* It is the chosen people who shall be ransomed from the power of the grave. Ephraim shall be redeemed from death. But within this hope for the chosen race is quietly enfolded, and growing all the time, the hope of personal immortality. One great impulse to the further development of this truth was provided by the experience which pressed ever more severely upon the minds of men, that justice is not always meted out in this world, that the wicked often prosper to the last day of their lives, and that the righteous do not receive here the full rewards of their labors. This old riddle of human experience cannot be solved unless we bring to it the key of this truth that the just shall live again. The righteous who have died, overborne by the judgments which fell upon Israel,—shall not they have part in the final triumph of the true Israel? So in the twenty-sixth chapter of Isaiah, the prophet struggles with this question, until he breaks out at last into the triumphal strain: "Thy dead men shall live, together with my dead body shall they arise. Awake and sing, ye that dwell in the dust!" This is the only possible solution of the problem of life; and it is the conclusion toward which the history of Israel, with its increas-

---

* Ps. cii. 24-28; Hosea xiii. 14. See Oehler, opus cit., ii. 240.

ing burden of suffering and death, presses on to Christ.

In the storms of the Maccabæan age, the belief in immortality rose more brightly than ever before.* The prophet Daniel, whose words, if not written in that age, were certainly for that age, holds up before the first martyrs of that beginning of persecutions the hope of shining as the stars forever and ever.

We find, then, the belief that there is existence after death involved in the fundamental religious conceptions of Israel.† But the truth of personal immortality is a truth struggling upward, a growing truth of the Old Dispensation; it is hardly a fully-formed hope, or ripened doctrine. It is in the Old Testament, but in it germinantly and potentially; it is the hope of the prophets in their highest moments of inspiration, but Christ must bring life and immortality to light before it can shine, a steady and transfiguring light of life, for the world.

It seems surprising that a truth so vital to religion, in our view, as the hope of immortality, should have been left in the background of the primeval revelation; and some Christian writers, therefore, can hardly credit the indications that the doctrine of the rewards of the

---

* Ewald: v. 306.
† For further proof see Prof. Mead, The Soul, Chap. vii.

future life, so essential to their conception of true religion, was not made one of the prominent, working truths of the Old Dispensation. In this, as in some other doctrines, they seek by forced interpretations to extract from the seed elements of truth which the God of the harvest left to appear in the fruit of revelation. They can hardly be restrained from reading the Gospel in Genesis, and finding the grace and truth which came by Christ in the law of Moses. All such overanxious and impatient interpreters need to be reminded again and again of Bishop Butler's sober reasoning concerning " our incapacity of judging what were to be expected in a revelation;" and our ignorance as to "whether the scheme would be revealed at once, or unfolded gradually."* But, though we are not competent judges beforehand of what course revelation ought to take (as some theories of inspiration dictate the terms of revelation), after the revelation has followed a particular method of development, we may discover some very probable reasons for its procedure. We can readily conceive some very good reasons why this truth of personal immortality should not have been pressed to the front in the Mosaic age. It was a hope overgrown with the ritual of

---

* Analogy, P. II. Chap. iii.

Egypt, and it was imperatively necessary for the whole future development of religion in Israel that the chosen people should be cut loose from every vestige of Egyptian superstition. Had Moses inscribed the word "Immortality" upon the ark of the covenant, the people very probably might have remembered "Osiris," rather than have feared Jehovah. The first duty of the hour was to separate from this world "a holy people," and consequently any truth associated with idolatry it may have been necessary to leave alone for a season. Besides, an earthly society was first to be raised up and secured as the firm historical basis for all subsequent revelation; and in order that the forces necessary to the consolidation of a peculiar people might have free play, it may have been necessary to keep at first other-world motives in reserve. Nor should it be forgotten that other spiritual truths of religion are first in order before the hope of personal existence after death can spontaneously blossom forth. The sense of the living God, of personal communion with him, and of fulness of life only in the presence and favor of God, must be gained before a worthy and exalting hope of immortality can spring up. Almost in proportion as the psalmists of Israel attain this sense of living with God, do they rise to the joy of the hope of living forever. (Ps. xvi., lxxiii. 23 seq.) And, at last, immortality is brought to light only through One who shows disciples the Father, and leaves them in the communion of the Spirit. The Bible, beginning with the fundamental truths of spiritual religion, ends in an apocalypse. We, certainly, who behold the glory of the finished temple, have no reason to complain of the Providence that has left some darkly-lighted passages, and chilling shadows, in the crypt.

These illustrations of the progress of doctrine in the Bible, in conformity with the requirements of a divine method of human education, are doubtless sufficient to give us a broader idea of what revelation is, than is commonly entertained.* The Bible is a living book. There is movement and life in it. Ideas grow in it. Truths blossom out, and come to their maturity in it. The purpose of love ripens, and bears at last its perfect fruit, in this sacred history. The Bible is not a

---

* I have passed over several illustrations of this educational advance of revelation, hand in hand with the history, which might be easily gathered, as, *e.g.*, the development of the doctrine of angels, and of the Satanic power ; and, also the growth of the idea or habit of prayer, and the new light gained for the whole conception of spiritual religion by the prophets of the exile. The educational office and work of the types of the Old Dispensation, ought not to be forgotten in this connection ; but their proper consideration would require more space than can be allotted here to an illustration of our general principle.

mere repository of the words of God, a receptacle of doctrines, like an apothecary's shop stored with the essences and abstractions of the products of nature, all labelled and ready for use, according to some favorite prescription. The Bible is not an abstract of useful doctrines to be administered by rule; it is rather, like nature, full of mystery, and full of life. We can follow, as it were, the whole course of the seasons through it—the springtime, the early days of promise, the time of sowing, and the times of waiting; the days when the growth seems checked, when the tares an enemy hath sown multiply; the dark days and the stormy, the hours of hurricane and desolation, as well as the days of blossoming and song;—and through all its changes, through the long succession of its ages, are to be discovered the steady advance and working out of one purpose, and the sure coming of the harvest. And, like the growth of nature, this progressive course of revelation, the gradual unfolding of its seed-truths, and the final and glorious fulfillment of its promise, are phenomena which imply the operation of higher laws, and greater forces, than the acts or the thoughts of the laborers who ploughed in hope, and scattered the seed, and looked forward, with prophetic expectation, to the harvest at the end of time.

The view which we have gained of the process of revelation lifts us at once out of many other moral difficulties which are often popularly urged against the authority of revelation, and which sometimes vex the hearts of believers. We need hardly follow them here farther into their details. The faults of the Old Testament are, as Herder said, the faults of the pupil, not of the teacher. They are the necessary incidents of a course of moral education; they are the unavoidable limitations of a partial and progressive revelation. If God chooses to enter upon a historic course of revelation, then that revelation must be accommodated to the necessities, and limited by the capacities, mental and moral, of each successive age. Otherwise, revelation would be a wild, destructive power—a flood sweeping everything away, and not the river of life. We cannot suppose that the Almighty can pour the Mississippi River into the banks of a mountain-brook. He can begin, however, with the springs and the brooks, and make in time the broad Mississippi River. We cannot expect God to pour the full Christian era into the limited moral experience of the patriarchal age. He may begin, however, with the first welling up of truth in far-off times, to prepare for the Christian era. He will not, by a too early flood, wash away the very possibility of an enlarging revelation. His stream keeps within its banks; his revelation never breaks through the appointed limits of a great historical influence. But this patience of the divine Teacher with man's slowly maturing capacity for instruction, this self-restraint of revelation, is itself the sign of a higher wisdom. It would have been like us to have hurried an Elijah on into a John the Baptist; to have spoiled Moses by making him into a Paul; we should have had no place or patience for the conservative life and the partial truth of an apostle like James, between Judaism and a full-grown Christianity. But with the Divine Instructor a thousand years are as one day. His unit of time is not the short axis of a revolving world, and his good providence puts no blessing in peril by unseemly haste. These very limitations, imperfections, and moral deficiencies of particular stages of revelation, so often alleged against the Bible, are among the signs which cannot be counterfeited of God's handwriting in it. The same powers of development, the same law of evolution, seem to have been followed, alike, in nature and in the Bible. The Koran is like a world made all at once, in the six literal days of some theologians. The Bible resembles a world that has been long in growing, and which may well be pronounced good when it is done.

In general, then, it may be remarked of many moral difficulties accompanying a progressive revelation, which our limits will not permit us to consider more specifically, that an earnest, true, moral purpose must use, at one stage of history, at some points in its progress, a certain roughness of procedure, a severity, at least, of judgment, which would neither be necessary nor allowable at another time, or in a more advanced era. Into the great mass of human ignorance and idolatry, God causes, in the call of Abraham, the sharp edge of his good purpose to enter; hard blows must be dealt to drive that thickening wedge in; and providence is too divinely in earnest, in its work of driving that wedge of Hebrew history into the tough resistance of mankind, to spare, when needed, strong, sharp, decisive strokes. Many vigorous providences were necessary and right in the divine order of history, as were the blows of the pioneer's axe and the smoke of his fires, when the forests were to be cleared and the wilderness made habitable. Moses and the judges, and the prophets, even, were God's chosen pioneers; and theirs was the rough, hard work of history. How much suffering and hardship does not nature relentlessly compel in the pioneer age! The necessities of the times determine the rights and the truths which must be made paramount and commanding. Thus, the right of the individual to life is an undeniable principle of morality; but, at times, the right of a race to its redemption may be more sacred. The rights of every individual Ammonite and Canaanite, slain by the children of Israel in execution of a divine mission, a just God cannot in the final judgment despise; but the right of the world to the coming of the kingdom of righteousness and peace may, at any particular crisis of history, outweigh all consideration of individuals in the scale of a just providence. Moreover, it should not be forgotten that the individual, who for the moment may be sacrificed for the good of the whole, has himself an immortality, in which the very good for which he was destroyed may return upon him in blessing. The stern, temporal measures sanctioned in the earlier stages of the Bible cannot be fairly judged except in the light of immortality thrown upon all the inequalities of human life by the finished Bible. Indeed, the very conception of a divine education of the race requires for its completion the thought of a future in which the final blessing shall be imparted to all who have passed away before its coming. All who at any stage of the process contributed to the result, or who have been, under temporal exigencies, severely used by the course of Providence, have their recompense in the final issue. Hence, we are never envious of the future, of coming days of greater good, because the future, too, as well as the past, is for all who fulfil aright their present part. The end of the world-age is for all the generations of man.*

Thus the revelator sees the kings of the earth bringing the honor and glory of the nations into the gate of the celestial city. The end of time is the blessing of that Messianic kingdom of which all the ages are the heirs. One would need, therefore, a view comprehensive both of the past and its exigencies, and the future and the final good, before one would be qualified to sit in judgment upon the public justice of Jehovah. The fact of history which does lie within our comprehension, is the fact that through it, and especially by means of the chosen people, a great moral purpose of human redemption has been pushed steadily forward, and with the stern mercy, at times, of nature's own laws of development.

We have thus far taken no notice of the

---

* See Lotze : Mikrokosmus, iii., pp. 50–53. The difference between this philosophy of history as a real working out of good—a process of human education whose fruits shall be at last for all generations—and the emptiness of the Hegelian thought-process, or any purely idealistic conception, is at once apparent.

significant fact that it is to the Bible itself we owe our own power of judging the Bible. The hard places in the Old Testament are revealed by the increasing light of the Bible itself. The Bible is its own commentary and corrective. When that which is perfect is come, that which is in part of itself falls away from the divine law. This very fact that we are able to judge the imperfections of the Old Dispensation by a more advanced standard, shows how effectually through all those ages of patient education the Spirit of Truth has pursued its work. The conclusive logic of facts shows that the divine policy of revelation has been successful. The real morality of the Bible is its final morality, the morality in the intention of the Lawgiver from the beginning.* The divineness of the whole process is evident from the very fact that it has taken place. Other nations "ended as they began;" no other ancient system of law and religion had in itself a principle of development, a constructive force, the power of passing on to perfection. In its very *evolution* we have a sign of the supernatural life in the religion of Israel. There is the continuity of a divine purpose here.

One other remarkable feature of the Bible,

---

* See Mozley's fine lecture on "The End the Test of a Progressive Revelation."

throughout, which indicates the continuous purpose and wisdom of a Divine Teacher in it, remains to be more distinctly noticed. Our view of the educational worth, and the pedagogical purport of Scripture, would be incomplete, did we not at least point out this characteristic in passing. We refer to the limits of the extent of revelation. The silence of Scripture is often one of the most superhuman characteristics of it. Not only, as we have shown, was the Bible, in the process of its formation from age to age, adapted to the receptive capacity of those to whom the word of God came—the commandment, as Augustine finely said, being in accordance with the heart of him to whom it was given—but also the Bible as a whole, in what it reveals and in what it does not reveal, is adjusted to the limits of the powers, and the moral necessities, of mankind. The light of revelation seems adapted to the eye of the human understanding in a manner so remarkable as to indicate a higher wisdom as the author of both. False prophets never know where to stop. Mahomet and Swedenborg know too much. But something seems to have laid a restraint upon prophets and apostles, and to have sobered them even in the midst of supernal revelations. There is a more than human wisdom in the silence of the Bible. It is divine as the silence of nature. Of the being and purposes of God, of the unseen world and its retributions, enough is revealed to us for the motives and duties of the present life ; but little or nothing to gratify curiosity. There is enough of both Heaven and Hell revealed for all practical purposes now, but nothing for merely imaginative or speculative uses. Revelation is limited by the moral ends of a system of education and trial; and in that adaptation of it appears again the thoughtful provision of the schoolmaster. Everything here seems to be fitted up to make this world a scene of discipline and moral education for us. Life is a school, we say, and from it only the suicide can play truant. A genuine message, then, from the author of nature might be expected to conform to the disciplinary or pedagogical purport of the present system of things. Precisely such a revelation we find the Bible as a whole to be. It is fitted wisely to the purpose of forming *character*. It is a revelation clear enough to render faith possible, and obscure enough to leave unbelief possible. It affords thus a trial or test of character. It searches the heart. Too bright as well as too dark a revelation might defeat the very end of revelation. It would bring the educational and probationary period of life to a close ; it would bring on the day of judgment. The very difficulties and limitations of revelation are adapted, also, to the conditions of moral growth. It requires, and it repays, toil. It tasks, and tries, and puzzles, and strengthens faith. It is like man to make everything regular, easy, and plain; but that is not like the God of nature, of history, or of the Bible. A revelation in which the way never could be missed; a revelation made level and smooth to our feet, would be like the work of man, but not like the builder of the mountains. Were there no Alps for men to climb; no ocean depths beneath the plummet's reach; no stars still unresolved; no Scylla and Charybdis waiting to catch up the unskilful voyager; no burdens of toil and sorrow laid upon our manhood; if this life were only the play of children, and all the days were sunshine: then, indeed, might we expect to find a Bible without difficulties; a Gospel without parables; a kingdom of truth without tasks for the athlete, and without rewards for the victor. But the God of nature, of history, and of the Bible, surely does not intend to people his heaven with a race of moral imbeciles. "To him that overcometh," is the promise—seven times repeated—of the crown of life.

Our whole discussion, then, of the morality of the Bible, is summed up in the conclusion that the development of the Bible has followed a beneficent moral purpose. We have given reasons for the belief, that in its growth, its historical influence, its unfolding of truth, and its limitations, the Bible follows the moral order of the God of history; flows with his purpose, and works out his design of redemption. The whole moral development of revelation, often against nature, across the grain of Israel, and in spite of all opposing forces, is to us an evidence of a higher than a merely natural revelation; it bears witness of a supernatural course of history.

CHAPTER IV.

THE GROWTH OF KNOWLEDGE AND SCIENTIFIC TENDENCY OF THE BIBLE.

But does not our conclusion leap too lightly over the scientific difficulties which have been heaped up against the Bible? How could a God of truth, it is asked, inspire a revelation which did not give the world a proper science of the creation, or, at least, which taught a very imperfect scientific conception of things? Moses should have had Herbert Spencer at his elbow, to have been an infallible guide to the laws of the creation; and the prophets would have been improved by a scientific course in connection with their theological schooling. If God's object had been to give, ready made, an infallible book containing, without error, all truth which man can know; Moses and the prophets, certainly, needed an enlightenment which they never received; and their inspiration has failed to give us a perfect and systematic epitome of the universe in our Bibles. We do not care to argue, however, concerning an imaginary

Bible. Our concern is to discover what God has done. The same broad, historical method of studying revelation which we applied in the last chapter to its moral contents and intention, we have now to apply to the scientific teaching and tendency of the Bible. Did the course of revelation, as we can trace it through the Bible, lend its impulse to, and help on, man's progress in knowledge, as it plainly has his growth in virtue? Does the Bible form, thus, on its scientific side, as well as its moral, a well-fitted part of the whole plan of a benevolent God for the education and redemption of the world? We have to do with a greater question than the interpretation or meaning of any single passage of Scripture. We are seeking for the main current of the stream, and its real direction; and we are not much concerned with the momentary whirls or eddies. We have to determine, in their relation to the growth of man in knowledge, the real tendency and the final outcome of revelation. We must weigh carefully the influence of successive Scriptures upon the science of their own times, as well as estimate fairly the proper relation of the finished Bible to subsequent scientific progress, and the position of the whole revelation toward the result of modern investigations. But to put the question in this way—the fair and reverent way of stating it—lifts us at once out of much controversial literature, and opens a larger and more fruitful field of inquiry than religious and scientific controversialists usually enter.

We must bear in mind the caution already given (p. 32), as we attempt this inquiry. While it is true that our interpretations of Scripture may be traditional, it is also true that much science is still only presumptive knowledge. Some theories advanced by competent scientists remind us of the dotted lines on our maps, where it is expected railroads will soon be laid, or existing lines will be prolonged. Time may see them completed; and it may see them built with important deviations from the projected course.

Our larger question with regard to the Bible and science involves two distinct inquiries; first, What are the historical facts as to the scientific teachings and tendencies of the Bible? and, secondly, How do these facts agree with God's method of human education, and the progress of man in knowledge up to the present conclusions of modern science? It will be convenient for us, however, and will prevent needless repetition, to blend these questions somewhat in the course of our reasoning, and to bring them both out together in our conclusion.

We notice, at the outset, one general characteristic of the biblical revelation, which has not had justice done it by many who reject, at first sight, the Mosaic account of the creation. The fact is that the Bible had in the beginning, and preserved throughout its whole development, one great scientific virtue. The biblical view of nature is singularly free from the mythological and superstitious conceptions of nature prevalent in antiquity. It is kept, in this respect, from one fatal defect of other early religious literature. It possesses, from the start, a virtue which made it capable of growth. The multitudinous personifications of other primitive religious traditions, and sacred hymns, are not to be found in the book of Genesis. Here is a variation from the prevailing type of religious tradition; here is a *specific* mark upon our Bible, at its earliest appearance, which we are at a loss to explain when we consider the historical environment amid which it sprang up. We have here a literary phenomenon certainly as remarkable, not to say miraculous, as would have been the appearance of man walking erect among the creeping things of the Mesozoic period. The contrast between the Chaldean Genesis, and our Genesis, is as marked as the difference between the " Miltonic conception," and Prof. Huxley's " American Addresses." The one could not have been the natural parent of the other. Prof. Smith's "Chaldean Genesis" is sufficient to represent the historical environment of the biblical tradition. It enables us to reproduce the historical conditions, in the midst of which the patriarchal interpretation of nature, preserved in our Bible, was born and grew up. But while these Assyrian tablets lend valuable historical confirmation, at some points, to the Scriptural tradition, and cast a useful crosslight over the Book of Genesis; and while they bear traces of their own descent from some purer and more ancient source; still, in a scientific point of view, they are as remote from the simplicity of the biblical conception of nature, as the science of our day is beyond the discussions in natural history which Plutarch used to carry on with his friends.

But, if Abraham did not bring this pure song of the Creation from the mythology of Ur of the Chaldees, may not Moses have found it in the wisdom of the Egyptians? But here, also, the contrasts go deeper than the resemblances. The study of Egyptology indeed, seems to be an inquiry in which the best scholars may find their judgments confused, and widely varying estimates of intervals of time, as well as of the nature of great dynasties, are entertained; as travellers often find their sense of distance deceptive in the peculiar air, and across the dry sands, of the Egyptian deserts. Enough, however, has been measured, with some degree of historical accuracy, by Egyptologists, to enable us to judge how great was the divergence of the monotheism of the Pentateuch, not only from the popular idolatry of the Egyptians, but also from the shadowy belief in the unity of the Godhead, which lay in the wisdom of the priests behind the polytheistic worship of the people. Ewald is of the opinion that the Egyptian culture must ultimately have repelled rather than attracted Moses.* Even the rationalistic Kuenen decidedly rejects the possibility of an Egyptian origin for the Javehism of Moses.†

The striking contrast between Moses and

---

* History of Israel, ii., pp. 55, 56.
† Religion of Israel, vol. i., pp. 276-78. " His one God stood outside of nature, as its creator and Lord ; not so the deity of the Egyptian priests, etc." Brugsch-Bei (Geschichte Aegyptens, s. 25) inclines to the opinion that Moses' doctrines were formed after the models of Egyptian wise men ; but, *per contra*, he also states (Ibid., pp. 551-52), that the influence of the Semitic-Asiatic hostages and captives made itself ever more predominant in the conception of God, custom, and speech, of Egypt. " The young Egyptian world, overshadowed by the traditions of centuries of a long-vanished past, found, to its taste, the fresh living power of the Semitic spirit, to which another far more attractive idea of the world gave a direction forward." Compare, also, R. Stuart-Poole, Contemporary Review, March, 1879, p. 757 : " The documents on both sides, do not, however, warrant the supposition that Hebrew monotheism had its origin in this esoteric Egyptian conception."

the magicians of Pharaoh, as portrayed in
the Book of Exodus, we must admit to be a
true historical picture of the opposition between two religions. We have then, in the
biblical account of the creation, a tradition
maintaining itself, and its own purity, against
its immediate historical surroundings. Whatever may have been its source, in its continuous contrast with the nature-worship and mythologies through which it flowed, it is singularly pure and refreshing. Its scientific virtue,
in comparison with the literature of its own
age, deserves prominent mention in any fair
judgment of the relation of the Bible to science.
One illustration of this scientific freedom of
the earliest Scriptures from the superstitious
conceptions of the powers of nature, universally prevalent in primitive ages, may be drawn
from its teaching with regard to the atmosphere and atmospheric phenomena. Principal Dawson, who has noticed this peculiarity
of our Genesis, justly remarks that "the
greatest gods of all the ancient nations are
weather gods, rulers of the atmospheric heavens;"* and Max Müller has made us familiar with the ancient habit of using the
more striking phenomena of the sky to sym-
bolize the religious sentiments of the Aryan

* Origin of the World, p. 171.

race. The disposition to deify the elemental forces is to be traced through all the "wild grown religions." But this thoroughly unscientific and superstitious tendency of the Gentile religions was resisted by the course of revelation from the beginning; and the mythologies of the air never became a permanent part of the Scriptures of Israel. The Bible never became hopelessly involved in this course of superstition; never in its poetry, even, became entangled in that glittering mythology in whose attractive, but fatal, meshes the religious spirit, and the poetic genius, of antiquity were caught and bound. The very names for God, which one after another became fixed in Israel, and which mark the rising tides of its deep religious experience, are not the names for objects in nature, like the many names for the Deity in the Egyptian worship, or the endless personifications of the Vedas. To the Hebrew poets and prophets, even the winds of heaven are sent forth by Jehovah to do his will; and they see everywhere, and in all the changing elements, the presence and law of One living and supreme Power. As revelation is free, throughout its course in Israel, from the natural tendency of man to personify and deify external objects, and elemental forces, so, also, no traces can be found in the Hebrew Scriptures of that later scientific superstition signified by the very word "Nature," under which we group all second causes, and which we sometimes use as though it were not a mere name, or symbol, but a real existence, or cause. We are not raising, at this point, the question as to the presence of historical legends in the Old Testament; but we insist that the comparative and well-preserved purity of the Bible from the mythological view of nature is a primary scientific virtue, and that revelation furnished in this respect one of the first conditions of scientific education.* If we may suppose the existence of a Divine Instructor whose intention it was in the course of time to open to the knowledge of man the secrets of the earth, and to educate the world at length into a thorough conception of the order of

---

* The account of the serpent (Gen. iii.) may be cited as mythological, and we do not forget that the negative critics find occasionally other signs of the growth of nature-myths in the Old Testament. We are not careful, however, to examine these alleged mythical passages at length, inasmuch as, even if we should yield far more than we believe a sober criticism can allow, our argument above would still hold good. The singular comparative freedom from mythology (not to say absolute freedom) is a most original characteristic of the Bible. Tayler Lewis's Six Days of Creation, Chaps. 23 and 24, argues forcibly the difference between the Mosaic Cosmogony and all mythical accounts of the creation—and the considerations he presents are not yet out of date. So Herder said, " How does this picture of creation so singularly distinguish itself above all the fables and traditions of Upper Asia? By connection, simplicity, and truth. . . . I thank the philosopher, therefore, for this bold amputation of monstrous ancient fables." (Gesch. der Menschheit, x., Chap. 6.)

nature; then we may say that he gave one of the first conditions of that knowledge, and provided one of the necessary preparations for that future education, by freeing the mind of man from subjection to the powers of nature, and setting the human soul above the world, as itself made in the divine image, and, in short, by first drilling patiently the human reason and heart into those pure monotheistic conceptions which distinguish the religion of the Bible. The cruel bondage of this world over the heart of man must be broken, before science can possess, undisturbed, its proper field. The world must be disenchanted by a higher faith before the age of science can dawn. And exactly this necessary work for the coming of the era of knowledge was begun by Moses and the prophets. Indeed the law-giver, the prophets, the poets, of Israel, stood in days of idolatry nearer the fountains of a pure science, and in their descriptions of natural phenomena observed far better what Prof. Tyndall calls the laws of the scientific imagination, than did the wise men of Egypt with their incantations, or Homer and Virgil with their stories of the gods, or even Dante and Milton with their classic mythology, or the whole brood of the frivolous court-poets and freethinkers hatched out in the artificial heats of the eighteenth century.

But the objection already may have occurred, as we press the scientific value of the preliminary work accomplished for human education by revelation,—" Did not the prophets of old believe in miracles, in the possibility of the sun standing still, in all manner of supernatural appearances?" Whether miracles have, or have not, their appointed place and day of power in the natural order and course of things, we need not at this point discuss; for it is enough for our present argument merely to affirm that, whatever may have been the Hebrew view of possible interpositions by the hand of the Lord, they admitted no power in nature save the One Divine Will, and regarded the creation as the orderly work of the divine hand; so that their admission of the supernatural did not, at least in their view of things, destroy, but, on the contrary, tended to fix and to confirm their belief in one all-pervading law, and one all-comprehensive order and kingdom of the Lord God Almighty; and that faith kept their interpretations of nature and history comparatively free from confusing and debasing superstitions. The fact that revelation caused in any way the idea of law and order and unity in the creation to rise as a majestic conception before men in an early mythological age, is the scientific merit of the Scriptures to be observed and emphasized. It certainly helped man to a better knowledge of nature. So far from hindering, it advanced the scientific education of the world. In Jerusalem itself appeared the first wise man of antiquity, of whom we have any knowledge, who made a descriptive catalogue of natural history; and his religion, and religious training, were no obstacle, but rather an impulse to him, in his scientific labor. The fear of the Lord, exorcising the world of its many gods, was to the wise man the beginning of his knowledge of natural history. It is true that in modern history the scientific age has been long in coming. But it was not the rod of Moses, or the staff of the prophet, that held it back. Nay, Moses and the prophets themselves must wait in modern history for the day of their true understanding and right use. The middle ages had their own providential calling and work. Much barbaric ore was to be broken up and fused, by the power of the Roman Church, before the modern nation and the age of freedom could emerge. Only, we cannot charge the long delay to the account of Moses. If the providential necessities of the middle ages had permitted the open habit of mind toward nature cherished by the prophets, and their consuming zeal against every form of superstition, to come to their rights in Rome, modern science might have been several hundred years older than it is. Moses might, indeed, have been wroth against a pagan and superstitious art. Elijah might have called down fire from heaven upon a corrupt Pope; but neither Hebrew lawgiver, nor prophet, would have forbidden Galileo to search the heavens which declare God's glory, or have bound the commandments of the Lord as fetters around the advancing feet of that knowledge which, in the latter days, they expected should be increased when many should run to and fro.*

This view of the real tendency of the Bible toward an enlarging knowledge, and in favor of a growing science, is confirmed by another general characteristic of the Scriptures which has not usually had justice done it by writers upon the warfare of science and religion. We find that the inspired writers possessed, in a surprising degree, a second essential scientific habit of mind—that of accurate observation of natural phenomena. The absence of superstitious fear gave them calmness and repose of mind in the midst of great natural phenomena. Their belief in the One God saved them from fear in view of the more terrible aspects of nature. They did not tremble before a host of nature-gods, and so they could become good

---

* Daniel, xii. 4.

observers. This primary scientific virtue of optical accuracy distinguishes the Old Testament from all other literature contemporaneous with it. The Oriental mind is not naturally exact; it abounds in extravagance of metaphor, and luxuriates in dreams. But, where in the Bible can a fanciful line of poetic description be found? Job, in his loftiest imagery, indulges in no extravagant characterization of nature. The laws of the scientific imagination are obeyed in these inspired Scriptures. One marked and frequently recurring feature of Hebrew poetry, as Principal Dawson has observed, is its sobriety and optical accuracy.* The present Professor of Poetry at Oxford asserts only what a comparison of the early religious writings of mankind would abundantly prove, when he says: "The accuracy of the Bible descriptions of these things is quite unexampled in other literature." † In this respect there has been an immense amount of hasty injustice done to the Bible. We have been too ready to take it for granted that the descriptive language of the Bible was accommodated to the erroneous conceptions of natural objects common in classical speech. "Will it be believed," says Principal Dawson,‡

---

* Origin of the World, p. 59, seq.
† Shairp: Poetic Interpretation of Nature, p. 140.
‡ Ibid., p. 62.

"that, with the exception of the poetical phrase, 'windows of heaven,' and the common forms of speech relating to sunrise and sunset, these instances of accommodation have no foundation whatever in the language of Scripture. It is said that among modern poets William Wordsworth has made not a single mistake in the description of natural objects. When we reflect how far astray from nature literature is apt to wander; how far from the simple truth of things poetry often has departed; the accuracy and natural realism of the Old Testament descriptions present a marked literary phenomenon; and some cause of it must be sought in the peculiar training of the chosen people. Here, also, amid the maze of idolatrous myths, we may find a thread by which we may be led to the truth of a self-revealing God in Israel, whose inspiration made the Hebrew poets truthful to a rare degree when they looked upon his works.

These more general reflections concerning the scientific influence and worth of the Bible, as estimated from an educational point of view, may enable us to approach, in a truer spirit, that particular passage of Scripture which, it is claimed, has been dethroned by modern science—the first chapter of Genesis. We have to view that chapter in the same historical light, and to inquire what was its fit-ness for the work given it by the Divine Teacher to do, and how successfully has it accomplished that work. Was it by its nature and scope, its position and limitations, a true opening lesson, a wise first step in a course of revelation and education intended to be continued from age to age? It will readily be granted that in the opening chapter the keynote is struck of the whole biblical philosophy of nature. The elementary truths of the creation taught in it lie at the basis of the whole biblical interpretation of nature. If the poetry of the sacred Scripture is free from nature-myths, and the vision of the prophets undisturbed by the apparition of gods in the successive phenomena of nature, and if, consequently, the natural history of the Bible is remarkably truthful and accurate, when contrasted with the allegorical representations of other contemporaneous literature—like the uncouth forms, half animal and half human, the eagle-headed and scorpion-men, and other monstrosities of the Assyrian tablets;—then, the source of this singular scientific virtue of our Scriptures is to be traced back to that primeval theology of the creation which has been perpetuated in the first chapter of Genesis. The whole marvellously truthful, simple, and pure poetry of nature in the Bible flows from that ancient fountain, and is the continuation of that primitive conception of things. That much controverted chapter, therefore, should be studied in connection with the subsequent literature of which it is the source, and which is the best commentary upon it.

Our first task in any fair examination of the scientific worth and tendency of this primeval Scripture should be to determine what was its immediate object, and the point of view which the nature of the lesson to be taught led the writer to take. The first thing always to be done in criticising any work is to gain the author's point of view. A mind destitute of imaginative sympathy is not fitted to be a critic. The whole work to be reviewed may lie in confusion before us, if we cannot stand, in judging it, where its maker stood when he looked upon it and pronounced it good. For instance, to take the first example which occurs to me from recent literature, John Ruskin counts it among the good deeds of his life that he has done justice to the pine. But from the point of view of the botanist, or the nurseryman, what has Ruskin done for the pine? He has not classified it, or made any useful suggestions as to the proper way to transplant it, and make it grow in a nursery. The traveller, however, who has ever seen the Alpine pines, massed in dense regiments along the skirts of some mountain, and throwing a line of hardy skirmishers up some seemingly inaccessible height, will understand how Ruskin has done justice to the pines. Words that have no place in a botanical lecture may be read with delight along woodland paths, or among the hills. Everything, then, in understanding a sacred Scripture, depends upon our sympathy with the author's aim, and our capacity to look upon his vision again as he beheld it, with the same background, in the same surroundings, under the same light.

Reading, with this object in view, the first chapter of Genesis, and recalling the literature which sprang from it, we shall hardly be at a loss to discover its leading idea and intention. We detect at a glance, upon the surface of the narrative, signs of a mnemonic purpose.* It was evidently arranged on purpose to be remembered. The form of the narrative, and the succession of days, are adapted to this purpose. It was a first lesson made easy for the memory. It might readily be transmitted and preserved from father to son. How important, and determinative of its form, this necessity of suiting early teaching to the convenience of the memory must have been, we hardly realize in these days of books and printing-presses. A more elaborate descrip-

---

* See Rorison: Replies to Essays and Reviews.

tion of the creation, a more detailed and strictly scientific classification of the successive epochs, and the appearance of the different species in the earth's history, might have proved a too burdensome tradition; might easily have been broken into fragments in the process of transmission; might have defeated the very object for which a primitive age needed to preserve from father to son a simple, grand song of the creation. What the times did demand of the divine Teacher, was not a complete text-book of God's manifold works, but a good religious primer—a primer of the creation so clear and certain, and easy to be remembered, that a chosen people growing up in the midst of superstitions and idolatries, might understand it, and teach it to their children, and by its unmistakable meaning be saved from the confused and debasing ideas of the Creator and his works, into which men all around them were falling. Now no other people had such a religious and scientific primer as this. Indeed, it would be hardly possible for any scientific teacher at the present day to invent a more suitable form for introducing a child into some knowledge of the successive epochs of the formation of our world, than that actually hit upon in this ancient instruction—the very simple method of dividing the whole process into the great days of the creative week. With the child's advancing intelligence and capacity, this scheme of instruction, this nominal scale of the creation, would not have to be thrown aside, but only enlarged, and the details of the whole process taught. Compare this sacred primer of the creation with the traditions in the midst of which it was given and handed down, and it certainly is a very striking literary phenomenon. If we are not ready to adopt the old explanation of it that its author was inspired, we must, at least, admit that he had a wonderful genius for teaching. He was centuries in advance of his age. But the stern laws of heredity permit no genius to be born a century too soon. Even Shakespeare was unmistakably an Englishman of the sixteenth century. What, then, was the far-seeing Power, and whose was the inspiring Spirit, that gave to the childhood of the Hebrew nation this simple, pure, enduring story of the creation?—a lesson in the origin and growth of things so far in advance of its times, so comprehensive and true to man's growing knowledge, that not until a few years ago did men ever think of putting it aside, and that it remains, even to this day, an influence and power in the world's latest literature?

But, more specifically, besides this apparent

mnemonic purpose, the point of view occupied by the biblical account of the creation is distinctively religious. The primary object is to impress upon minds sadly in need of knowledge of the one God, a true, religious view of nature. So far as a natural history of the creation is called for by that paramount object, it is given; but the immediate and distinctive purpose is to bring out, and to bring out in an effective popular way, certain religious truths which are involved in the very make of things. The history of the rise and growth of worlds, of the great days, and the orderly succession of life upon the earth, is here followed by a religious eye, from a religious motive, and with a religious end in view. This is evident not only from the relation of this first lesson concerning God in nature to other teachings of the Scriptures which continue it, but also from the general purport of its contents, as well as from some particular points seized upon by the prophet's eye, and made prominent in his narrative. Thus we notice this significant fact that, in the description of the creation of animals, special mention is made of one only, and that one no more noticeable than many others from a naturalist's stand-point. "And God created great whales." The great whale of our version may refer to any amphibious monster, and it is

OBJECT OF THE FIRST LESSON. 149

very probable the mention of it would have carried the mind of an Israelite, in Moses' day, back to the animal worship, and particularly the worship of the sacred crocodile, prevalent in Egypt;* and so, by one stroke, the inspired seer sweeps away the whole idolatry of animal life, with which the Israelites had become familiar in the land of bondage. It may have been exceedingly important for him, as a religious man, to single out the creation of the sacred crocodile, though a naturalist, with a purely scientific object, might have given a different classification of living creatures. The paramount religious motive in the Mosaic account of the creation appears, also, in the emphasis laid upon the statement that the great lights were made for signs, and for seasons, and for days, and for years.† Many who have not stopped to gain Moses' point of view, have stumbled at this statement. To no one writing of the formation of the solar system from a purely astronomical motive, would it occur that the sun and the moon were made simply for earthly uses. But for five verses, in this brief account, the ministry of the great lights is made prominent by a teacher who knew how the Chaldeans studied

---

* See Speaker's Commentary, in loco. Also Dawson: Origin of World, p. 215.
† Compare, also, Jer. xxxi. 35 ; Ps. civ. 19.

the aspect of the stars, and how easily the heavenly luminaries might take the place of the glory of the Invisible God in the wondering eyes of men; and who meant, therefore, by this emphatic and repeated mention of the creation of the sun, and the moon, and the stars, and their earthly uses, to do away at once and forever, among his people, with that ancient and most natural form of idolatry, and to keep Israel true to the worship of the one Creator, who said, "Let there be light, and there was light." Judged, then, *historically*, or in view of the requirements of the times upon a religious teacher, all falls into order and becomes plain in this first great lesson given at the beginning of Israel's schooling into a true religious view of nature.

In consideration of this evident religious purport of the natural history of the Bible, it has often been said, but too loosely said, that it is not the office of a revelation to teach science; that we have no reason to expect the several Scriptures to be in advance of the scientific attainments of their day, and that the religious infallibility of the Bible is quite consistent with a multitude of sins against the truth of nature. These statements, however, need closer definition. We can conceive a progressive revelation from the God of Truth to be free, at any one point of its course, from the obligation of teaching science far in advance of the knowledge of men living at that particular time; but there is one scientific obligation which would seem to be incumbent upon revelation at every period of its development, and that is, the obligation of helping on the advance of the human mind in knowledge by its whole tenor and spirit; and this obligation involves a wise precaution and method in the accommodation of its teachings to human ignorance from time to time, so that the permissible and necessary adaptations of revelation to an early age may not become fixed as barriers in the way of progress in a later age. Providence cannot be expected to outrun its own work, and to violate its own benign law, which makes knowledge always the reward of labor; but, on the other hand, we should expect a providential revelation so to frame the first lessons of human childhood that the world, when come to age, would not have to unlearn them. While it was enough for Adam, or man, to begin by giving their names to things, if man was from the beginning under divine instruction, that first lesson and schooling in natural history should not stand in the way of subsequent science. We should expect, then, in a primitive revelation, imparted primarily for a religious purpose, that it would not teach a false scientific alphabet of things, and that its reflex influence, at least, all along would be helpful to growth in knowledge. We should expect to find in it the principle of its own correction; and its whole influence, if it came from the God of nature, would help on, rather than stand against, a growing knowledge of the mysteries of the creation. If it would be absurd to require the teacher of a child to explain the higher mathematics to a mind incapable of comprehending a simple algebraic equation, it should be required of the teacher of the elements that he should not introduce error into the multiplication table; that his instructions on any subject, and at any point of the course, though incomplete, and accommodated to the pupil's intelligence, should be so far truthful and *stimulative* as to set the child's mind moving on in the right direction. The moral, and spiritual, and natural, alphabet of things, first given by revelation, must be a truthful and helpful alphabet, though the whole language and literature of God's wonderful thought may belong largely to a higher course of education than this earth can possibly afford even to the wisest and the most advanced. Providence, in Moses' day, could have done little more with our physics and astronomy than a mother with her child in her lap, just beginning to talk, could find use for an "Unabridged Dictionary," with its definitions. When the good Providence which held humanity with all its hopes in its hand, began to teach the rudiments of that Divine wisdom which shall be the study of man forever,—that thoughtful and far-seeing Providence was content to teach the simple alphabet of nature first, and to put into one short chapter, which a child can commit to memory, the first truths of the creation, whose manifold wisdom the human mind is to contemplate through all generations, and to begin, perhaps, to comprehend after it shall have fully come to age in eternity.

The whole vexed question, then, of the scientific truthfulness of the Bible seems to us to reduce itself to simple inquiries like these: Is the scientific alphabet of the Bible good? Do the Scriptures teach the few first principles of nature so well that man has not been compelled to unlearn them in order to acquire the language of nature? Did the word of God, as it was spoken from age to age, work for man's enlarging knowledge of things? If so, the Bible fits admirably into the process of revelation, and is wisely adapted to the whole broad plan of the divine education of man. If, however, in any particular accent of its rudimentary scientific speech, the Bible fails of this test, and should give a false sound, there we may be sure we should hear the stammering voice of the pupil, and not the word of the Divine Teacher. But if, in the confusion of tongues, in the idolatrous ignorance of the nations, to one people was given the alphabet by which the heavens and earth are to be read; if a few leading words of the knowledge which in the latter days shall run to and fro over the earth were correctly spelled out; and if this elementary scientific training prevented this chosen people from corrupting the very first principles of any true knowledge of nature, and running into fetichism, and superstitions; then we have something in this peculiarity of it which at once arrests attention, and commands our admiration; and in proportion as we are unable to explain the rise and power of this remarkable virtue of the Bible from the conceivable conditions of the world's childhood, we have in it an indication of the working of a higher than human wisdom. And this is what we claim we do have in the science of the Bible. This is the great phenomenon which did appear in history in the Mosaic account of the creation. Such is the work for man's better knowledge of nature, the elementary and most necessary work for a true and ever enlarging science, which has been accomplished by the natural philosophy of the Bible. We do not deny that good men may often have taken divine accommodations to the weakness and ignorance of a past age, and thrown them as shackles around the advancing morality and knowledge of their own times. We do not deny that the Bible may be so abused as to be made an enemy of progress. But our concern at present is with the real scientific worth and tendency of the Bible, not with the work of the Roman Catholic Church, or with the untenable positions which an over-anxious Protestant apologetics from time to time may have assumed. We are content to affirm that the following elementary truths, which belong to the alphabet of nature, and are essential to all proper scientific speech, are to be found in our Scriptures; and the fact that they were put there, has proved a great help to man's growing understanding of nature.

The opening verse of the Bible gives the Alpha, the true first letter, of any real science of things. It declares, with no uncertain sound, the spiritual origin of all material phenomena: "In the beginning God created the heaven and the earth." Have we been compelled, by any advance of positive knowledge, to give up that teaching? What has our latest science to say to that Alpha of the biblical alphabet of nature? Herbert Spencer says there is an unknown Power, but that there never was a beginning of things; for "evolution negatives the supposition of a first organism."* Prof. Tyndall is confident that life never stirs within the glass cases of his experiments, in the Royal Academy, unless there is some life already there to stir; but, as a man of science, he does not pretend to say what was in the beginning. Haeckel, however, almost knows what was in the beginning, and is willing to teach all that he knows in the schools. In the beginning was an atom of homogeneous matter; and it stirred, and became different from itself; and it multiplied; and, behold, the earth, and its beauty, and its fruits, and man! The atom begins at last to think of spirit, and to dream of God! and thought, and conscience, and love, and God—the world and all things therein, the heavens and all their hosts—come forth in succession from this one homogeneous beginning, this all-comprehensive protoplasm; very much it seems to us wondering and unsophisticated spectators, as we have seen all imaginable things emerge from under the cover of a magician's sleeve! We forget, however; the magician is banished by this science;—but is not his magic after all only transferred to nature itself? Do not extremes meet here? Haeckel, with his monistic theory, and the old supernaturalist, with his creation out of noth-

---

* Biology, Appendix.

ing? Do not both unconsciously give a magical theory of nature? the only difference, after all, being that the one puts the magic outside, and the other puts it inside the creative process? The story is told of the singular feat of a Japanese magician, who "took a flowerpot, filled it with earth, put a seed in it, placed it on the table, and commenced fanning it. Soon the earth was broken, the plant appeared, and in a few minutes grew before the spectator's eyes into a bush, budded, blossomed, and the performer picked off the blossoms; and gave them to the spectators." So the supernaturalists, as our evolutionist of Haeckel's school might tell us, would have us believe the world was brought forth in a day by a Being who conjured it into existence. Science has banished the thought of a divine Magician. We are glad that it has; only we do not see what is gained, if the magic is taken from the magician and left in his pot. We have, on any hypothesis, the miracle of the creation, the great wonder of the world. If we attempt, with such scientific imagination as we can command, to realize Haeckel's visions of the past, and see just how the world grew, we confess we cannot help wondering what strange magic is concealed in the pot. We turn with relief to the simpler statement— which yields indeed no explanation, but which suggests no wand raised over the creation, or no occult art of transformation hidden within it, but which does leave reason resting at least on the idea of a sufficient cause—"In the beginning God created the heaven and the earth." What do we know, if anything, concerning the first cause, or necessary beginning, of material things? Do we know anything by which we may convict Moses' elementary lesson of falsehood? We have, in many respects, a far better knowledge of the secrets of the dim past than Moses, or the prophets, ever dreamed of possessing. We have opened the long-sealed records of the earth, and followed, step by step, its history through cycles upon cycles of ages before ever the mountains were brought forth; and traced, as we suppose, the slow growth of the present earth, teeming with life and fruitful civilizations, back to its beginning in a mass of nebulous light, thrown by some unknown Power into the midst of space. We have searched for the last principle of matter, until human ingenuity has attained a skill in measuring the infinitely small, the results of which human imagination utterly fails to follow. Science has pursued the molecules by its measurements until they have left, in which to conceal themselves, a space no larger than the five-hundred-millionth of an inch; a rise in temperature of the eighty-eight-hundredth of a degree centigrade has been detected; and, more amazing still! the presence of the hundred and eighty-millionth part of a grain of soda has been revealed by the spectroscope! And not content with this, we have sought to penetrate into the secret dwelling-place of thought, until, in a bit of brain-tissue which one might hold on the point of a needle, there have been disclosed wonderful groupings of cells, and lines of communicating fibres, which rival, in their adaptations and perfectness, the order and rhythm of the heavens. But the deeper into the secrets of nature we pierce, the farther back toward the beginning of the creation we penetrate, the nearer are we brought to the old mystery of a reality beyond all knowledge, before whose presence and power our imaginations must drop their last images of things, and reason must give place to faith. We feel our dependence upon the Infinite God around us. Faith is the sense of the pressure upon our being of the Infinite Being in whom we live. It is the beginning and end of reason. Science, searching for the origin of things, cannot find it in things themselves, and is compelled, after all its endeavors, to give the creation over to reason and conscience for its final interpretation. It knows nothing by which it can gainsay their assertion that on the other side of the atoms is God. Beyond the last conceivable subdivision of matter, beneath the last imaginable centre of force, is the One substance—the continuous, indivisible, omnipotent, spiritual ground of existence, the living God.

That we are not indulging in the mere assertions of the metaphysicians (though we cannot, if we would, silence the daily assertion by the spirit within us of its own nature) ; but that our latest science is incapable of detecting any false sound in the Mosaic speech of the Creator; it would not be difficult to prove from the often unconscious testimony of the most pronounced materialists. A short, and not unfair, method with the materialistic denial of spirit and God, would be to show the impossibility of becoming a materialist from the lives of the materialists themselves ; the impossibility of materialism from the writings of its believers; the impossibility of living, thinking, and writing at all, without confessing more than materialism means to confess. If physiological materialists should claim, in mitigation of their frequent unintended lapses into spiritual modes of expression, that the metaphysicians have so thoroughly saturated human language with their conceptions that the difficulty of avoiding them is not the fault, but the misfortune, of the new science; then, they are refuted again by their own principles. For, according to their own physiological laws, the metaphysicians have not made the brain dream of spirit and entity, but the brain has made the metaphysicians spin their endless discussions of supersensible things; and if the brain has dreamed a great historical dream of a spiritual life, and if matter still persists in thinking the philosopher's idle thoughts, and the physical organism compels language itself to enter into the service of the metaphysicians; then, surely, they are not to be blamed by the physiologists for following nature out to her spiritual conclusions.

Dr. Maudsley ought not to berate the metaphysicians so soundly for what, upon his own showing, is a purely physiological process. Let the brain, whose cells have worked together to produce the language of the soul, do its work over again, and to better purpose; let the brain, in its nineteenth century evolution, create, if it can, a language in which Dr. Maudsley can write a book on "Physiology of the Mind," in which the very words which he binds together in his sentences shall not, by their inherent meanings and inherited force, transmit more spiritual significance than he wishes to let into his conclusions;—a language which shall not at every turn, whether we will or no, send our thoughts off, far and wide, in contemplation of things unseen, things not dreamed of in the materialist's philosophy. Until materialists can make language work steadily in the traces of their logic, we cannot help being borne by their own words farther and wider than they would have us go. So impossible, indeed, is it for a thinker to be a materialist, even when fully determined to be one, that Dr. Maudsley—in a passage intended to be a conclusive illustration of the assumed fact that reasoning may be an organic process, a piece of mechanical brain-work; that a man, in short, might be as good a reasoning machine without as with consciousness—is obliged, in the very sentence in which he makes this assumption, to bring in the supposition of another instrument (besides the reasoning-machine) more delicate than the microscope, or the galvanoscope, as the means of "reading off the results of his cerebral operations from without."* He is obliged, that is, in order to conceive of man as a reasoning-machine, to fall back upon the subsidiary hypothesis of a "reading-machine;" though the brain be the agent, and does all the work, there must be, also, a reader, or witness, of its operations; though there is no such entity as

---

* Physiology of Mind, p. 26.

a thinking mind—and Dr. Maudsley is indignant at the absurd metaphysics which is still enamored by that old delusion—nevertheless, our determined materialist cannot get through with his own physiological reasoning without calling in the aid of something to witness his performance. We claim Dr. Maudsley as a metaphysician in spite of himself! Indeed, mere physical thinking is an impossibility of thought. Metaphysics, driven out of one window, flies back through another. Drop metaphysics from your substantive, and it insinuates itself into the adjective; expel it from the subject of a sentence, and it lies coiled up in the verb. Metaphysics even our mental physiologists find to be a ghost which will not down at their bidding. No man, while breathing the breath of life, has succeeded in being a materialist. To accomplish that feat he must first think in a vacuum—that is, stop thinking.

Not only do we find that would-be materialists cannot deny extra-physical facts, without at the same time implying their existence; but also, it is true, that to deny the spiritual origin of matter is in no way necessary to positive science, and the great body of scientific men are not fairly chargeable with materialistic extravagance. Thought, though baffled at many points, hard pressed and confused, ignorant of its own origin and destiny, is nevertheless not going to commit suicide in our day. The "Microcosm" of Lotze represents a modern spiritual philosophy which is on the flood, and which may yet pour its refreshing power over the English positivism. For the explanation of the very mechanism of things; for the possibility of their actions and reactions; for the origin and continuance of the very order of nature; Lotze is led to fall back upon the reality of a living spiritual Being and Omnipresence. The ultimate fact of the universe is not an atom, or a group of atoms, but that Unseen Presence by whom all things consist. The first and the last fact of human experience, is Intelligence and Will. Matter, pressed to the utmost, declares itself to be Force. Force, pressed to the utmost, declares itself to be Thought and Will. And Thought and Will, pressed to the utmost, declare that they are the breath of the Spirit of God. The Alpha and the Omega of human experience is Spirit. Our science, when it has held up the world to the most searching scrutiny, must drop it back again into the hand of the Almighty, from whence it came. Reason, following motion from star to star, and into the infinite past, cannot escape the necessity of looking beyond the bounds of the visible universe for the First Cause, which it always seeks, but never finds, within the limits of the seen. We can bring nothing, then, from the whole domain of knowledge to contradict the Mosaic vision of the spiritual origin of all created things. The prophet of old, so far as we can know, made no mistake in the first letter of his alphabet of nature. It enters into our latest and best speech of the creation. We cannot think without it. At the end of all our science, at the summit of all our philosophy, we stand to-day where, in the dim antiquity of an almost prehistoric age, one stood in the spirit of the Lord, and said: "In the beginning God created the heaven and the earth."

Secondly, the opening chapter of the Bible refers three existing phenomena directly to a spiritual cause. It selects three points in the creation as special points of divine activity. Other links in the chain of existence may be dependent upon these points, but these three are held up by the hand of God. These direct acts, or constant modes of divine activity, are, according to the Scriptural account of the origin of things, that divine act by which matter exists; that divine act by which life comes forth from the earth; and that divine act by which a human soul thinks and worships. The creation of the heaven and the earth (the matter of the universe endued with force); the springing up of life on the earth; and the birth of the soul of man, are the results of divine interpositions or words. God calls them forth—from what, or how, the Scripture does not presume to say.* The distinction between these initial acts, or more immediate points of divine efficiency, in the creation, and other intermediate stages of the creative process, is indicated in the Mosaic Genesis; but it is not defined, or explained, in the biblical philosophy of nature. The Bible does not take sides on the disputed question of the nature of vital force. It would be but the repetition of an old and mischievous error of over-zealous theologians, should we impute to Moses the intentional teaching of a specific vital force in his account of the supersensible origin of life. The one does not necessarily involve the other. One mistake Moses certainly did not make; he did not seek to determine, as spiritual truths, questions which are matters of scientific investigation. A positivist in theology, he was not a dogmatist in physics. Leaving the modern question concerning vital force untouched, the Mosaic account does commit itself, however, unhesitatingly to the assertion of the spiritual origin of matter, life, and soul. Other parts of the

---

* Notice the use of the strongest word for "to create" in verses 1, 21, and 27.

creation may follow of themselves, when these are once given; but these three, at least, come from without, are phenomena of supersensible origination; they are acts, or modes, of divine efficiency. The account of the creation in the book of Genesis, and the whole subsequent natural theology of the Bible, agree in regarding these three phenomena, at least, as made from something which does not appear. The Bible looks without nature for their origin and cause.

The pure monotheistic faith of the Hebrew prophets, indeed, is never careful to distinguish between first and second causes; and not only the elemental forces, but human actions are often referred directly to the will of the Lord. Life especially is always attributed to God—He is its author, and source. In the biblical doctrine we may say that these three form the ancient and sacred " trinity of the creation"— matter, life, and soul; they are the related and coexistent, but underived distinctions in the creation; each existing in and for the others; neither complete without the others; partaking of the same Divine creative principle, but each having its own distinction of being. We do not mean that this trinity of the creation lies as a doctrine fully formulated anywhere in the Bible; but that the biblical philosophy of nature can be legitimately reduced to this expression of it, and that in the Mosaic Genesis these three great, distinct, yet related, acts of the Creator are indicated. Moses is fairly responsible for this much of scientific teaching, that matter, life, and soul, are of extra-physical origination; that they come from without the present creation and are of God. Was he wrong in this elementary teaching? Are these letters of the biblical scientific alphabet to be superseded? Experience brings us daily before the mystery of this sacred trinity of the creation; but can scientific scrutiny either remove the mystery, or resolve this trinity of existence into any primal unity? Can we find anywhere within the bounds of the physical universe the cause, can we overtake anywhere in the endless transformations of energy the original force, from which these ever-present distinctions of being have proceeded? In order to avoid repetition, I reserve for a subsequent chapter —where in connection with the inquiry into the existence of an Unseen Universe these questions must be considered—the further justification of this primary lesson of the Bible in a scientific conception of nature. The biblical premises for a philosophy of nature have not yet, at least, been proved false or defective. Matter, in its present form, is not eternal; and life is, if anything is, a constant mode of the divine energy; and mind, on the lowest admissible hypothesis, is the supersensible side of matter—whatever Mr. Lewes may mean by that. Reduce matter, life, and mind, to the simplest possible scientific terms, and they still remain the unknown quantities of the equation by whose laws reason is to solve the problem of the universe; they are the original terms, given in the very statement of the problem, and their meaning and value are to be sought elsewhere than in the course of the equation itself. So Moses thought when he represented them as given by God. Science cannot forbid us from seeking for their real significance outside its own processes; and reason, and conscience, and our own spiritual sense, urge us to write before each one of these three original terms of the creation, what Moses of old wrote—God.

Thirdly, the Mosaic account suggests one other primary scientific truth. It reveals the fact of a continuous creative process; it implies a law of development in the creation. This world, according to the Bible, was not finished in a day; it was not thrown into existence ready made, and fitted up with all the modern improvements. It was a progressive work. These are the *generations*, or growths, of the heavens and the earth when they were created (Gen. ii. 4). Herbert

Spencer may have been misled by chance passages from the theologians, but he does not read his Bible to good purpose, when he satirizes the belief in a special creation as "a carpenter-like theory." Moses, in his vision, saw no Almighty hand building up the stories of the creation; he heard no sound of hammer, or confused noise of the workmen;—the spirit of the Lord moved upon the face of the deep; chaos took form and comeliness;—and before his inspired vision the solar system grew through a succession of days to its present order and beauty; and at last, when all things were ready, man came forth out of the dust. There is absolutely no warrant in Scripture for us to regard the world as an extemporized manufacture; on the contrary, the Bible lays from the beginning firm hold of a scientific principle, not grasped by other primitive traditions of the origin of things, viz., that there was an orderly process of creation, a continuous development of a creative purpose or law, some of the main steps and advances of which it sketches with graphic power. It gave details enough of this unfolding, creative purpose, to fix an orderly conception of it in the mind and memory of a primitive age. This distinguishing, and, for an unscientific age, singular virtue of the Mosaic Genesis ought to win for it the admiration, instead of the ungrateful and hasty rejection, of scientific lecturers. How happened it that amid the grotesque myths which were the current beliefs of antiquity, this one clear, authoritative assertion of creation by law sprang up and maintained itself in Israel? How happened it that the doctrine of an ascending order of life was put into the religious primer of Israel? How did it come to pass that a Jewish patriarch and lawgiver knew, to some extent, the fact of the orderly development, the "increasing differentiation," the progress from type to type, and to ever higher forms, of the creation? and that, too, centuries before the accumulated results of the laws of heredity in the brain of a Herbert Spencer had recorded themselves, through his physiological organization, and for the wonder of a late age, in his "First Principles?" If not more than a century or two ago some genius had grasped clearly the idea of evolution, and, in order to accommodate it to an unscientific ecclesiastical generation, and to plant it so that it might grow in the mind of his contemporaries, had hit upon the expedient of using a week, with its mornings and evenings, as the scale of time by which to set forth his speculations, and had filled up those days with tolerable geological accuracy, —that genius would have been more than a

Lucretius to our modern science—he would be venerated by Tyndall and Huxley as a thinker of the first magnitude! But some Jewish prophet was in some way enabled to do that in a remote antiquity ! Were the first chapter of Genesis some newly-discovered remnant of Arabic literature, or a hieroglyphic just deciphered from some Egyptian monument, it would be hailed as a remarkable anticipation of some of the chief results of modern science; and, even though it might be shown to be the writing of some priest, Dr. Draper would have exulted in it as a scientific trophy, and have found some way to show that religion suppressed it. Really, Moses ought to have a seat of honor in the scientific pantheon ! How happened it that this wonderful Mosaic conception of a growing world, an unfolding creative work, burst upon the mind of man at that early day, long before the knowledge of the Copernican system, long before man's acquaintance with fossil records, centuries even before the earth had been mapped, or measures of time or space, greater than a few leagues of an inland sea or a few generations of men, had become familiar? When the human mind, awaking with the whole world to question, was confused by a thousand nursery stories, and still wondered and dreamed like a child; what simpler, more impressive, and more easily-remembered scale and method for teaching the truths of a process of creation, and an orderly progress of it, could have been devised? Did it not occur in a book held to be sacred, would not Moses' creative week be regarded as a wonderful stroke of genius? Is not the wisdom of a Divine Teacher displayed in the method of the lesson?

But we may be interrupted with the question, Did not the method of the Mosaic teaching involve falsehood? has it not served to fix for centuries an erroneous idea of the origin of the world? It certainly has not kept a single erroneous idea in place after science was ready to become an authoritative teacher of the truth; and the "nominal scale" employed by revelation, as Herder aptly designates it, involved in itself no untruth, while it proved useful in fixing first truths necessary to the very beginnings of right knowledge. No science ever could have grown out of a Chaldean cosmology. As knowledge grows, the biblical philosophy of nature does not, when rightly interpreted, stand in the way of scientific truth. Indeed, from the educational point of view which we have all along taken, and which seems to us to be the proper historical point of view, the controversy which has been so hotly urged as to whether the days of

Genesis are literal days, or designations of vast æons of time, becomes a matter of very little importance. For the length of time occupied in the course of the creation was not the subject of this first lesson concerning the creation by God, and according to law. In either case, whether the word day is to be taken literally or largely, the divisions of time, the mornings and evenings, are only the scheme, so to speak, of the lesson—the method of the teaching. In neither case is the designation of time the end, or contents, of the instruction, but the means, or best available method, of the higher truths to be imparted. Definite information as to the lapse of time since the beginnings of the present system of things was not given, or so much as attempted, in the primary lesson of a true religious science. Here, also, we have another illustration of the patience of the Divine Teacher, of the self-restraint of revelation. One of the most difficult things for a child to do is to gain any idea of past duration. The Mosaic Genesis, with great sobriety, abstained from the imaginary conceptions of past duration which were attempted in other primitive traditions of the creation. Other cosmogonies, like that of the Hindoos, with their repeated circles of conjectural numbers, and their fabulous ages of imaginary gods, resemble the child's often absurd efforts to form some idea of the days before he was born. There are no incongruous guesses at time in our Genesis.* It is left indeterminate by a revelation intent on impressing upon the growing mind of man the first simple, essential truths of a religious view of the creation. Any adequate conception of past duration must be gained, if at all, by the practised scientific imagination. It is the wisdom of God not to teach a lesson which would only confuse and throw into foolish conceptions the imagination of man in his childhood. It is left for us, in our matured knowledge, to determine, if we can, how long the Mosaic days must have been. But we should not expect a divine Revelation to work a miracle in order to anticipate science, and to cram the brain of Adam with the knowledge of the Encyclopædia Britannica. The difficulty which our most brilliant scientific lecturers incur in the effort to make their immense generalizations popular, might teach us caution, lest we

---

* Contrast, with the sobriety and abstinence from guesswork of Genesis, the following scientific opinion of the much-lauded Lucretius:—" But, as I am of opinion, the whole of the world is of modern date, and recent in its origin ; and had its beginning but a short time ago. From which cause, also, some arts are but now being refined, and are even at present on the increase ; many improvements are in this age added to ships, &c. (B. v. 330). How happened Moses, with grand simplicity, to avoid all such labored scientific blundering ?

captiously require impossibilities of a primitive revelation.

It will not be necessary for us, therefore, from our educational point of view, to examine, at length, the reasons for or against the literal translation of the word day, in the Book of Genesis. It is sufficient to observe that the writer himself uses it with different significations, as a flexible word, in different places.* Why should we contend for, or regard as of any special significance, a word which the writer evidently regarded as of so little importance that he neither defines it, nor attaches to it any one constant meaning—a word, in fact, which he employs as a natural help, a flexible and convenient means, for imparting the higher truths with which he is concerned? If the word has since been fixed in theology, and made to bear the burden of a false science, that was not the mistake of Moses, but a limitation put upon revelation by the ignorance and perverseness of the human mind.

It is noticeable that the modern theological abuse of the Mosaic word day—so admirably chosen for its purpose—does not occur throughout the Bible itself. Revelation, that is, does not misinterpret itself, or use, so as to perpetuate false notions, its own accommoda-

---

* Compare verses 5, 8, and 14, and these with Genesis ii. 4.

tions to man's limited intelligence. Those passages of Scripture which are the later commentaries and expansions of this primeval Hebrew "Song of the Creation," contain no sign or trace of any six-day theory of the making of the world. On the contrary, the question as to the time-element involved in the creation was a question kept in the background of revelation; * it does not come to the front among the truths of God's power, law, and omnipresent efficiency, which occupy the foreground of revelation. It is a scientific question reserved for a scientific age, and we are still very much at sea with regard to it. The only important reference in the Bible to the days of the creative week occurs in the retrospective sanction of the commandment to keep the Sabbath holy; and there the reference is to the seven-fold division of time, and to the finished work at the end of the creative week, and not to the length of the day. But, while the time-element is nowhere made prominent in the Bible, we do find, growing and bearing fruit in the Hebrew literature, the grand primitive conceptions of the Divine power, and law, the Divine wisdom

---

* We may say, however, with Tayler Lewis, that in some passages of the Old Testament "there evidently is a laboring to set forth the immensely prolonged antiquities of the proceeding."

and order, manifest in God's many wonderful works.*

Thus far, then, we have found nothing in the great leading truths of revelation, or in the manner in which they were taught, and the providential order of their development, which brings us into conflict with established science. We find, rather, the alphabet of a true religious science, and the elements of a growing and helpful philosophy of nature. We find anticipations and hints of the coming wisdom, and a great impulse to a reverent but unsuperstitious study of the manifold works of the Creator. Since we have, in the Mosaic Genesis, a rapid and most suggestive sketch, for our religious use, of these few great outlines of God's creative work, we are not careful to answer concerning any mere question of detail. The fact that to some prophet of old such a panorama of the past was opened, the first principles of things disclosed, the order of the heavens and the great outlines of the vast drama of life revealed, is the fact which arrests our attention, and which compels the confession that the Spirit of God, and not the grovelling spirit of the age, inspired this grand prophetic vision of the creation. The

---

* A remarkable illustration of this appears in the one hundred and thirty-ninth Psalm, verses 13 to 18.

historical wonder to us is, not that the prophet did not see the succession of life with a naturalist's eye, but that days followed days at all in his vision; not that he did not fill in with minute exactness the details of the picture, but that he beheld so much as the outlines of God's ways in the creation, which we are not yet able to follow far with scientific precision. No more should be required of what is aptly called this prophecy of the past, than we are accustomed to demand of a prophecy of the future. We have no more good reason to suppose that Moses, or an older seer, saw or knew the particulars of his vision of the past so that he might have fixed each detail with a precise word, than we have to suppose that Isaiah, or Daniel, not only foresaw a general course and certain divinely ordained conclusions of history, but also knew the successive actors, the battles, the specific groupings of events, and the times and the seasons for each successive coming of the Son of man in history. They, at least, who regard the literalistic intepretations of the Second-Adventists as a confusion of the tongues of prophecy, ought not to apply their crass methods of exegesis to the sublime Mosaic prophecy of the past. The outlines of God's ways in the past or future, the leading truths and commanding principles of the Divine government, determine the scope and limits of revelation, whether of the beginning or the end of things. Providence makes no premature waste of its gifts of knowledge. It was necessary for Israel to know—it was necessary for the mission of Israel in the world that it should know—that in the beginning God was the Creator; that He is the author of life, and the Father of man's spirit; that His work was a work of order, and the execution of a divine plan; but it was not necessary for Israel to know the secrets of the depths of the earth, in order that it might be thoroughly furnished for its providential mission. The Creator has left many revelations of his glory latent in the nature of things until man shall need them, and then Providence brings them forth. Some are coming forth—coming like new words of the Eternal —in these latter days.

We are not anxious, then, from our educational view of the scientific side and tendency of the Bible, to enter into a particular comparison of the Mosaic account and the last geological table. They who are curious to learn the latest discrepancies and coincidences between geology and Genesis, can find the subject treated in detail in Principal Dawson's recent book on the "Origin of the World." Some of the coincidences which are to be found between the two, such as the Mosaic account of the existence of light before the creation of the sun, the comparatively late appearance of mammals on the earth, and the indication that the great geological periods were completed and the world given over to the operation of existing causes on the fourth day, would seem to be important confirmations of the truthfulness of the Mosaic account. Our chief hesitation, however, in resting the argument for revelation upon these anticipations of science in Genesis, is the reflection that neither Moses, nor our present science, may in these respects be infallible; and we have much still to learn concerning the order of the creation. These coincidences are indeed remarkable, and confirmatory of revelation; but neither the special agreements nor disagreements of the two records are to us the final and commanding considerations. The former are not necessary to, and the latter need not be inconsistent with, the educational work and progress of a revelation. Indeed, a caution is taught us here by the unconcern of the revelator himself with regard to the grouping of the particular parts of his vision; for he is not careful to follow in two connected verses his own arrangement of facts —in the twenty-fifth verse he does not copy the arrangement of animals just given in the twenty-fourth verse. Surely we have no right to demand even of an inspired writer an exactness which he does not profess to give; nor are we to test a revelation by truths with which it is not concerned.

Let us gather up, then, the separate threads of our reasoning in one conclusion. The biblical account of the creation meets the necessities of the elementary instruction of a race chosen from idolatrous surroundings to become the bearer of a divine Gospel to mankind. The teaching of the Bible, on its scientific side, is so free from superstition, so correct in its understanding of the alphabet of nature, so retentive in its grasp of the elementary truths of the creation—its spiritual origin, its unity, continuity, and divine order—that, altogether, it presents a unique literary phenomenon,—one which must have a cause, but whose cause does not appear in the conditions of the times, or the historical environment of the Bible. The simplest explanation of this literary wonder of antiquity (if upon other philosophical grounds we are not prevented from giving it) is, that some special divine providence was at the source of this marvellous life in Israel; that, in some manner provided for in his own laws, the God of history gave to the children of Adam these greatly needed rudimentary lessons; himself, in some of his many open ways of suggestion to the soul of man, taught the human reason these elementary truths of the creation. Instead, therefore, of assuming an apologetical or dogmatic attitude toward the science of the Bible, as though it were something for believers to stand up for against the apparent truths of nature, or else to drop quietly out of sight, we would advance the scientific tendency of the Bible, and its educational work, as a unique literary fact, which affords a strong presumption that the Bible was a special object of care on the part of the Divine Instructor. We see here significant evidence, when all things are fairly considered, that with one chosen race, selected for a special divine training for the ultimate blessing of the whole world, there was present from the beginning a higher than human wisdom, schooling it, bearing with it, educating it with divine forethought in those truths which man needed to learn by heart before he could be fitted to pass on to the toils, and responsibilities, and knowledge, of the ages to come.

We may feel some of us personally toward the first chapter of Genesis, in particular, very much as one might feel toward an old friend whom for a time he had come to suspect, and to wish out of sight, and from whom he grew all the more estranged by the indiscreet claims of others in his behalf; but whom at length he has learned to know better, and to take at his real worth, and has found after repeated trial to be a friend indeed. Cleared of false interpretations, relieved of the suspicions cast upon its truthfulness by imprudent defenders, known in its genuine worth, and prized for its really exceptional virtues and grand character, the Mosaic Genesis is found to have been all the while the firm, steadfast friend both of science and religion.

The moral progress of the religion of the Bible which we considered in the preceding chapter, and the scientific tendency of the Bible which we have just been estimating, taken together, indicate a great historical process of revelation. There seems to be a historical development of something which is not given by history itself. Within the natural, there are signs of a supernatural evolution. A divine life is in the world, working through history, and in a special and altogether unique manner in Israel, for far-off ends. We have seen, thus far, the signs of its workings; we have still to behold this divine power in its perfect historical manifestation, and to follow this supernatural evolution to its last and highest consummation.

CHAPTER V.

THE CULMINATION IN THE CHRIST: I. THE UNIQUENESS OF JESUS.

THE great surprise of human history was the coming of Jesus Christ. The uniqueness of his person is an ultimate fact of Christianity. Whoever would deny the presence of the divine power in human history must first reduce the character of Jesus of Nazareth to the level of the possibilities of common human nature. He is himself the greatest of his miracles. If by close historical scrutiny, or critical questioning, we fail to resolve the miraculous character of Jesus—the ultimate fact of Christianity—into the common, known elements of our human nature; if the laws of heredity prove insufficient to explain his generation; then, the further question will at once arise whether there may not be other than natural elements present in human history, which come to their perfect flower in Jesus of Nazareth; whether we may not find in the laws and the forces of a supernatural evolution the sufficient explanation of his miraculous person. If the appearance of Jesus is not natural in comparison with other lives; if the Christ of the Gospel seems to be a miraculous fact contrary to human experience; then, before we throw aside the historical evidences which centre in the uniqueness of his person, and flow from the originality of his life, we are at least bound to inquire whether there may not be a broader view of human history, and a deeper science of the creation, in which we may find revealed an unsuspected and larger naturalness in this greatest miracle of the ages—the personality of Jesus Christ.

We have, then, at this point of our application of the new idea of evolution to old faiths, to take into consideration, first, the uniqueness of Jesus, and then the perfect naturalness of the Christ as the fulfilment of the whole development of the creation.

The originality of Jesus appears the very moment we bring the narratives of the New Testament into juxtaposition with the known lines of previous history. There is an apparent break between the two. The former cannot, without historical violence, be bent into a mere continuation of the lines of the latter. A fresh start is made in Christianity, under a new impulse, in a changed direction. The portraiture of Jesus, as drawn by the Evangelists, does not seem to be that of a Jewish face, or a Gentile countenance; nor does it seem to combine the peculiar features of both in its own striking originality. A mere glance at the delineation in the Gospels awakens this feeling of surprise before Jesus of Nazareth. If, amid the ancestral pictures which hang upon the walls of some old English manor-house, and which betray the same noble lineage through many generations—the features of some far-off ancestor reappearing, perhaps, in the last portrait hung among those of the dead —we should notice a face unlike all before it, having eyes of southern fire, or beauty of another clime; we should at once conclude that the strange countenance represented some other line of descent; that its presence there could not be explained by the laws of heredity, working through the English blood; and that an altogether new element, at that point, had come into the family line. But in the world's gallery of illustrious persons, we find introduced, in the portraiture of the Evangelists, a countenance never seen before on earth. It is neither a Jewish nor a Gentile face; it resembles none before it; it is like itself alone. From whence did it come into the human family?

Looking at it with the closest scrutiny, we are unable to remove the first impression of strangeness which the portraiture of Jesus in the Gospels makes upon us. We cannot by any known law of heredity explain its origin as a possible Jewish face. There were elements in the life of Jesus which were not of Jewish origin. Even Strauss felt obliged to look beyond Judea for the explanation of the life of Jesus.* The laws of descent fail utterly to account for the coming of Jesus as a mere Hebrew child. He was unlike his mother and his brethren—so unlike them that his brethren did not understand him, and his mother wist not what he would do. Though he grew to manhood in a quiet Israelitish home, no man ever thinks of calling him a child of Abraham. Though living all his life among his father's people, he never became a Hebrew of the Hebrews. Though inheriting the traditions of Israel, the Son of David was known as the Son of man. Though never walking beyond the mountains of his native country, he lived a life which belongs to the whole world. The contrast between Jesus' character, and the fixed Jewish type, appears at once when we view beside it the greatest of the prophets who came just before him, or the chief of the apostles who followed after him. We cannot mistake the manner, the garb, the voice, of the Israelite in the Baptist. He is

---

* Leben Jesus fürs deutsche Volk, s. 206. 167.

a figure stern and wild, a prophet from the dim past, who stands with foot advanced upon the very threshold of the new Dispensation—his strange garment half hidden in the darkness of the night, but his face catching the glow, and his eager hand pointing to the light within, where the Bridegroom rejoices with his friends. It was not permitted him to cross the threshold of the new; but the contrast between that unmistakable Jewish form, standing with his disciples just without, and Jesus sitting at meat with his disciples within, the kingdom of God, marks the great divergence between the most advanced Hebrew character, and the new humanity of the Son of man. In this freedom from distinctively Jewish characteristics, Jesus surpasses even the apostle whose Hebrew habits had become most thoroughly revolutionized. St. Paul, long after he had become accustomed to speak of himself as a new man, to whom all things had become new, still shows incidental signs of his Hebrew descent. The Israelite appears, every now and then, in the Christian. Had he not told us, we might have known from the peculiarities of his language and manner in his pleas for the freedom of the Christian man, that once Paul had been a Pharisee. The great Apostle of liberty is as unmistakably a Hebrew of the Hebrews, as Luther was a German of the Germans. But such inborn marks of nationality, which manifest themselves unconsciously in St. Paul, never attract our attention in the Son of man; and that, too, although our portraiture of him was drawn by rude Jewish hands. Even while Jesus keeps the passover of his people, he is more than an Israelite. Even when he observes the most distinctive Jewish customs, he keeps the law not as a Pharisee; and while he uses the Aramaic dialect of his people, he speaks not as the scribes. If the laws of heredity have unbroken sway, Jesus was not a mere Hebrew child. If natural evolution be established science, Judaism does not explain the birth at Bethlehem of the Son of man. The Christian type is a new phenomenon in Jerusalem. We must look beyond its immediate historical environment, beyond Judea, for its origin.

We are equally at a loss if we seek to derive the originality of Jesus from the influence of the Gentiles. We do not even know that Jesus, during his quiet growth in wisdom, ever came under the influence of Gentile modes of thought. The whole outlying world did not contain a philosophy, or a religion, of which we can say his doctrine was the natural heir. The leaven of the Gentiles in Judaism was not the leaven of Christianity. Jesus' doctrine of the kingdom of God had no spiritual father in antiquity either in India or Greece.

But if the Son of man was neither Jew nor Gentile, may we not suppose that his originality may have been the natural product of some peculiar blending, or exceptional union, of the better elements of both? Here again the historical facts prevent the explanation of the person of Jesus as the natural child of two races. We can still trace in history and philosophy the line where the two civilizations, the East and the West, and the two minds, Plato and Moses, met; but that line which marked the meeting of two great historical currents, flowing from the opposite quarters of the world, does not denote the course followed by the new and mightier wave. Christianity is a rising movement which crosses all existing currents of thought, coinciding with none except at few points, and pursuing with gathering force its own original impulse. The apocryphal books of Ecclesiasticus, and the Wisdom of Solomon, mark the first influence of Hellenic culture upon Hebrew faith. In their form, at least, we may, with Dean Stanley,* regard these writings as " connecting links " between the earlier Hebrew literature and the later Christian epistles; and in this first meet-

---

* Jewish Church, iii. 296.

ing of Hellenism with Judaism we may recognize with Ewald,* "a premonition of John, and .... a preparation for Paul, like a warm rustle of spring, ere its time is fully come." But we know with historical certainty that the natural offspring of the union of Grecian philosophy and Hebrew wisdom was not Christianity, but Alexandrian Judaism. Its own child was not the Apostle to the Gentiles, but Philo, the Jew. The first logical outcome of these two great historical tendencies was the allegorical wisdom of the Alexandrian Jew— not the mind that was in Jesus of Nazareth.† What the last possible combinations of the ideas and tendencies of the two worlds were, became manifest toward the close of the first Christian century in the many-colored philosophies of the Gnostics. The attempt to patch together the beliefs of the Jews and the ideas of the Gentiles resulted in a philosopher's cloak of many colors; the doctrine of Jesus, like the garment which the soldiers divided, was woven without seam throughout.

We are reasoning from the observed forces and laws of human nature. Take the known

---

* History of Israel, v. 484.

† For an exhaustive discussion of the radical antithesis between Philo and the Christian idea, see Dorner, History of the Doctrine of the Person of Christ, i., pp. 19, ff. The points of opposition are more popularly defined in Pressensé's Life of Christ, pp. 77 ff.

tendencies of Judaism, and the known ideas of the Gentile world, and combine them in every imaginable manner, and Christianity in its unity of design, and transcendent beauty, will never come out in your historical kaleidoscope. Many incongruous philosophies, many bright, grotesque fancies, did result, when time shook these variegated materials up together in the Roman Empire; but the Gospel which Jesus began to preach in the villages of Galilee never arose from the dissolving of the old Hebrew faiths, together with Gentile superstitions, in the great crucible of the world's unbelief.

Grant, even, that in the age which the historian may recognize as the fulness of time, materials for a new nation and a higher religion had been brought together from thousands of years; and that these elements, gathered from the four quarters of the known world, were waiting in the great alembic of the Roman Empire to be recombined in some new form of society, and purer faith;—whence shall come the electric flash, the heavenly spark, that shall precipitate from these confused and turbid times the new era, and occasion the crystallization of a purer worship and a perfect form of society? History may explain everything in Christianity, except the Spirit of Christ. If it can number the elements of this world which were met in Judea, it has still to account for the force which organized them in the Church. The new Life is beyond the analysis of historical chemistry. The creative Spirit that was in Christ is the super-historical and divine principle of Christianity.

As a last possible naturalistic explanation of the appearance of the Son of man in Judea, it might be suggested that the spirit of the older prophecy was raised from the dead in Jesus to newness of life; that Christianity struck its roots down deep through the traditions of Judaism into the living fountains of Israel's earlier and better faith. We are far from denying the relationship between the spirit of Christ and the spirit of prophecy; we shall return to this again in our account of his appearing. But the spirit of prophecy affords no explanation of the historical Jesus. The laws of heredity forbid the supposition of a leap, even of spiritual genius, entirely out of the conditions of its own age, across centuries, into alien and vanished modes of thought. The Book of Isaiah does not yield a sufficient cause for the actual Messianic life of Jesus. He was not another Elias, nor is Christianity to be conceived of as a return to the great prophetic age of Israel;—as the Protestant Reformation was a return to a more primitive Christianity, and as Luther had the work of the great Apostle before him for an example. Jesus brings in his own Gospel the truth which unites, and makes alive, in one personal reality, the broken conceptions, the scattered members, of the prophetic image of the Messiah. His life was not a copy of any Messianic portrait. It was the original in comparison with which all the portraits of the coming Messiah drawn by the prophet's hands look like copies, themselves imperfect, and not alike, and marked by discordant features. In the Divine original alone all incongruities of the copies are harmonized. That, says the Evangelist, who had beheld his glory, was the *true*, that is, the *genuine*, the *original* Light which lighteth every man that cometh into the world.

It may be said, indeed, that Jesus possessed the exalted spiritual genius to see and to satisfy the deepest want of his age, and of all ages. But even a happy phrase is not of itself sufficient to solve a great historical problem; and our problem is, whence came, and of what manner of spirit was, this unexampled religious genius of Jesus? It is true that the scholasticism of the rabbis did not meet the wants of the people; and the uprisals of the zealots had only plunged into deeper despair the national expectation. It is true that in the gathering gloom, here and there, the old Messianic hope seemed to be rekindled. But our question, which cannot be put aside by a form of words, is, how did it come to pass that a religious enthusiast had the "spiritual genius" to rise above all ancestral limitations; to see that the only way to save the life of his nation was to lose it; to teach a salvation of the Jews so novel in its conception, and so alien to the tradition of the law, as to unite both the learned and the aristocratic parties at Jerusalem in a common hatred against him; and to seek to attain the hope of that salvation by methods so unworldly as to cause the patriotic zealots to forsake his standard, and to lead the priests and people in their disappointed rage to fill the court of the Roman governor with the despairing cry, "We have no king but Cæsar," "Crucify him, crucify him!"*

But let us bring these first and general impressions of the superhuman originality of Jesus to more searching proof.

The power and life of Jesus were neither Jewish, nor Grecian, nor a combination of the diverse elements thrown together by the Ro-

---

* As Pressensé has observed, the "Fourth book of Esdras shows ... the chasm which separates the ideal of Jesus Christ from that of the Jews of his time. The book of Enoch represents the popular conception in its designation of the Messianic reign as the era of the sword.

man state; but they were above and beyond the known tendencies and forces of human nature in the following striking particulars:

1. We begin with that aspect of Jesus' ministry in which he was most like others—his moral teaching. In the broad historical retrospect, now clearing up before the new science of comparative religion, it is certainly a pleasure for one who believes in the omnipresence of the Spirit of Truth, and in the religious nature of man, to discover that the large, catholic prophecy of the last of the Hebrew prophets * was not wholly a vision of distant futurity; that, even while he heralded the coming in Judea of the "messenger of the Lord," "from the rising to the setting of the sun," the "incense in every place" was ascending, and many "pure offerings" were brought to the adorable name which all religions strive to express, and which the chief of Apostles confessed that he knew only part.

But, among those chosen of God from every nation, Jesus is *the* Teacher sent from God. His inimitable moral originality appears to the best advantage when compared with those very fore-gleams and reflections of his teaching which bear the closest resemblance to it. Print in parallel columns the choice sayings of

* Mal. i. 11.

those who have served God in every nation, and the words of Jesus,—and, as we read, the very similarity reveals the difference. A spirit not of this world; a light from afar; a subtle quality, not easily defined, but felt as the very life of Jesus' moral teaching, lead us instinctively to recognize in him One who spake as never man spake. The precepts alike of the rabbis and the philosophers, when taken up in Jesus' teaching, receive a different setting, and a more heavenly light is in them. A diamond in a dark or dimly-lighted room is not the same thing as a diamond in the track of a sunbeam. We see in the Gospels the purest morality of the Gentiles taken out of darkness and uncertainty, and held up in the light of a new revelation. Jesus' teaching is man's moral truth with a ray of heaven playing through it.

A recent writer* has gathered the results of nearly ten years' study of the Talmud into a collection of those rabbinical sayings which have any analogy to the Gospels. The Sermon on the Mount, when read thus, in the midst of the rabbinical lore, seems like the new wine when put into the old bottles. The best morality of the rabbins smacks of a

---

* Wunsche : Neue Beiträge zür Erlauterungen der Evangelium aus Talmud.

prudential virtue; it is not better than the wisdom of Solomon; but the Sermon on the Mount imparts to morality the essence of spiritual truth. A greater than Solomon is here. The Talmudic literature yields but a distant and indistinct echo of the blessing pronounced upon the pure in heart; and if we seek for any approach in the traditions of the scribes to the simple yet deep ethical truth of Jesus, " Whosoever will save his life shall lose it," we can find nothing better than Hillel's clever warning against the ambition of the pharisee overleaping itself, " Whoso spreads out his calling shall lose it." The negative precept of the Grecian sage, and of the most human of the rabbis, Jesus makes the golden rule of the world.* While the scribes were repeating the saying of Hillel, " No uneducated man easily avoids sin; no man of the people can be pious;" the common people heard gladly One who made publicans and sinners his disciples and friends.

If we compare, not merely single precepts, but the moral doctrine of Jesus as a whole with the ethics of the Gentiles, we observe that, while separate threads may be easily matched, and particular sayings may corre-

---

* Stanley's Jewish Church, iii., p. 507. Dean Stanley hears, amid the trivial casuistry of Hillel, " faint accents of a generous and universal theology."

spond, still the general pattern of his teaching is unlike any other; the design is original; and the whole fabric is taken out of uncertain and confusing lights, and held up in the sunshine. The one-sided intellectualism of the Greek ethics; the inability of the Pagan morals to rise above the barriers of natural condition and race to a true spiritual conception of man's birthright, unity, and destiny; the essentially political conception of the brotherhood of man, when the instinct of humanity did lead to the Stoic idea of the one universal state; the want of the idea of a kingdom of God, or power to realize any spiritual conception of man in society; these, and other limitations like these, mark the radical and world-wide difference between the best moral teaching of antiquity, and the new, transforming doctrine which Jesus began to preach in one of the obscurest provinces of the Roman Empire.*

Greece had perfected a crystalline language to contain the new truth; the philosophers brought much beaten oil; but Jesus by the power of His spirit converted the oil into light.

And, above all, the absolute peculiarity of

---

* See Neander's thorough discussion of "The Relation of the Hellenic to Christian Ethics,"—Wissenshaftliche Abhandlungen.

Jesus as a teacher was the manner in which he made the knowledge of truth the means to something beyond itself, and never the end of his teaching. Truth with him is not an end; it is the way to life. Truth is like the light which shines, not that it may be seen, but that in it we may see the realities of the world. The philosophers were content to show the truth; Jesus, *through* the truth, shows the Father. Hence everything in his Gospel is intensely personal and real. He is himself, in his oneness with the Father, *the* doctrine. Trust in his Person, not belief in a dogma, is the condition of discipleship. In his Gospel nature answers to nature, and God is at one with man. Jesus leaves his disciples in the communion of the Spirit; and this divine realism of his teaching (if one may put into a single word this marvellous characteristic of it) made a vital impression upon the hearts of the disciples, which they never lost, for henceforth with them " to know the truth " was to have " eternal life."

2. The moral ideal of the Gospels was peculiarly Jesus' own. The good man of Jesus' parables was not the good man of the world's admiration. His ideal was different even from the ideal righteous man of the prophets, for, according to his own saying, the least in the kingdom of heaven was greater than the great-

est of the prophets. The central and formative principles of Jesus' ideal of goodness were not those upon which any type of character had ever been created before. Not merely higher degrees of virtue, but, in some respects, a new kind of goodness sprang up in the path of Christianity.* Humility, with Jesus, is the lowly source of the virtues. The two connected words, repent and believe, marked the two polar duties upon which the new Christian type of character was to be formed; but the centre of the whole is love. Love is the central and formative virtue of Christian ethics and theology,—not the Platonic idea of justice, nor the magnanimity of Aristotle, nor the self-abnegation of Buddha. Love is the divine centre of the moral ideal of Jesus, and around that living heart of goodness the virtues grow in their order and perfectness. It is an evident historical fact, that Jesus introduced a new creative principle of character. Distinct and clearly outlined as the Christian character has been, and is, in comparison with all other types of goodness, Jewish or Gentile, ancient or modern; so unique and divinely original was the first creative thought of it in the mind of Jesus of Nazareth. What science

---

* See Matheson: Article, "Originality of the Character of Jesus Christ," Contemporary Review, November, 1878.

shall declare the generation of that creative thought of Jesus?

3. The constructive method of Jesus was comparatively new. It is one of the redeeming merits of Matthew Arnold's "Literature and Dogma," that it brings out clearly this new and distinctive method—"the secret of Jesus." He begins his work within the heart. The later prophets had been taught something of this natural method of righteousness, but in Jesus the new method of the heart comes to perfection. It is that perfect method of righteousness which substitutes good for evil in the heart. Religion, with Jesus, not only sweeps the house, but it opens the windows and lets the sunshine in. It peoples the soul with new purposes. It makes its chambers echo with new and innocent joys. It brings in new affections. The coming of religion to the soul is like opening a deserted house, and filling it with the laughter of children's voices. This, at least, was Jesus' own method, however men, in later ages, may have lost his simple art of winning souls. The fact that his own Church has too often forgotten his secret, and that his own prophets never fully attained to it, shows how divinely original Jesus' perfect method with his disciples really was. But how, we ask, could one in whom, on the supposition of a merely natural evolution,

were accumulated, by the inevitable laws of heredity, the traditional methods of generations of scribes, and the marked peculiarities of the Jewish race, have fallen all at once, easily, to the utter astonishment of his contemporaries, into the new method of Jesus? It had not been treasured up in the customs of his people, nor could it have been learned in the schools. Even his chosen disciples were slow of heart to understand it. It was Jesus' own method; it came to him spontaneously, as the flowering of a plant. It was the natural blossoming of his own life,—what science shall tell how it grew?

4. The plan of Jesus was original. Its object was the establishment of a kingdom of which no one in the world but Jesus had dreamed. The first step in its execution was the refusal of the usual modes of winning success. Judas was soon disappointed and provoked by the utter strangeness of the Master's manner of gaining a kingdom. Jesus, from the first, marked out for himself a way of life which was sure to cross, again and again, the paths trodden by all other men. He followed out his singular plan of life by rejecting the favor of the chief among the people, and turning from the temptation of the kingdoms of this world, and choosing for his helpers and friends men without power, wealth, or influ-

ence, who possessed nothing but the desire to learn of him, and the willingness to receive the training of his spirit. He finished his novel plan of life by giving himself up to death, when one single word of denial of his mission would have set him free. So anomalous, so contrary to all maxims of common-sense, was the plan of Jesus, that some recent writers have endeavored to regard him as a religious enthusiast, a good man deceived by his own dreams, and allured by some wild illusion to a life which a soberer judgment might have foreseen would surely end in disappointment, rejection by the world, and death; and that too, although we are told by those who were best acquainted with him that he knew what was in man, and though, from beginning to end, his life, through all its eventful scenes, seems to move on full of purpose, and with thoughtful anticipation, to its tragic close. His was a plan which looked calmly forward to the end of time. Everything in Jesus' words has this far look forward. His plan of life involved his death, and the coming of another dispensation. Rationalism can escape from the impression of divine originality left by the plan of Jesus only by making the mind of Jesus a chimera, a psychological impossibility.

5. The life of Jesus as portrayed in the Gospels was unique in the absence from it of

traits common to other lives. There are certain negative characteristics of the teaching of Jesus, as contained in the New Testament, which, on the supposition of a merely natural evolution of Christian doctrine, are, to say the least, very curious. It remains for naturalism to explain how certain peculiarities and limitations of the prophetic teaching quietly disappear from the perfect law of the New Testament; and also how it happened that there are no traces of certain prevalent Aryan conceptions to be found in Gospels which naturalism would account for as the product of an age in which Aryan and Semitic ideas met in new combinations. How happened it that Jesus' doctrine of sin, for example, escaped the taint of asceticism, and of that conception of evil, then not unknown within as well as without Palestine, which regarded matter as the abode of corruption?* The negative virtues of Christian doctrine are a peculiar excellence of the teaching of Jesus, with regard to which much more might be said. It is, to say the least, singular, if Christianity were the natural product of the age in which it sprang up, that it escaped so much evil and error which were in the very soil, and in the air, of the land where the Gospel was first preached.

---

* Tulloch : Ch. Doct. of Sin, p. 109.

I might notice here, also, the absence of any appearance of eclecticism in the character of Jesus. Had the Gospel been originally, as some modern critics labor to make it, a mere patchwork of sentiments of the philosophers, and notions of the sects, put together by many hands, after the general Roman idea of a world-empire; it would have shown upon its very surface the seams and the stitches, the signs and unmistakable marks of its fabrication from materials so diversified; it would never have deceived the world as the *simple* Gospel. Whatever Jesus of Nazareth may have been, he certainly was not a religious eclectic.

But I turn from these minor, yet significant, negative considerations, to view that characteristic of Jesus' life which, by common consent, is one of the most superhuman peculiarities of it—his sinlessness. The marks of passion, of weakness, of pride, of the love of popularity, and the consequent lack of moral courage, of a thousand infirmities of the flesh, some of which we notice in all other men, are certainly not obvious, or any where forced upon our recognition, in the life and conversation which is mirrored in the four Gospels. On the contrary, Jesus was not only followed and loved, but, by those who knew him best, he was worshipped before he died.

The apotheosis of this man took place in his lifetime, and not as an empty imperial honor, but as a real adoration of the glory beheld in him by a disciple who leaned upon his bosom, and among the friends who were acquainted with his whole manner of life. For him no friend ever apologized; and no enemy convinced him of sin. Modern infidelity must be pushed to extremities before it will venture to turn and cast any reproach upon the name which still, in the reverence of the Christian world, is above every name, full of an ideal light. But how shall the laws of natural descent declare the generation of a seemingly sinless character? Let any one read some careful scientific statement of the laws of heredity, and then read Ullmann's classic book on "The Sinlessness of Jesus;" or, better still, read the Evangelists' simple portrayal of his daily life; and either he must deny undeniable science, or overcome the weight of historical evidence, or else seek for some other than physical cause, some deeper than natural necessity, for the coming to this earth of the sinless Son of man.

6. It is the unique life in its power. Whatever may be our belief concerning miracles, enough of the Gospels, on the most unfavorable view of their authenticity, must be admitted to be historical, to show that we have

to do here with a life full to overflowing with peculiar and wonderful power. Even if we should discredit the narratives, and be disposed to regard them as myths or legends, nevertheless their peculiarities as myths would point to a Being at the source of them wholly without parallel or example in the catalogue of great legendary heroes. The kind of wonderful works related, the circumstances and conditions, the objects and moral aim, of the miracles which Jesus is said to have performed, constitute a group of events which, even on the mythical hypothesis itself, distinguish the Gospels sharply and broadly from all other mythologies. The peculiar moral quality, the unearthly virtue, of the miracles of Jesus at once arrest attention, and stamp them with a signature all their own. Moreover, another singular characteristic of these narratives is the self-restraint and perfect poise of the miracle-worker amid his wonderful works. No word or hint of excitement or surprise on the part of Jesus at his own mighty works has come down to us, although the narratives are often so detailed and graphic as to reproduce his very gestures and tones. Jesus never was seen standing for a moment in surprise before his own miracles. They seem to be perfectly natural to him. He does them apparently as easily and as naturally as we perform our everyday acts of interference with the general laws of nature. The disciples, upon their first exercise of the Master's power, came running back in excitement, rejoicing that the spirits were made subject unto them. Jesus does not share their astonishment, but calms and hallows their thoughts by reminding them of a better reason for their joy. He never seems to have mistaken his power; to have attempted more than he could perform; or to have been astonished at his own success, when all men marvelled at him. It is remarkable, also, that one who could do so much as Jesus is reported to have done, should not have done more mighty works. The self-restraint of Jesus in the exercise of his superior power is one of the signs of the divineness of his power. He never performs a miracle for mere effect; never uses his signal power for display; never abuses it to strike terror into his enemies, or even to save himself; always holds it under the control of his higher spiritual purpose, and makes miraculous power serve heavenly love. This moral control of marvellous power, preserved throughout the ministry of Jesus, is an indication of the divine originality of his life of great significance.

But, irrespective of the miracle-working of Jesus, his power is altogether an unparalleled fact in history. A new era dates from his birth. His coming, as Dr. Sears has well said,* was "a new influx of power." Jesus seems to concentrate in his own person the great constructive forces of religion. Prophecy, before him, had been more than a destructive energy. It had begun to build. Prophecy in Greece was only "a voice, a song:" in Israel it was an architect and builder.† It founded a nation; built a state; made straight over mountains, and across valleys, a highway for the Lord. These creative forces of religion in Israel culminate, and are endowed with new and marvellous power, in the ministry of Jesus. His spirit is the great constructive principle and power of modern history. It was his wonderful work to create in the Roman Empire a new faith, a new hope, and a new joy. The belief in immortality became through him in Judea, what it never had been at Athens or Rome, a living, working faith, which transformed this earth, and transfigured death. The greatness of this change, and the marvel of the power which wrought it, may be appreciated at a glance by the traveller who walks through that corridor in the Vatican, where, upon one wall have been placed pagan burial tablets and in-

---

* The Fourth Gospel.
† Mozley : Ruling Ideas, pp. 17, 18.

scriptions, with symbols of the pursuits in which the departed delighted before death quenched life's torch, and words of fond recollection of earthly scenes scarce broken by any anticipations of joy among the shades below ; and where, upon the opposite wall, have been placed inscriptions taken from the Catacombs, with their benedictions of peace and their emblems of hope, the ascending bird with the olive bough, or the ship sailing into the sky.

This unexampled power of Jesus was creative, likewise, of a new humanity. It poured its fresh, renewing streams through all the channels of social life. Modern society, as well as modern history, dates from the advent of Christ. We ought to glance, at least, in this connection, at the contrast between the moral decrepitude of the pagan world, and the Christian restoration of society. Ecclesiastical writers have sometimes been accused of indulging in a too sweeping condemnation of the popular morality of the pagan world; and there is certainly a brighter side of life in the later Roman Empire, which Mr. Lecky and other writers, who are disposed to keep as much as possible on the sunny side of the street in their walks through Rome, will not suffer us to overlook. But the pages of Tacitus grow dark with the increasing gloom of a history of crimes, and St. Paul's condemnation of Roman morals finds its confirmation in more than one revelation of the buried life of Pompeii. "Could we have seen depicted the inner life of that brilliant period," so Prof. Jowett* thinks, "we should have turned away from the sight with loathing and detestation." Undoubtedly there were better elements in the midst of the growing corruption, and, in that age of easy divorces, inscriptions on some burial tablets still tell the pleasant story of life-long faithfulness and affection. But the sentiments of the philosophers, and examples of individual virtue, were powerless to pervade a fermenting and decaying society with the leaven of a new spirit. While the rabbis of Jerusalem were uttering fine praises of humility, the Pharisees were making broad their phylacteries. While Hillel's voice still was heard in the temple, reminding the prudent disciple to take his seat one or two places below the position belonging to him, the scribes were jostling one another in their eagerness to seek the uppermost seats in the synagogue. While the philosophers at Rome were discoursing loftily of virtue, vice was growing too common to be talked of as a scandal.†

---

* Ep. of St. Paul, p. 77.
† Mommsen, iv. 618.

While the rhetoricians were preaching morals, slavery was heaping up its iniquities, and labor sinking into disgrace. While the Roman law was giving woman greater rights, the family was losing its sanctity, and marriage becoming a commercial contract. While the poets were still singing of fidelity and love, divorces from marriages, which had been contracted without the bonds of religion, were matters of daily occurrence; and men immersed in sensuality, and overwhelmed by extravagance, could hardly be induced to take wives even by the bounties decreed to husbands by Augustus. While sentiments of humanity were cultivated in literature, even Cato did not scruple to sell his old and worthless servants; not infrequent exhibitions of cruelty gave occasion for Juvenal's satirical picture of the mistress who, in a fit of hot temper, crucified her slave;* and the popular brutality was gratified by the bloody spectacles of the Coliseum. We do not forget, in this rapid survey, the temporary revival of the better elements of Roman faith and virtue in the age of the Antonines—that Indian summer of the Empire's fading glory. But neither the new Platonism of Alexandria, nor the later Stoicism of the Roman metropolis, could prevent

---

* Sat. vi.

the decline of the world. "It was an old world," says Mommsen, as he closes his history, "and even the richly gifted patriotism of Cæsar could not make it young again."* It was the peculiar power of the despised Nazarene to call forth, by a mighty voice, a new civilization from the grave of the old. It may be said that philosophy rolled away the stone; but to restore life was the miracle wrought by Christianity.

This originality of Jesus' power was signally exhibited in the rise and rapid growth of the Church. He created a new kind of society —in this world, as Jesus himself said, but not of it. What science of natural forces shall explain the advent, in the midst of its historical environment, of this new type of humanity? The Church, as a great and surprising historical result, requires as its cause a person of most original power. The rise of Christianity presents a problem in history which resembles the problem of motion in astronomy. If the motion of nebulæ and worlds be once granted, then our physical science may find some possible solution for the succeeding phenomena of the solar system; but the difficulty is to account for that first impulse of the nebulous mass, for the originating motion of the

---

* Hist., iv. 738.

order of the spheres. Once admit an original divine impulse, a new formative, constructive power sent from without into human history, in the person of Jesus Christ, and then the spread and growth of Christianity becomes an intelligible historical study; but it is difficult to find in history a natural cause for a supernatural movement, a material source for a spiritual life. This original, new creative power of Jesus of Nazareth is itself a miracle continued through history, and at work before our eyes to-day; and though one after another of his many mighty works be explained away, this historical miracle still remains to show forth his glory.

6. Another altogether unique characteristic of the person of Jesus was his self-consciousness. An apostle has expressed in a single phrase a peculiarity of Jesus' self-consciousness which distinguished him from all other men : " In him was Yea." (2 Cor. i. 19.) The absence of self-contradiction and questioning, the continuity and wholeness of Jesus' own self-conscious life, are marvellous in our eyes; for we are daily contradicting and questioning our own hearts; we find different kinds of men bound together in us from our birth—spirits of light and of darkness, of doubt and of faith, of evil and good; angels of God, and demons of the flesh, struggling within us through life for the

mastery. But Jesus never seems to have been an enigma, a question, to himself, as we are often half-solved riddles of existence to ourselves. He knew whence he came. He knew whither he should go. This calm, assured self-knowledge of Jesus, as it was preserved in his conversations with his friends, and through all the hurrying scenes of his life, was something never witnessed before or since in man; something that seems more like God the more we think of it and realize it. As he never stood in surprise before his own miracles, so he does not seem to have gazed in wonder into his own soul. The most wonderful thing in the world to every man is himself. All the mysteries of the creation meet in our own consciousness of self. But while men marvelled at him, and most strange things were happening in Jerusalem, this Man possessed himself in perfect faith, in calm, serene self-knowledge; even from boyhood living his wonderful life as naturally, as spontaneously, as simply, as a child in his Father's house. This unbroken and undoubting "Yea" of Jesus' self-consciousness manifests itself throughout his teaching. His doctrine is never a question and a weary doubt; it is an uninterrupted affirmation. The manner or kind of his positiveness in teaching is peculiar. It is not the assurance of education, or habit, or ignorance:

it is not the dogmatism of the scribe. His authority puzzled the scribes, for it came not from Moses' seat, nor from a prophet's vision; but it was the authority of his own kingly soul. His manifestations of himself are his revelations of God. The singular positiveness of Jesus makes a powerful impression upon us when we consider the nature and the extent of the questionings which he answers with an unwavering "Yea." In order to appreciate the wonderful range of his answers, and this distinctive positiveness of his teaching, pass quickly from one to the other of the verities which he points out to his disciples. Is there another than this earthly existence for us mortals? Yes: I am the resurrection and the life. Are there other spheres of being? Yes: In my Father's house are many mansions. But can man know the Father? Yes: If ye had known me, ye should have known my Father also; and from henceforth ye know him and have seen him. Is God thoughtful of his creatures? Yes: Your Father knoweth what things ye have need of. Does the great Creator care for me? Yes: The very hairs of your head are all numbered. Is prayer a power with God? Yes: Ask and ye shall receive. Will justice ever be done—justice now mocked, and trodden under foot of men? Yes: Many that are first shall be last, and the last shall be first. Is conscience, then, a true prophet as it proclaims law and predicts future retributions? Yes: He shall reward every man according to his works. But can we be forgiven for our sins? Yes: Son, thy sins be forgiven thee. But can we, though forgiven, ever lose the memory of our shame, and rejoice unrebuked among the sinless? Yes: I will see you again, and your heart shall rejoice, and your joy no man taketh from you. So Jesus dwelt daily among the great verities of God's kingdom, and his teaching is throughout a constant affirmation, a most positive Gospel of glad tidings. It was in Judea, it has been for eighteen centuries, it is to-day, the great affirmation of the human soul, and of all that the human heart can hold dear. Whence did man born of woman derive this wonderful consciousness of truth? What science of natural descent can declare its generation? And, besides this, there are expressions which fell from the lips of Jesus, of a still higher self-consciousness, a certain divine sense and knowledge of oneness with the Father, which transcend our experience of ourselves, and leave us wondering what manner of man he was.

7. One more mark of the divine originality of Jesus our rapid summary would be singularly incomplete should we leave unmen-

tioned, viz. : his position toward the sin of the world. Sin finds in him a new and diviner law of judgment. He stands, indeed, on the common Hebrew ground in his teaching with regard to sin; but he rises in his doctrine far above Moses and the prophets; and in his presence we feel that we are in a changed and clearer moral atmosphere. He has more than a prophet's divination of the evil nature of man. He feels with a peculiar sensitiveness the presence of sin in the thoughts of those whose conduct fulfils the law. His superior knowledge of the evil hidden in the heart of man, his instantaneous detection and unerring judgment of the wrong concealed behind the masks and within the customs of men, and of the evil dispositions lying at the root of many questionings even of his own disciples, are a frequent surprise to us, as we read the narratives of his conversation with men. No man ever saw or felt what sin is, as this man saw and felt it. Though dwelling among us, he seems to have looked down into the depths of the human heart as from some higher sphere, and he knew what was in man. When our eyes are near the level of the sea, we can hardly look beneath the glimmer of the surface; but, from some higher point, we can discern the sunken rocks and tangled sea-weed amid the broken ledges : so, as from some higher plane, Jesus looked down, and saw, beneath the smooth surface of men's lives, the hidden purposes, the wild tangle of desires, the hard, selfish thoughts of human hearts.

But we are lingering with the more outward peculiarities of Jesus' relation to the sin of the world. The resemblances between him and all others diminish, the contrast deepens, the further we penetrate into the significance of Jesus' redemptive work. The altogether unique and original personal position which Jesus assumes toward sin is the distinctive doctrine of his Gospel. It is evident that, from his baptism to his cross, Jesus regards himself as holding in the Father's plan of the world a peculiar place, and as having a work to do, in regard to the sin of the world, which separates his life from all others. The Son of man, he says, has power on earth to forgive sins. The mere fact that he exercised that power, and as by some divine right inherent in his own person, separates him, in his own self-consciousness, from all the prophets and priests who were before him. Not merely to teach that sin is in its nature forgivable, but actually to forgive it as by a divine right of forgiveness dwelling in him,—that was the new, startling word which aroused the synagogue against him. In the charge of blasphemy, which was brought against the Son of man who forgave sins, we have a genuine historical sign of the absolute originality in Jerusalem of the life of Christ. We need not, for our immediate purpose, enter farther into the nature or meaning of Jesus' personal relation to man's sin. We may call attention, however, to the fact that, for our knowledge of the peculiar significance which Jesus attaches to his life and death for sinners, we are not dependent entirely upon his words, or the reports of his words in the Gospels, but upon a great undisputed historical fact, which was and is, itself, a new and distinctive Christian institution—the Lord's Supper. Looking at the last supper simply as an historical event, regarding it merely in its relation to preceding Jewish rites, as well as in its place in subsequent Christian history, we certainly are surprised by it, as an occurrence without precedent and without parallel. It followed the Paschal supper; but can we conceive of a John the Baptist, or even of an Isaiah, the prophet of the Man of Sorrows, as having instituted it? The very idea of the last Supper was Jesus' own. He only could have superseded the Passover by making himself the sacrifice. We need no evidence of the correctness of the narration of the evangelists here. No disciple could have dreamed of the action which

Jesus performed when he took the cup, and blessed it, as the new testament in his blood. The account of the Lord's Supper could only have originated from the actual occurrence of it. But whence came Jesus' own idea of it? What science that does not admit the inspiration of the Spirit shall account for its suggestion? Consider the amazing significance of this unheard-of action — that a human being, like ourselves, calmly, quietly, with prayer to God, while pronouncing a farewell blessing upon his friends, in the very presence of death, where usually the masks which may have been worn for a lifetime are suffered to fall off, and all deception ceases, should, nevertheless, have made himself the passover of his people, both the mediator and the mediation of the sin of the world! Surely this action of Jesus is contrary to human experience—a miracle not to be believed, according to Hume's famous argument—yet Jesus did it; and we know that he did it, for we have the sacrament of the Lord's death observed by the Church in memory of him unto this day. The Church and its sacrament are the faithful witnesses, through all the intervening centuries, of the divine originality of Jesus Christ.

We have given above a rapid survey of those characteristics of the Christ of the evangelists which distinguish him from all others, and leave us wondering and worshipping before a being altogether unique, original, and superhuman. These supernatural elements in the life of Jesus are so inwoven with the commonest incidents as well as the greater events of the Gospel; they appear and reappear in so many scenes of the sacred story; they are elements so constant and so natural in the narratives of the evangelists, as to preclude the idea of any intentional invention or artificial production of them. The impression made by Jesus upon his age—the impression of a divinely original being which we receive from merely reading the Gospels—is not broken, and cannot be done away with, by any questions or doubts raised by the critical school concerning the time when our present Gospels were written. Whenever and wherever our Gospels received their present, final form, the real historical fact to be accounted for is the great original of their wonderful portraiture. Human imagination never literally creates—its pictures are new combinations of existing objects; but here we have a portraiture of a character and a life which, if we look at it simply as an ideal picture, we are at a loss to explain as a happy combination, a marvellous union by genius, of any known features, or virtues, ever seen before on earth. The portraiture of the Christ of the

Gospels is a work beyond the power of the philosophers, certainly then beyond the imagination of fishermen of Galilee. We know that they could not have originated it, as we know that Peter could not have chiselled out of the marble the beauty of the Apollo Belvidere, or Paul have painted that wonder of art, the Sistine Madonna. We know it, that is, not merely by reason of critical inquiries into historical records, but by the simple application to the Gospels of the common laws of the human imagination. The original of the evangelists' portraiture of Jesus would remain the great wonder of humanity, even though it could be proved, as it never has been proved, that our Gospels are copies of copies. Our conclusion depends upon the historical necessity of believing in the Person whose appearance was the creative cause of the New Testament literature, and the Christian tradition, and the rise of the Church; it does not depend upon any question as to the authenticity or inspiration of some particular Christian writing. We have reason, indeed, to thank the rationalistic critics that, as one result of their microscopical study of the beginnings of Christianity, it is becoming more difficult for us to conceive of the spontaneous generation of the Church from the historical conditions of the first century; and we are gaining, on the other hand, a clearer apprehension of the divine and ineffable impression produced by Jesus of Nazareth upon those who beheld his glory. The miraculous conception of the image of his character in the mind of some unlearned Galilean of the first century, or some unknown writer of the second century, would be a greater tax upon our credulity than any of the mighty works recorded in John's Gospel. The image of God which the Church of the second century possessed in the Christ of its worship, would be itself the greatest of wonders, if the first century had not witnessed the miracle of his very person. Rationalism must excuse faith from rushing into belief, in psychological miracles, wrought in the highest realms of the spirit, and supported by no historical evidence, in order to avoid belief in miracles, wrought in the lower realms of nature, which are confirmed by much historical evidence. Christianity, in short, in all that is wonderful, unique, powerful, and creative in it, leads directly back to the historical Christ. And the character of Jesus Christ rises before us from the midst of history in solitary and unapproachable grandeur.

In the northern part of Maine there is a mountain which springs from the midst of the forest, unapproached by lesser heights, lifting its solitary peak into the clouds. Floating down the stream which flows by it, between the overhanging banks, suddenly, at some turn of the river's course, I have seen Mount Katahdin, standing out from the interminable forests, its grand lines sharply defined, its single, sublime peak rising alone into the sky. Often that mountain vision seems repeated, as I am brought before the character of Christ. Above the interminable levels of common human nature, across the intervening distances of history, an image of solitary majesty stands out before the mind; and the view of that sublime character, rising from the midst of our low, monotonous human attainments, clearly outlined against the soul's horizon, in its wonderful elevation, is an inspiration and a joy, awakening the whole moral enthusiasm of our being!

But no sooner have we reached this conclusion, which has been fairly gained upon its own evidence, that Jesus was a person of divine originality, than we find ourselves violently thrown back upon our reasonings by the force of another conviction equally positive and powerful. Science can admit the appearance of nothing original in the world. If, putting entirely out of mind for the moment our preceding reasonings, we start again from our observation of the course of nature, we shall find no exceptions to the uniformity of nature. We see nothing rise above the horizon of our own experience, which has not had elsewhere its setting. We know that there is nothing new under the sun. All things that appear to us, seem to come to pass in the regular operation of natural laws. We know of nothing which is separate from all other things, nothing absolutely unique in the world. The solitary peak has its foundations deep in the common earth. Genius rises from the people. There is nothing so singular, so exalted, or so separate, that we are not to seek for its origin and its cause in the general system of nature. Every thread of life is inextricably looped with a thousand other threads; nature never breaks her web, and no science can find the beginning nor the ending of so much as a single thread of her ceaseless spinning. The force of this scientific conviction we would neither avoid nor abate. We accept the law of continuity as a law of things which it is infidelity to truth to deny. We believe in the uniformity of nature as we would in a word of God. What, then, are we to do? Here are two conclusions, each fairly reached, each standing impregnable upon its own ground; yet they stand facing each other; we cannot pass from the one to the other; they rise, separate and opposite, and equally commanding. What are we to do? Possibly there may be deeper ground where we may find, at the bottom of things, a way from the one to the other of these confronting truths. But we are not to seek for the harmony of science and religion by levelling either to the plane of the other. Two conclusions, both positive and substantial, are brought over against each other. On the one hand is the person of Christ—the ultimate moral fact of history—whose origin cannot be derived from the past by any of the known laws of heredity—a sublime historical phenomenon, unexampled and unexplained—a mystery of being and of influence, whose spell has been upon all the passing generations—a name, above all others, which grows not less, but more adorable, as the ages come and go. On the other hand is the unbroken order of the creation, and the law, older than history and more ancient than the stars, which binds all things that come and go into one continuous whole. What then?· Give up either conclusion on its own ground, we cannot. To sacrifice one truth to another truth is never reasonable. Scepticism may look about and see oppositions, and raise questions, and create doubts; but it is the very essence of infidelity to give up truth; and, whether the truth sacrificed be a truth of nature or of the spirit, of science or of religion, it is always infidelity to give up any truth to any other truth. There may be believing as well as atheistic infidels, if the essence of infidelity be the giving up of truth, even though as an offering to some other truth. Faith is often refusal to surrender truth to truths—the holding fast all feelings, or perceptions, of truth—and waiting. When, therefore, a moral phenomenon and a physical law are made to confront one another —as the divine originality of Jesus stands over against the uniformity of nature—is not he who should bid us deny either for the sake of the other the real unbeliever? We refuse to abandon the scientific principle of continuity in reading the life of Christ; we also decline to give up the witness of history and the testimony of the human soul to the supernatural person of Christ at the command of the principle of continuity. We know that contradictories cannot be true. It would be infidelity, again, to truth to hold that the same thing can be true in religion and false in philosophy. But we know that we do not always know what are opposites in the nature of things. And we would wait until eternity, believing in apparent opposites, rather than deny, for the sake of mental peace, one apparent truth. But need we do either? May we not in this instance find truth enough already known, to indicate that there is no real contradiction between nature and Jesus Christ?

May not the opposition of convictions in our minds result simply from the narrowness of our view of both truths? Is there any larger view in which these two great conclusions— the oneness of nature, and the divine originality of Jesus Christ—shall both appear to be parts and results of one and the same comprehensive and far-reaching design? May we not have in the person and life of Christ the very culmination, the highest union, of two great processes of God's activity, of two evolutions, which have been working from the beginning towards one far-off and glorious consummation? I believe that there are divine processes, great supernatural laws and forces of the natural economy of things— traces and results of which are to be found in the visible worlds and in human history— which culminate and are manifestly fulfilled in the person and work of the Christ; and in relation to which his supernatural being may be seen to be most truly and profoundly natural—the end of the creation, and the consummation of history, prepared from the foundation of the world.

CHAPTER VI.

THE CULMINATION IN THE CHRIST.—II. THE NATURALNESS OF CHRIST.

ONE evidence of this deeper naturalness of the incarnation, of this higher harmony of the life of the Christ with the whole system of things, comes to us directly from our consideration of those characteristics of Jesus by which his uniqueness is made obvious. Though without parallel, his life is in perfect accordance throughout with itself. All its characteristics seem natural when grouped together, and looked at, each in its relations to the others. Though we have never seen one like Jesus, yet Jesus always seems like himself. Any one marvellous word or deed, related by the evangelists of the Son of man, does not appear strange if we read of it in connection with all the other alleged facts of his life. Or, in other words, if all the circumstances related of Jesus be admitted, they form together an orderly and consistent whole. Though Jesus is the great miracle of history, he is a self-consistent miracle.

The importance of this consideration can hardly be overstated. It has great evidential force, and is significant both of the genuineness of the life of Jesus, and also of his place in the larger nature of things. It shows his life to be a true life, and a life, however wonderful, not out of the divine order. We need, therefore, to look closely at this unity of Jesus' life and its significance.

The fact that the particulars of any narrative, although very strange in themselves, form together a perfectly consistent and straightforward story, gives credibility to the whole account, and reflects back the probability of the whole upon each incident of the story. This is a strictly legal principle of evidence. A witness, we will suppose, begins with an improbable statement. He adds another and another singular incident. We shake our heads in incredulity, but we begin to notice a method in his madness. His very improbabilities begin to combine themselves into one growing probability of truth. If any one incident happened as he narrates, it is possible that the whole event, or series of events, occurred. The unity of all, and the consistency of the whole story, furnish strong presumptive evidence, at least, of its truth, which can be set aside only by positive evidence, or stronger probabilities, to the contrary. The fact, therefore, that the several scenes in the life of Jesus fall into order and make one continuous, beautiful whole, if all the reports of the evangelists be substantially true, is certainly a striking evidence of the truthfulness of the evangelists' strange story. Taken as a whole, it looks natural.

It is a strictly scientific principle of judgment which we are using. If, for instance, we should discover a single fossil bone which looks as though it might belong to the anatomy of some bird, yet is so large, or curiously shaped, as to make it impossible for us to refer it to any bird we have ever seen or heard of, we might say: "This could not have been what we supposed at first; it must be something else." But if, one after another, several strangely formed bones should be found, and if, when put together, it were discovered that their very peculiarities match, and that they form the skeleton of a bird, complete in itself, though unlike that of any bird known to us; then we should be obliged to admit that the fossil remains, taken as a whole, prove that the strange bird once really existed; and if we had no place for it in our science of organic forms, we should simply have to revise our science and make room for it. The completeness of the whole, that is to say, enables us rightly to interpret the parts, and to view as a natural series, or connected system, peculiarities which might otherwise seem contrary to experience and unaccountable.

Similarly the confirmation of the parts, given by the whole of the Gospel, ought to have recognized scientific value. What looks unnatural by itself, becomes a natural part of the entire order of events or system of truths. The several supernatural occurrences, related in the Gospels, form one natural order, if regarded as successive manifestations of one divine process of revelation. Thus we begin with a strange story of the nativity. It would be incredible if it were followed by an ordinary life. We could not believe it if the song of the angels had announced the birth of a man who should prove to be only like one of us. But we read on, and find that the life, scene after scene, year after year, corresponds to the strange story of the birth, and the end confirms the beginning of the Gospel of the Son of God. A marvellous effect equals a marvellous cause. As we pursue the narrative, we find upon almost every page the report of some wonderful work. We might be utterly incredulous, did we not notice, as we proceed, that they all seem to be manifestations of one and the same power, and the agreement and correspondences of the works would indicate some one efficient principle common to them all. We read on, and are amazed by the words to the women, "He is risen." But in our surprise, while the testimony of different witnesses is brought to us confirming the marvellous fact of the resurrection, we remember that his very birth was miraculous, and his daily life a growing wonder. And, again, miracle answers miracle, and all seems to be the continuous manifestation of a more than human presence. These many testimonies to his resurrection would be contrary to experience, and seem incredible, if related of one of our friends whom we had just buried; but are they contrary to the experience the world had already had of Jesus? Are they contrary to human experience of the Christ? He who appeared to the disciples, risen from the dead, is One whom they had already followed, wondering, in the way; One whose life with them in Judea and Galilee had been full of surprises; whom they had already found to be not as other men are. The resurrection was not contrary to their experience of Jesus. We read on to the end, and the Gospel concludes with the strange story of the ascension from Mt. Olivet. Of any other a close of life like that might seem incredible. But the whole preceding narrative makes it a natural scene at the close of Jesus' life. We expect a wonderful sunset at the end of a rare day in June. Read the description of the ascension, after reading the whole Gospel before it, and it ceases to seem surprising that Jesus should have vanished in a cloud of glory from the eyes of his disciples. His miraculous conception, and his ascension into heaven, seem the fitting and natural beginning and ending of the unearthly life that lay between. The deep, wonderful harmony between Jesus' person and his life, between his character and his works, is to us the almost irresistible proof of the genuineness of both. We are asked to believe in no disconnected miracles; we may trace the unbroken continuity of a divine life with man. We are bidden to put our faith in no momentary and evanescent gleams of something mysterious and unearthly; we are called upon to follow humbly and reverently One who from the first scenes of his boyhood moved upon a plane above us all—a daily wonder to his friends—in thought and life, as well as word and deed, the continuous miracle of his age; and all the events in his exalted life require each the others; and though, when taken singly, they are seemingly incredible, together they form one consistent whole, itself not inconceivable as one divine process of self-revelation.

Besides this naturalness of Jesus' life as a whole, and the agreement of its parts among themselves, there is perfect correspondence between being and influence in the life which the evangelists portray, and in the continuation of its power in Christianity. The influence of Jesus is most natural, if his person is what it was represented to have been; and his person is natural when viewed as the cause of the effect which, it is alleged, was produced by his dwelling among men. The law of cause and effect is not broken, the harmony of being and influence is not interrupted, if all the alleged facts be granted. This, also, is a significant appearance of the Christ of the Gospels; for the law, which is fulfilled in his life, of the direct relation, or correspondence between being and influence, is one of the universal laws. It would be hard to conceive of a miraculous violation of it, for it is a law of nature which contains in itself, also, a moral truth. What anything does is determined, and ought to be determined, by what it is. "Of such as they have" all things give unto us; the solid earth of its gravity; the air of its breath of life; flowers of their fragrance; birds of their songfulness; the moon of her silvery light; the sun of the gladsome day. The whole science of physics and of chemical equivalents rests upon the primal law, that what any molecule of matter does is in direct ratio to what it is.

The work done never exceeds the measure of force represented by the quantities of nature's constant equation. Nothing gives what it has not first received. There is always absolute truthfulness in the charity of nature. So, also, in human society, men give of what they have in themselves; their influence is the exponent of what they are. What goes forth from them of good or evil, of hurtful influence or of healing virtue, is the expression, the moral equivalent, of what they are and have in themselves; of the goodness, or the sin, which is formed in their own hearts.

In the long run this law of personal influence proves itself to be true. Our doing is measured by our being. This, also, is one of the fundamental principles of the philosophy of history, that being and giving, what men and states and civilizations are, and what they do, form a direct historical ratio, and each is the explanation of the other. We simply apply this universal law of influence to the life of Christ, when we seek for the adequate explanation of what he has done, and is doing, in the world, in the mystery of his own person; and, conversely, in the ineffable glory of his person, see the wonder of his influence in human history made plain. Each is the natural correlate of the other. We apply this principle to his miracles. Was he who wrought these miracles himself such a person that they seem natural works for him to do? The surprise, then, of his works disappears before the greater surprise of his person. If he, himself, has a supernatural consciousness, then, by the established and universal law of influence, his miracles follow as a matter of course. The ultimate reason, to thoughtful minds, for belief in the miracles of Christ, must be faith in the higher nature of Christ's person. Given either as historically probable, and the other is conceivable. Either makes the other natural. The miracles, as related in the Gospels, are simply a part of Christ's self-revelation, in consistency with the whole, and with each other, showing throughout the same power and moral quality, and in perfect keeping with all other parts of his self-revelation, manifesting his glory. If the life of Jesus was the evolution in nature, in human nature, of a higher power, the development of an incarnate divine life, it is, from beginning to end, in entire harmony with itself—one continuous and orderly revelation.

We may apply the same general law of influence to the teaching of Jesus. He spake as never man spake, because he was as never man was. The originality of Christ's doctrine has its counterpart in the uniqueness of his self-consciousness. One peculiarity of Jesus' authority, to which we have already alluded, finds in this manner its only explanation. There seems to be a difference in kind between the inspiration of Jesus and the inspiration of the prophets. Jesus was inspired from within —not from a God without himself. The Delphic priest must go and consult the oracle for the response; the Hebrew seer must bind around him the Urim and the Thummim; the later prophets declare the words of the Lord which came to them: a voice calls them; a sign is shown them; a scene of strange import appears as a vision of the spirit; they wait, and look, and listen, and then go forth to the people, or enter the king's palace, with some message with which they are sent from the Eternal;—but Christ does not seem to go without himself, beyond his own self-consciousness, for his revelations. He knows the Father. He declares what the Father makes known to the Son. As he comes to the knowledge of himself, he comes to his knowledge of the Father. His own thoughts are God's thoughts. His revelation of God is the manifestation of his own glory. His word from the Lord is given to him through his own life, and in showing himself he declares unto his disciples the Father. This is altogether exceptional and marvellous:

both the inspiration and the truth of Jesus are unlike anything ever witnessed before in Judea, and contrary to human experience; but they *correspond.* The teaching and the person of Jesus, as the evangelists represent each, are at one, and each is the witness of the genuineness of the other. So all the other peculiarities of the teaching of Jesus, at which we have glanced, are in accordance with the image of the divine human person, of which the disciples were the witnesses.*

The same correspondence between being and influence in Christ, it should be noticed, is illustrated and confirmed by the historical work of Jesus, or, what we may justly call, the continuation of the life of Christ in Christianity. "Lo, I am with you alway even unto the end of the world," was his word to his disciples as he vanished from them; and what the evangelists say that he is, and what he has been doing through Christian history, correspond. But we shall recur to this correspondence between the Christ of the Gospels as a cause, and Christianity as an effect, in another connection. At this point we desire to

---

* The same law of the direct ratio between being and influence should be applied to the Christian doctrine of the atonement; what Christ did for us upon the cross is determined by what he was when dying upon the cross: but to enter upon this suggestive subject would carry us too far from our immediate purpose.

dwell upon the special significance of this agreement among themselves of the several parts and successive events of Christ's life; of this thorough harmony between the work and the being of Jesus; of the naturalness of his supernatural life when viewed as one whole, complete in itself. Such appearances indicate that this strange life was not out of order, or without law—an anomaly of nature— a causeless and incredible miracle in the regular course of human experience. The very orderliness, symmetry, and perfectness of this life might lead us to suspect that it may have been lived in fulfilment of diviner things in nature than we have dreamed of in our philosophy. There is a method in the miracle. There is a spiritual design worked out in the course of this divinely human life. It is a life that manifestly follows its own higher law of development. It is throughout the orderly unfolding, the natural growth, of a supernatural principle and a superhuman soul. Its several moments, epochs, and manifestations, inexplicable by our self-knowledge, and contrary to our experience of ourselves, seem to be the successive stages of some diviner unfolding than we know, and the whole development follows its own hidden and spiritual law. The life of Jesus, in a word, unnatural and inconceivable on any other hypothesis, becomes natural and conceivable the moment we regard it as the development of an incarnation.

The question, then, at once springs up: Are there any signs elsewhere in the world of a great supernatural movement, a higher evolution, whose natural culmination may be the divine human life of the Christ? Original and unaccountable as were his coming and his appearance, in the order of nature,—is there a larger, deeper, higher, diviner order of nature and history in the midst of which Jesus has his own proper place and dominion? From the consideration of the naturalness of the life of Christ, when viewed as one continuous process of divine revelation, we are led further to ask how that unique person stands in relation to the divine processes in history which had already, before his coming, been working out providential designs? As the fulfilment of a divine life in the world, as the culmination of a divine energy in human history, may not this wonder of the ages, this miracle of humanity, become again to us a most profoundly natural phenomenon—a manifestation of God in harmony with the deepest truth, and highest law, and largest design of the creation— verily foreordained, as the Scriptures say, before the foundation of the world? We believe the uniqueness of the Christ to be but the half truth of history; the naturalness of the incarnation is the whole truth of the creation.

In attempting to enlarge our horizon, and to rise to this broader philosophy of history, we have then, first, to regard Jesus Christ as the end of a special historical development, the power and law of which were from above. As such, Christ is the natural conclusion of a supernatural process, the signs and evidences of which we have traced, in preceding chapters, in the history of Israel—in the historical growth of the Bible and the religion of the Bible. Judaism of itself did not produce, as its natural flower, the beauty of the Gospel; Judaism by its own forces could not develop into Christianity, or account for the Christ standing among men. He is unique. But he appeared as the end of a supernatural evolution, which we can follow as a great, special providential preparation through the history of Israel. Jesus is the realized Christ of the Old Dispensation. Without the coming of the Messiah, the divine light, glimmering and growing through the Old Dispensation, would be as unnatural and inexplicable as a dawn that should purple the mountain-tops, and, while all the meadows and valleys lay hushed in expectancy, ready to break forth into song, should go out in darkness, and end in no day.

The early Christian fathers, as they reasoned

with the philosophers, or laid their apologies for Christianity at the feet of emperors, placed great stress upon the fulfilment of prophecy in the coming of Christ. The argument from prophecy was a favorite argument of those early writers who had awakened from the broken dreams and disappointed visions of the pagan philosophies into the clear light of the new Christian hope. Justin Martyr found in Christianity the true philosophy, in which the words of divine wisdom, the seeds of the Logos, scattered among the gentile religions were comprehended and fulfilled. The Word, he believed, was in the world before Christ came in the flesh : " the Word of whom every race of men were partakers; and those who lived reasonably," * he said, " are Christians, even though they have been thought atheists, as, among the Greeks, Socrates and Heraclitus, and men like them ; " and Justin Martyr, accordingly, commends his Christian faith alike to Jews and Gentiles as the consummation of all philosophy and the fulfilment of direct testimonies of the Hebrew prophets. Similarly a genial, classical student and historian of the last century finds in the New Testament the key to all his studies of the past. In the year 1782, Mueller wrote these words in a letter to

---

* With reason, or " with the Word." First Apology, 46.

a friend : "I have been reading the ancients, without excepting a single one, in the order of time in which they lived. I know not why, it occurred to me, two months ago, to take a look into the New Testament, before my studies had advanced to the times in which it was written. I had not read it any more for many years, and before I took it in my hand I was prejudiced against it. How shall I express to you what I found therein? The light which blinded Paul on the way to Damascus was for him not more wonderful, not more surprising, than was for me what I suddenly discovered there, — the fulfilment of all hopes, the highest perfection of philosophy, the explanation of revolutions, the key to all apparent contradictions of the physical and moral world, life and immortality. I have read no book over it, but hitherto there has always failed me something in my studies of the early times, and first since I knew our Lord, all is clear before my eyes; with him there is nothing which I cannot explain." * Matthew Arnold † regards the argument from supernatural predictions as a line of evidence which gives way at all points. But Mr. Arnold's literary methods touch only upon the surface of the great prophetic stream and

---

* Luthardt, Fundamental Truths. Note, 17, Lect. iii.
† Literature and Dogma, p. 114.

tendency of history. Criticism may readily enough convict Justin Martyr and the early Apologists of laying undue weight upon particular predictions of the prophets; but the argument from prophecy goes deeper than the text of Scripture; and the preparatory significance of all pre-Christian history, which made so profound an impression upon Mueller, is its inner and abiding sense. Single texts of the Hebrew Scriptures, and definite predictions of the prophets, may still, according to a critical scholarship, be more important, and less easily dissolved into general moral platitudes, than Mr. Arnold would allow;* but the question of a divine life in history, specially revealed through Israel, and finally incarnate in the Word, is not a mere question of proof-texts and interpretations of particular Scriptures. In the argument from prophecy we have to do with a forest, not with a single bough or a basket of leaves; with the whole trend of a coast, not with single headlands or inlets of the sea; with a zone of constellations, not with scattered stars. We have to do with the whole tenor of Scripture, with the pro-

---

* The critical discussion of particular prophetic predictions would carry us beyond our bounds; we cannot, however, dismiss with Mr. Arnold's gracious wave of the hand several prophecies which seem to have been remarkably fulfilled. We are not always satisfied with the rationalists' short method with prophecy; viz.: the bringing the writer down to the times of which he writes.

longed course of centuries of history; with the multitudinous testimonies of the human soul in many generations; with the arrangements and combinations of many events in one continuous and resplendent revelation of the glory of the Lord. Not only, as Justin Martyr, with a more catholic sense of Christ in history than is sometimes manifested among ourselves, thought, was the Word with all who lived reasonably, but, also, Israel was itself a prophet, a messenger sent to prepare the way of the Lord. The history is itself strangely prophetic. Mr. Arnold lays down as the first law of reasonableness in our judgments that we should be acquainted with the best that has been thought and said; but nothing to better purpose has been said concerning prophecy than Herder's word that the "whole Old Testament with the nature of its religion is to be regarded as one great prophecy;" or than Dorner's comment upon Herder's saying, that "thereby whatever is lost in untenable verbal predictions is richly renewed;" that with "a prophecy of words" we have "a prophecy of reality." * Through the perspective of biblical history we look down a real line of prophecy. The angel in the Apocalypse had a broader and better understanding than Mr.

---

* Geschichte d. prot. Theologie, s. 861.

Arnold of the argument from prophecy when he said : " The testimony of Jesus is the spirit of prophecy."

In this larger view of prophecy two leading lines of evidence, two great courses of historical development, can be traced to their point of meeting in the Christ. The one is the progress of the educational purpose of the God of the Bible. There is a growing revelation of truth, the signs of which all point to the coming of the great Teacher with his final doctrine. In a preceding chapter we have marked the signs of a great process of divine education of man going on through the unfolding history of Israel. If our reasoning has not been all in the air ; if we have been dealing with divine ideas that passed into institutions, laws, customs, types ; if we have been following, in one word, a real historical revelation,—then we ought to view the life and doctrine of Christ in its relation to this vast educational and reformatory work of God in Israel ; and, beheld in that relation, he who spake as never man spake comes, nevertheless, not as a sudden wonder of history, but as the fulfilment of the whole truth of God implanted and growing through the past. All that has been said of the educational methods and design of God in the Old Testament is in keeping with the manner in which Christ comes not to destroy, but to fulfil, the law and the prophets. His voice startled the synagogue, and his word destroyed the temple; but the wisdom of God, which had been struggling through all the errors of the dark, clouded past, was made perfect in his Gospel. Scribes and rabbis, as we have seen, could not have deduced his new truth from their Scriptures or their traditions; but when Christ brought it from heaven it was found to be the perfect expression of all that the Holy Spirit of education for generations had been trying to say. Christ's word, when once it is spoken on earth, is the divine word which completes the broken words of the prophets, and fulfils the Scriptures. That which was partial in the divine teaching heretofore, disappears. The defects of the preparatory stages are removed; human misunderstandings of the earlier lessons are corrected when the end is reached, and the mystery of the ages is revealed. When the revelation of God is fully come, old truths, but dimly seen, or half revealed, or strangely confused, in the twilight of an earlier hour, are seen in the distinctness of the day. As many objects of a landscape appear as shadowy forms in the first glimmer of the dawn, the distant and the near being alike indistinguishable — far-off and lofty objects starting suddenly like spectres out of the mists just before us; but when the sun is risen all things assume their true proportions, the horizon recedes into the distance, and all confusion of vision ceases: so the truths of God's kingdom and its vast prospects lay half revealed and half concealed before the prophets of old; the present and the future often seemed to them alike close at hand; far-off events were dispensations impending over their own times; dim visions of distant ages rose unexpectedly before them, near at hand, out of the great wonder and awe in which they walked;—but Jesus' coming brought out into clear certainty the kingdom of God and its verities; and his disciples, the children of the light and of the day, went on their way rejoicing in the revelation of the mystery of the ages. The Gospel from above fulfilled and dismissed the preparatory truth and teaching, and ushered in the new dispensation of the Spirit. Viewed, then, as the culmination and end of a great supernatural course of human education—of a course of divine historical object-lessons, of truths embodied in events, and enforced through the providential guidance of a chosen people—the life of Jesus, separate though it is from all other lives, and his doctrine, in all its originality, seem no more to be an isolated and incredible phenomenon; but the mission of the Teacher sent from God has its appointed place and necessity in the very plan of the God of history.

But here, also, we must rise above the defects of a merely intellectual conception of history and revelation. Life is more than a process of thought, history is richer than a development of the Hegelian idea; revelation is a larger and diviner gift than the inculcation of a system of truth. It is, as we have seen, a manifestation of God in deed as well as in word; an impartation to man through a continuous giving, from generation to generation, of God's own Spirit and love; it is the life of God in man, and with man, and for man. And in this largest and divinest sense the history of Israel is as a whole a prophecy of the incarnation. Christ came as the most perfect possible impartation and revelation in human form of the very life of God with the world and in the world; and all that God had been graciously doing and becoming in history, as well as teaching and saying, reaches its perfect result, bears its final fruit, in the Son of man. He was the life, says the beloved disciple, and the *life* was the *light* of the world. Jesus Christ was a divine fact, in the eyes of the disciples, before Christianity became a doctrine of their understandings. Christianity was a divine fact, full of life and power, before it was a creed of the Church. And for this final divine fact of revelation all the preceding events and dispensations were fitted up and arranged. This is the other aspect of the argument from prophecy to which we referred. The providential arrangement of the historical scenes for the coming at last of the Son of man, is the great supernatural fact of history, which rationalism can never quite explain away. Though we may regard event after event, and life after life, as merely natural occurrences, yet, after all that should be admitted, another more marvellous fact remains, and one more difficult of explanation. We have to give a reason for the order of the facts, for the perspective of the history. The combination of events, their adaptations and progress, and the deep design running through them all, and making all tend towards one far-off end, one divine result,—how shall they who have no eyes for the working of spiritual powers, and for the presence of God in history, account for these things? As one entering some mansion might readily understand for what purpose its several chambers and connected apartments had been provided and fitted up, but would wonder what was about to take place, should he observe that the whole house was put in order apparently for some great event—all its rooms being lighted and in waiting—and his wonder would at once cease, and all become clear, should he hear the sound of music from the hall, and the bridegroom's voice among his friends: so we pass from scene to scene through this great history, and all things seem prepared and waiting for some coming event, and we understand at once the meaning of it all when we hear that at last the bridegroom is come, and all things are now ready for the marriage supper of the Lamb.

The design of the whole is the real prophecy of Israel's career. The particular letters of this message may belong to the ordinary alphabet, but they are arranged in an intelligible order, for an extraordinary communication. The arrangement is the ultimate supernatural fact. It is not enough for criticism to tell us that particular predictions are meaningless. We are not anxious to dispute about the letters or the types. The history, as God has put its letters together, spells the adorable name of the Messiah. Christ, therefore, in his divine originality, is, nevertheless, as the Word made flesh, not a sudden appearance —a causeless miracle of history; for in this view he is seen to be the real unity of the Old and the New Testaments. The New Testament is not evolved from the Old, yet it cannot be separated from it; for both proceed from the same divine life which has been with man in all his history of ignorance and sin, and which is the true light which lighteth every man that cometh into the world.

As the Son of man seems no more a stranger, but the expected heir, when we look up the perspective of Hebrew history, and behold him as the fulfilment of its whole prophecy; so also, when we look back through the history of his Church, the incarnation seems to be the necessary beginning, the natural cause, of the continuous life which has been in the world since he came. Take the divineness from that life, and whole series of events are thrown into confusion, and men and women, in every generation since, are made to live in a manner unaccountable and most absurd. Take that one hour at Bethlehem out of human history, and eighteen centuries of hours are left but partially explained. The scepticism which cannot see the divine in Jesus Christ, becomes blind to the human in Peter, and John, and Paul. In order to look upon Jesus as altogether like one of us, it is compelled to view the disciples in unnatural lights. In order to escape from the difficulties of supposing miracles in the realm of nature, it invents miracles in the realm of mind and morals. In order to avoid belief in special manifestations of the supernatural in nature, for which we can render a reason, and which we may bring under a more general law, it introduces anomalies of human conduct, for which we can give no good reason, and which we cannot bring under any known law of experience. When faith in the supernatural in Christianity is thrown away, the key is lost which can unlock the meaning of the Acts and the Epistles of the apostles, and open passage after passage of Christian history. Here, also, the combinations of the forces of Christianity, the grouping of events, the arrangements of the historic stage, indicate a higher ordering and a divine power. Though the five causes which Gibbon has assigned as the reasons for the spread of Christianity may be intelligible on natural grounds, nevertheless, as John Henry Newman* has strikingly shown, the coincidence of these causes is left by Gibbon unexplained;—but this coincidence of causes, and this combination of forces, the result of which is a continuous, growing Christianity, constitute a residual providential part of modern history—they are the undeniable and living witness of Christianity to Christ.

We have gained, then, thus far a view of the naturalness of the person and life of Christ, when considered as a whole, complete in itself,

---

* Grammar of Assent, p. 445.

and also when contemplated in its appointed place in the midst of a divine order of human history. But our horizon enlarges as we proceed. Human history is only a brief span of time; the existence of our race is only for one day of God's thousands of years; and the process by which the worlds are made embraces vaster cycles of ages. When we endeavor to place ourselves in imagination nearer the beginning, and to gaze down those vast vistas of time, through those great creative processes, on to the advent of man, and the coming of the Son of man,—how then does the Christ appear? unexpected, unheralded, a causeless wonder, or as the appointed heir and natural head over all? The apostle who more than any other possessed a Christian philosophy of history, in several passages,* represents the Christ of his faith as the head of the creation. He seemed to see the whole creation summed up and perfected in the second man, the Lord from heaven. The time had not then come for that germinant truth of the Pauline Epistles to obtain in the thought of the Christian world its full development. It is but beginning to obtain it in the theology of to-day. The great apostle lacked the scientific knowledge of the world's whole prophetic past which

---

* Ep. i. 10, 22; Col. i. 15–20; 1st Cor. xv. 25–28, 45–47.

might have enabled him to carry out in a grand apostrophe his own inspired idea of the natural headship of Christ. Subsequent theology has labored to grasp the natural relationship of Christ to the human race as an essential element in the Christian doctrine of sin and redemption. We believe that Paul's great truth is not yet exhausted, and that a scientific age will eventually leave it still farther advanced, and possessed of commanding authority over reverent minds. Already Paul's idea of Christ has begun to triumph in the midst of the spoils of our sciences. It was not many years ago that Hugh Miller advanced Paul's truth to still larger honor as he read from nature's own indelible records a mute prophecy of the coming of the perfect man. The lower dynasties, whose records the geologist reads in the tables of stone, give place to the higher, and never return. The dynasty of the future, which shall not pass away, for beyond it progress cannot go, is to be the kingdom of God himself in the form of man. "We find the point of elevation never to be exceeded meetly coincident with the final period, never to be terminated—the infinite in height harmoniously associated with the eternal in duration. Creation and Creator meet at one point, and in one person. The long ascending line from dead matter to man has been a progress

Godwards, not an asymptotical progress, but destined from the beginning to furnish a point of union; and occupying that point as true God and true man—as Creator and created—we recognize the adorable monarch of all the future."* But the authority of Hugh Miller is already outgrown; does the advance of science since his day compel us to leave his interpretations of the "geologic prophecies" with the discarded biblical expositions of the theologians who mistrusted him? or does it enable us to say with clearer confidence that the ways of the Creator through the creation slowly yet surely converge towards, and only can find their destined meeting-point and end in, some form so perfect and complete as to be the crown of all God's works, and the express image of his person? In one word, are we warranted in believing that the creation can stop short of the Christ? Can the creative process stop short, and return upon itself, when the human race is reached, and man's day on earth shall be finished? or does the manifest destiny of the creation point to something still human, but diviner?

The question just stated is partly a question of fact. But it is also more than a question of fact; it is a question of interpretation.

---

* Testimony of the Rocks, p. 178.

Natural science must determine the facts;—determine them as her own legitimate work, and without interference. We have no right to disturb by so much as a heart-beat the scientific investigation of the facts of nature. Feeling has no business in the laboratory. Clear, precise, careful perception is the first duty of natural science. But when the facts are once seen and determined, their interpretation is another matter. Other, and higher, powers must enter upon this work. Natural science must pass her facts over to moral science for the final interpretation of them. Scientific perceptions are to be taken up into metaphysical and moral conclusions. They cannot be rationally co-ordinated, and really understood, until they are. And it is possible that a strictly scientific determination of the law of evolution may just miss the truth, and fail of the real secret at nature's heart, because it refuses to call in the aid of the spirit that is in man, in order to divine the interpretation of its visions.

Our first concern, then, must be to go to our natural sciences for any facts which may bear upon our inquiry. Two results of modern science claim at once our attention as of possible spiritual significance. The one is the ascent of life. The mode or laws of that ascent may still be matters of scientific questioning;

for, notwithstanding the positiveness of the pronounced evolutionists, there are still writers whose scientific attainments we cannot question, who are not yet satisfied as to the mode and manner of evolution. Whether the ascent of types has been a gradual rise, without leaps or breaks, or any gaps in the evidence; whether it should be represented by an inclined plane, or by a succession of steps; whether catastrophic upheavals, and the introduction of new forces, or forms, at marked epochs, into the creation, should be admitted on strictly scientific grounds,—we are neither concerned nor qualified to determine. We cannot find these questions determined for us, or put beyond all doubt, by those who do seem qualified to judge. At least the teachers differ among themselves. Perhaps a far broader and more patient induction of facts may be still necessary before man can write, what an inspired prophet did not attempt to write, a thorough and perfectly correct natural history of the creation. It is possible that there may be more "incident forces" to be taken into the account than appear in Herbert Spencer's diagrams. The last word of science is not yet spoken. But certain results, however, may be regarded as established; and the gradual ascent of life is an observed fact. Whatever the manner or the law of it, the fact of it is beyond question. Whatever may be the ultimate form of our evolutionary philosophy, the fact is that this world is one great development. Alike in the physical constitution of the globe, and in the forms of life which have appeared upon it, each age has surpassed the preceding, and prepared the way for the better age to follow.

The other result of modern science, which is significant in this inquiry, is the fact that the development of the creation has all along been a process of differentiation and individualization, a process the tendency of which throughout has been to evoke ever more highly organized specific and individual forms. Indeed, according to the evolutionists, some favored individual of one species constitutes the variation which is the beginning of a new species. The line of progress is through chosen individuals. All things conspire together to produce the highest, best, most richly endowed individual form, and that brings in the new species. If this law, therefore, is to continue, the goal of the creation must be not merely some supreme type in which all the energies of the creation exhaust their power, but rather in the most specialized and perfectly organized specimen, or individual realization of that last highest type. Our scientists have grasped firmly this great law of differentiation and individualization which runs through the creation, and determines the succession of life upon the earth; but possibly they may not have fathomed the deeper moral significance of this first principle of things, or divined the Christian fulfilment of their own leading truth. Herbert Spencer, who has made the law of differentiation a guiding principle of his thinking, asks of the theologians if it is not just possible that there should be a higher form of life than that of which we can gain a conception from our own personality.* We follow the struggle of existence upwards from dim nebulous beginnings to substantial worlds, and animate forms, and sensibility, and the dawn of consciousness, and the rich personal life of man; and we, too, ask, if the process shall stop there? if the ascent of life shall end in the broad level of humanity, or reach one crowning point? Is it not "just possible" that there may be a higher and diviner realization of nature and humanity than our personal consciousness? Have we reached in the type of the human soul the last possible goal? Is there still to come the One in whom the whole prophetic ascent of life, through ever more favored individual forms, shall be fulfilled—

---

* First Principles, p. 109.

the second man, the Lord from heaven? Clearly it would be in accordance with the whole analogy of the previous ascent and differentiation of nature, if, after the common plane of humanity has been gained, the process of selection should still continue; if we should find evidence within the historic period of the natural selection of an Abraham and his descendants; if a thousand forces should combine to call forth a peculiar people; if upon that highly favored stem should appear at last humanity's consummate flower! It would be in accordance with the whole course of nature, and a working on to still higher issues of its organic law of differentiation, if the coming of man should be followed in the fulness of time by the advent of the Son of man, who should introduce a new reign upon the earth, a kingdom of God in which all should be fulfilled. We take the "just possible" of Mr. Spencer's question as a scientific permission to look up through nature's evolution to a still diviner issue than a human soul; and we do but follow nature's innate prophecy when we seek for our Lord. Viewed through the perspective which our evolutionary science has opened, the glorious form of the Son of man is not unnatural, not a miracle; no more without preparation and heralding than the coming of any higher type in the great ascent of life, or than the advent of man. If the momentum of life makes the birth of man possible, so that a being possessed of sufficient intelligence, in some earlier geological age, might have confidently predicted man's coming at some future time: so equally the momentum of the creative purpose makes possible the introduction of a reign beyond the kingdom of man, so that before Christ came in the flesh a superior intelligence might have read from the succession of life on the earth, and the advance of human history, a prophecy of the day of the Messiah. The apostle may have gained the widest generalization, and the last philosophy of the creation, when, in a great moment of inspiration, he saw first the natural order, and afterward the spiritual; and learned that the first man is of the earth, earthy, but the second man is the Lord from heaven. It is just possible—to use again Mr. Spencer's permission—that in a personality which is human, yet more than human (as man sums up in himself all the life in the earth before him, yet is himself more than all beneath him), the goal of the whole creation may have been attained, and that through him who is appointed heir of all things a new kingdom which shall supersede all the kingdoms of this world has been already ushered in.

If it be objected that it is impossible for us to conceive of a divinely human personality, we may fall back again upon Mr. Spencer's assertion, and apply to the Messiah, in whom we believe, the words which he uses of his imagined superhuman personality. "It is true," Mr. Spencer says,* " that we are totally unable to conceive any such higher mode of being. But this is not a reason for questioning its existence; it is rather the reverse."

But we have already passed to a question of the interpretation of the appearance and laws of nature. And no Scripture, whether written on the rocks or on parchment, is of any private interpretation. The specialist is never the best interpreter. A more general culture, a broader discipline, the habit of exercising many powers of our complex being, are indispensable to the art of interpretation. Our scientific specialists are in danger of giving us only the private interpretation. Something besides scientific training is indispensable to the broad and larger interpretation of the Scripture of nature. After the evolutionist has discovered a law or course of nature, by the very limitations of his special studies, and the acquired habits necessary to his work, he may be incapacitated from acting the part

---

* First Principles, p. 109.

of an interpreter of nature's truth, and of discerning the relation of what he has discovered to spiritual phenomena and the moral order of human history. We ought to read the facts of physical science in the light of moral science, in order to obtain a philosophy which shall be more than a private interpretation of nature, and life, and destiny.

It remains for us, therefore, to interpret this law of ascent and individualization of life in connection with moral and spiritual experience; to ask whether the prophecy of nature, and the prophecy of the human soul, combine in one growing Messianic hope. Positive science cannot stop us on the threshold of a moral interpretation of its phenomena by any denial of the possibility of an influx of spiritual or divine influences into the heart of natural processes. To claim that evolution necessarily excludes any impulse from without, or the permeation of nature with spiritual force, is to beg beforehand the very question of fact at issue, and to shut out of the world, upon the testimony of the senses, forces which, were they operating ever so powerfully before our eyes, we should not be able to see; and of whose presence, or absence, in any phenomena, therefore, the senses are not competent witnesses. Science, thus, would exclude religion by irrelevant testimony. The final question is, in general, not whether the creation *appears* to be a continuous natural evolution, but whether, as moral and rational beings, possessed of our own unseen life in self-consciousness, we must not give to that which appears a higher and diviner significance? The immediate creative or preservative activity of a personal God would not make any change in the *appearance* of things. They would seem to the senses to come of themselves, though a God called them into being. If the Creator should make a new world before our eyes, we should see only what the astronomer sees when a new star shines into his telescope. Though the Almighty stretches forth his hand, the finger of God is never visible save to the spirit of the prophet. Our special question at present, then, is, whether when we attempt as moral, spiritual beings to interpret natural evolution, to realize its invisible moral side, to divine the real purpose at the heart of things, we are not led on to the hope of some high spiritual fulfilment of the whole course of nature; and whether the coming of the divine life, in the form of man, is not the goal and end of the creation prepared for from the foundation of the world? To answer this question, we must bring to this apparent evolution of life and struggle of nature upwards towards the most individualized and perfect form, reasonings and divinations which we draw from other sources than those of natural science. We must go and consult the oracles of our own hearts; we must read nature in the spirit's light. Our moral intuitions, our religious feeling, have a legitimate place, and work of their own to do, in our final philosophy of the creation.

The true moral interpretation of the course of nature is indicated, first, by the testimony of the human soul to the need of a Messiah. We do not fall back in this assertion simply upon the familiar argument of man's need of a mediator, which may be drawn from the universality of religious sacrifices. We appeal, also, to the general desire of mankind for some embodied ideal, some realized example of what is truly adorable and divine. Seneca acknowledges the need of a moral ideal, a pattern by which conduct may be shaped.* It is a singular and significant moral fact that people in general do make for themselves some Christ. Something takes the place to them of Christ, and they find their life in it. They cannot live without imagining something which, however vaguely or imperfectly, shall be a substitute in their expe-

---

* Fisher, Beginnings of Ch., p. 174.

rience for faith in the Christ of our Gospels. These objects of veneration and devotion, which are made to answer in the thoughts the place of the Messiah, vary with different temperaments and degrees of culture—from the rude idol of the untaught savage up to the refinements of hero-worship, or the surrender of self to some worshipful idea. It is not wholly a pious fraud that has raised the saints into objects of worship. The human soul in many an hour of its truest, deepest life must have some altar of devotion. The Christ-want of the soul has led many to bow down before pictures of saintly beauty. The Christ who knows the heart may find himself ignorantly worshipped where the Protestant, passing among the devotees prostrate in cathedral chapels, and gazing coldly at the pictures over the altars, may see only superstition. A deep Messianic desire lies, also, at the bottom of hero-worship. Even in these modern days of cold intellectualism, it is said that incense has been offered to the bust of Goethe, and the apotheosis of some master of philosophy or poetry in the conversation of his disciples is hardly an unknown phenomenon. Others still, who call no man master, have made for themselves a religion of some inspiring idea, and found their substitute for the Christ of history in that ennobling ideal. Their idea may have assumed to them almost visible form and shape, and they have loved it with an almost personal devotion, and followed it with a sacred enthusiasm. Liberty has been to not a few noble souls as the very glory of the Lord, and they have sealed their faith in it with their blood. To others, more calmly intellectual, the Christ-need has assumed a more shadowy form, and the vague conception of humanity has become the object of their worship. The future of humanity represents to their minds the promise of the Messiah. They, too, follow a vision, undefined and changing as the cloudland of a western sky, but a vision of light, the evening glory of humanity's long day of storm and darkness. Their ideal of humanity is also an emanation of the soul's deep need of the Christ. A want inherent in the nature of man is disclosed by these habits of semi-worship so often to be observed among many who profess no faith; a necessity inwrought into the very constitution of the human soul is revealed by these Messiahs of the imaginations of men—these Christs of the thoughts of the heart, which are of yesterday, or to-day, but not the same forever.

What do they really mean? What does this inwrought and ineradicable Christ-necessity of the human soul prophecy? The fact that the most thoughtful, best, and noblest souls must have a Christ of some sort; the fact that men have been always saying, "Lo, here is Christ, lo, there,"—shows that we need for the inspiration of our lives a diviner form than we have seen, and indicates that the Christ-want is a constitutional want of the soul of man. But are not our constitutional wants prophetic? They carry in them, if the whole analogy of nature be not false, the prophecy of their own satisfaction. The want, if constitutional, is itself pledge of its fulfilment to come. So far as we may reason from analogy, the deep, universal Christ-want in human nature is an intimation that the coming of Christ is provided for in the nature of things. For the constitutional wants of every creature in the ascent of life up to man have been met in the conditions of their existence. Up to man there is a well-balanced law of demand and supply, of need and satisfaction, in the struggle of life and the conditions of existence. Constitutional wants, up to the needs of man's spiritual nature, have been provided for and met in the constitution of the world. Capacity and environment correspond. Where the geologist finds imbedded in the rock the fossil bones of a fish, the veracity of nature warrants him in saying that there, some time, the waters must have flowed; for the make of the fish required stream or lake. The make of a bird requires free air, and not until the heavy vapors of the carboniferous age began to be dispelled, did the birds appear with wings to beat the breezes above the tree-tops. The make of a mammal requires solid earth upon which it may find footing. And the mammalia came into existence upon an earth condensed from the infinite spaces for their dwelling-place. Nature is true up to the heart of man;—shall nature become suddenly a false prophet there? That would be, indeed, a dreadful breach of the principle of continuity—a loss of the divine veracity in nature which would put all our faculties to confusion. No creature that exists requires for the development of its life aught that it does not have, save man alone. Does the flower need a voice, or the bird desire a book? No creature that is made, save man alone, seeks for what it cannot find provided for it in the very conditions of its existence. Want and environment meet, and ever adjust themselves to the perfect equilibrium of the economy of nature. The whole analogy, then, of created being supports the prophetic interpretation of man's constitutional, spiritual wants. They are signs of that for which we are made, and which, when our wings are grown, we shall have. They are intimations to us of the purpose of the faithful Creator. "Thou openest thine hand," so long ago the Psalmist of Israel sang, "and satisfiest the desire of every living thing." All analogy gives us reason to expect that this Scripture will prove true of man's highest needs. Is it scientific to regard man alone, in his spiritual nature and hope of immortality, as an exception to this continuous law of the development and satisfaction of life? In proportion, therefore, as the Christ-want of the human soul can be shown to be a simple human want, a universal need, underlying the heresies as well as cherished at the heart of the faith of the Church; coloring the dreams of the gentile religions as well as glowing in the visions of the prophets; in proportion as the words of the disciples, "All men seek for thee," can be proved to express the desire of the nations—in that proportion the Christ-necessity, or the constitutional Messianic need of mankind, becomes the prophecy and pledge of its own ultimate satisfaction. We may legitimately and confidently bring, then, the light of this inner moral and spiritual prophecy of Christ to help us interpret those signs and processes of nature and history which seem to point on and upwards to the coming of a higher Presence, and the reign in the last of the creative ages of the perfect man. Seen in this light, the advent of Christ is, at least, not unnatural, not an unexpected miracle; on the contrary, Christ's coming is natural, as the rising of the sun to one watching for the morning.

But a profounder and more satisfying view of the naturalness of the incarnation may be gained. The human heart, with all its passions and its impurities, is still the truest mirror in which we can behold the Invisible God. It is related of Thomas Erskine, of Linlathen,* that once meeting a shepherd in a lonely path in the Highlands, he greeted him with the question, "Do you know the Father?" and without waiting for the reply, he passed on his way. Years afterwards he met the same shepherd among those same hills, who recognized him, and gave him the answer at last, as he passed, "I know the Father now." That knowledge he had found in the experience of a human life. It comes to us, if it comes at all, through those years of learning and of waiting, in which our human hearts are both humbled and exalted, both made empty and enriched. That knowledge is the knowledge in which all moral experiences sum up their wisdom of life, and it cannot be taught, for it is a revelation coming through the life of man, through all his affections, needs, trials,

---

* Dean Stanley, History of the Church of Scotland, p. 184.

satisfactions;—a knowledge of the heart which cannot be taken away. Thus the Bible sums up its revelations of the Father in one intensely human word, God is love. The most womanly mother, brooding over the child sleeping in her arms, may give us a truer idea of what God in his good providence is, than we might gain from all the abstractions of our philosophy. If, then, in our reasonings concerning the possibilities of the creation, we start from any word less thoroughly and perfectly human than the biblical word for God —Love—we shall surely fail to understand the nature and course of things. If we begin by conceiving of God as the Supreme Law, or the Absolute Reason, or the Almighty Will, we shall not understand nature's truest speech of God's glory, and we shall throw all the prophetic voices of history into confusion; for we shall begin by refusing the simple key which God gives every child to his wonderful works, and by neglecting the one all-harmonizing word of revelation—God is love. In thinking, therefore, of the ways of God which meet in the incarnation, our all-illumining conception must be derived from the purest human experience of love. Whatever seems natural, or to be expected in that light, we are justified in regarding as in accordance with the law of laws, and in unison with the very heart of the nature of things. Now, human love—that charity which is the bond of perfectness—has in it three essential elements; there are three primary colors in love's perfect light; and these three are, the giving of self, or benevolence; the putting self in another's place, sympathy, or the vicariousness of love; and the assertion of the worth of the gift—of the self which is given—self-respect, or the righteousness of love. Under the conceptions of vicariousness and the assertion of its own worth involved in perfect love, the Christian doctrines of atonement and redemption need to be regarded; and when considered from any lower point of view, as that of law or government, the sacrificial work of Christ is hardly lifted out of difficulties and shadows into a pure moral light. But at present we have to do directly with the doctrine of the incarnation; and that is seen in its truest light when it is regarded as the final and complete work of the first element, or energy, of God's love—the giving of self to the utmost. The unselfish giving of self to the utmost belongs to the very essence of love, and it is the divine necessity, therefore, of the incarnation. The self-imparting energy of love is the first cause of the creation. The divine love must create, because to give of its own being and life is of the very nature of love. The creation is throughout, from beginning to end, a giving of self, a self-imparting act, of God. It is not an emanation of divinity, for it is a *moral* work—an unselfish giving of God, not a mere outgoing, or exercise, or play, of the divine Thought or Will. It is a self-impartation of God, by which he really gives of his own life, places something over against himself with which he enters into relations; it is a self-limiting act of God. We have, then, as the nature of things, as the principle of all principles in the creation, the divine law of self-giving, of self-imparting love. But if this be the first principle, the ultimate law of the whole creation, where shall its work stop? At what point shall the divine energy of self-imparting love be satisfied, and return into itself? When shall its last possible work be done? its final word spoken? What is the highest, fullest, conceivable self-impartation of the Infinite God? Surely not an atom, or a star! Not an angel, or a human soul! Nature, herself, strives for something beyond our mortality. The answer of the Bible, the answer of history, is, The incarnate Lord! The Word made flesh is the utmost gift of God in the creation. The second Man, the Lord from heaven, is the last conceivable, perfect, and final self-impartation of God; and if the divine creative process, ever advancing to more perfect works, should stop before He came who is God's own image, Immanuel, God with us,—then the creative love of God would seem to fall short of its own purpose from the beginning, and fail of its own divinity. The necessity of love which began the work would not be satisfied to leave it unfinished and uncrowned. The creation without its supreme end, the creation without the Christ, would it not be a disappointment to God himself, for God is love?

If we bring now this most human and most Christian conception of the law of love to the interpretation of scientific facts, and historical events, all becomes plain. We behold revealed the mystery of the ages; the first stepping forth of a material universe from the unseen—God's thought placed without himself, God's idea given a life of its own from God;—then the development of that creation according to the divine ideas implanted in it; the formation of a habitable word; the ascent of life; the typical forms reaching their perfection in the coming of man; the impartation, whenever the creation was ready for it, not only of existence from God, but also of the gift of reason and spirit, God's own image; the marvellous union of these higher gifts with the lower in man; and then—God still imparting his own spirit and life so far and so fast as the soil of nature was prepared for its reception—the selection of a special race, a divine training of his people; and, at last, the crowning gift, in which all others were made complete, and love finished its perfect work, the Incarnation. In his wonderful fulness of divine life, and in his unique oneness with the Father, the Christ stands among men as the head of the creation; and his reign is the coming of the eternal kingdom of God. From lower and less human points of view, the God-man may seem contrary to all experience and his miraculous life a thing incredible; but not from the highest conception of God as love. All is changed in that light. Bring to Paul's truth—Christ the head over all—John's light of the spirit—God so loved the world,—and everything unnatural or incredible disappears from the person of Jesus Christ. "God so loved the world that he gave his only begotten Son;"—if we are able to rise to the height of this biblical conception of the incarnation, we shall at once find ourselves clear of shadows which seem impenetrable from lower and less worthy ideas of the creation; and if the truth reflected in those words of the evangelist has risen upon us, Christ's presence and mission on earth will seem no more unnatural than the sunshine in the valleys does when the sun is in the sky above. Christ is on earth the most perfect possible manifestation of what God is in heaven.

Our reasonings concerning the naturalness of the fact of the incarnation when considered as the goal and manifest destiny of the creation, in the light of the highest moral conceptions we can form of the divine nature, are not invalidated by any difficulties we may have in conceiving of the mode of the incarnation. The place of Jesus in nature and history is one thing; the manner of his unique union with the Father, or the metaphysics of the divine-human consciousness, is another thing. The one may be a fact which we can know; while the other may transcend reason. Our view, however, of the naturalness of the incarnation, in the larger, divine order of things, may be freed from needless difficulty by considerations like the following. If it be said that a unique person, such as we are obliged to confess that Jesus was, is seemingly contrary to our own experience of the possibilities of human nature, we should remember that the very distinction of human nature is its capacity for God. The essential characteristic, and the innermost power of human nature, are its capacity to receive the divine likeness, and its ability to enter into communion with God. Man is by nature the son of God. We know not, therefore, to what largeness and perfection this human capacity for God may have been brought in One in whom our nature attains its utmost development, and is bound in final and indissoluble union with the Godhead. We fall back not entirely upon our ignorance, but upon our partial knowledge of man's inner relationship with the Father, and creation for a divine life, when we find refuge from questions we cannot answer concerning the incarnate Son of God in the old Lutheran saying, that the finite *is* capable of the infinite. Morally and spiritually, in its innermost principle and life, human nature is more capable of the infinite than we may imagine in our physical philosophies. And one other reflection may come to our aid here—not indeed to enable us to understand the metaphysics of a divinely-human consciousness—but to prevent us from investing the personality of Jesus with needless mysteries. Our whole reasoning has made us familiar with the idea of processes of revelation, and the self-manifestation of God in nature and history. The incarnation is relieved of some difficulties in our conception of it, if we regard it in the same manner as a process—a growing union of God and man—begun indeed at the nativity, but finished, carried to its last possible height, in the glorified humanity of the ascended Lord. The mediation of a human life, as well as birth, would seem necessary to the perfect and final union of the two natures in one person. Thus ample room is left for the growth of the child Jesus, and for his humanity to be made perfect; while the incarnation, which was real at the beginning, and continued through his life as fast and so far as the human nature developed, is finally made complete and glorious in him who sat down at the right hand of the Majesty on High. So we can see in Jesus, amid his temptations and sore trials, our elder brother, while he becomes more and more divine to those who follow him to the cross; and, at last, after he had risen, just before his ascension, the very doubter can say: "My Lord and my God!"

We do not disguise from ourselves, moreover, the fact that our view of the naturalness of the person of Christ, in the creation's larger meanings and deepest purpose, leads us towards the further conclusion that the incarnation is not the consequence entirely of the fall of man. The idea of an incarnation, irrespective of sin, as the natural or predetermined end of all God's ways in the creation, seems to go but little, if any, beyond the Pauline doctrine of Christ as the first-born of every creature, for whom all things were created. It seems to be only a philosophic statement of the evangelist's truth, "Without him was not anything made that was made." The whole creation is first for Christ, who is then for the whole world. Had there been no human history of sin, so, we may suppose, God's love would still have finished its perfect work, and given of itself to the utmost, in One in whom the creation itself is taken up to the very bosom of God; only then his advent would not have been in humiliation and shame, but in glory and honor. A gleam of light, at least, is thus thrown over the dark abysmal question, why did God create at all, if creating made possible a world of sin? For evil is only the incident of creation; it is the passing mote in the sunshine, while the light is abiding. Sin is but for the day of human history, while the Son, the perfection of God's glory, is the necessary, the eternal will of the Father. And redemption is, thus, not an afterthought of the Creator, but a possible work of God's love prepared for in the very nature of things; the Lamb is slain from the foundation of the world. The incarnation has absolute worth in itself, and is for God's own sake as well as for our sakes. It is not, in this view, an accidental truth of history, but a necessary truth of the divine love.*

---

* This conception of the necessity of an incarnation for the completion of the creative purpose (the form of it being historically determined by sin and the necessities of redemption) is an idea which seems always to have been hovering in the atmosphere of Christian doctrine, though it has never been distinctly recognized by the creeds of the Church. For the history of this idea

The incarnation, we hold, therefore, may seem to us a thing incredible only from the narrowness of our horizon of thought, and from our failure to see this central and culminating fact in its place in the divine order and development of the creation, in its real connection with the thoughts and purposes of the Eternal. They whose own spiritual experiences have given them other than physical views, and lifted them above the horizons of the mere understanding; they whose lives have opened boundless meanings in the words, "God so loved the world,"—will pass without sense of strangeness to those other words, part and substance, as they are, of the same divine truth, "that he gave his only begotten Son." Our most speculative theology, it is true, can only skirt the shores, and sound the shallows, and measure the inlets, of that revelation of infinite fulness, God is love. But even the little which our human hearts can teach us of what love is, and its infinite possibilities, and its great constraining law of self-impartation, may cause a thousand perplexities of the understanding to vanish before the

---

see Dorner, History of the Doctrine of the Person of Christ, passim ; also, Ullmann, Reformatoren vor der Reformation, ii., pp. 339–401. This conception has been again brought into prominence in recent German theology. See especially Dorner: opus cit., II. Div., iii., p. 236 ff.

divine mystery of the incarnation. Love's revelation of the nature of God makes the voices of the angels, heralding the advent of the Messiah, sound as welcome and as natural to the listening spirit of man, as do the songs of the birds at early dawn when at last the summer is come.

Let us gather up, then, the threads of our reasonings thus far in one conclusion. We have found in the Bible, and the religion of the Bible, a great divine process of revelation. We have marked by many signs, and followed to ever larger results of good, a supernatural development of history, a more than natural evolution. We have seen in the midst of the days the great wonder of history. No natural science can declare the generation of Jesus Christ. But the principles of scientific thought permit us to believe in no uncaused miracle. If Jesus be the Christ, his coming must be the fulfilment of a supernatural order, the consummation of a divine course of creation, the goal of all development. We find that there are facts and laws of nature, as well as groupings of events in history, of which Jesus Christ is the centre and harmony. These growing Christian probabilities of nature and history become moral certainties when we interpret them in the light of the spirit, and behold them to be ideally true.

That which in the last and fullest sense of the word is natural, is not simply true to the facts—true, as we say, to the life—but also true to the idea of things. This ideal truth of the creation we seek for through our own constitutional wants, and moral intuitions, and in the revelations which our human hearts reflect of the nature of God. Whatever is seen to be in harmony with love is natural, is true to the idea, true to the heart of the nature of things. It may be supernatural, but nothing in unison with love can be unlike God, can be really, that is, unnatural. And in this ideal, yet most real, view, the Gospel of Jesus Christ seems to us as natural as it is for love to be love, and for God to be God.

CHAPTER VII.

THE UNFINISHED WORLD, AND ITS COMPLETION.

He who fulfilled the past came preaching the Gospel of the kingdom of God. His advent ushered in a still higher reign than the age of man. Our review of old faiths in the light of the idea of development will not be complete, therefore, until we read the signs in nature of the ages to come, and look forward through the whole perspective of revelation to the last things of the creation. And if we shall find reasons for believing that the future course of the world shall carry on to perfection the development of the creation which we have observed up to the coming of the age of Christ, and that there is a continuous supernatural evolution of the natural whose issue is the kingdom of heaven,—then these probabilities of the final completion of the cosmos will confirm our preceding reasonings; our argument will be cumulative in its force; the unity of our view, and the continuity of our vision, will assure us that we have followed correctly the outlines of God's thought, and have not mistaken the ultimate design of things.

The first broad sign upon the very face of things of something still to come, is the manifest incompleteness of the present world. We live broken lives in an unfinished world. Our earth in some respects, it is true, is already completed. Nature in some directions seems to have come to an end of her progress. As a world fit for the abode of human life the earth is finished and pronounced good. The ages which consolidated the crust of the earth; laid up vast beds of coal; fixed the bounds of the sea; determined an equable temperature; produced fruit-bearing trees; made the earth ready for the grass and the flowers; and cleared the air of heavy vapors for the breath of life, and the songs of the birds;—those creative ages finished their work of preparation when man at last awoke in an earthly Paradise. The world as a stage for the great drama of human life, its comedy and tragedy, is done. The human body, likewise, seems to mark the end of one long course of nature. The goal of a slow, toilsome physical ascent is reached in its perfection. Nature has made, so far as we can see, the best use of her best materials in the organization of the human body. In this direction the creative process has come to a pause; the earthly elements, in their combinations within the human brain, seem to have been brought to their last conceivable refinement of organization. For six thousand years—for we know not how many ages past—nature has been able with all her chemistry to show nothing higher, nothing more marvellous, than the human brain. It is not probable that nature can bring protoplasm up any higher than the sentient organism of man. Another step would be a step beyond existing nature. Some gate, now closed, must be opened before organization can be carried farther than the present physical life of man.

Moreover, the arrangements of human society seem in some respects to be completed. The natural basis of friendship and love is finished. We cannot conceive, at least, of any better, or higher natural basis of spiritual affections than the relationships of the family. Any attempt to advance beyond the institution of the family, as the ground of all social organization and life, is a reform against nature, which falls back into chaos.

But while the world in these and other respects is obviously done, there are still many signs around us that this is an unfinished world. The evidences are daily pressed home to our hearts of the incompleteness of the present visible order of existence. This world, and human life in this world, seem complete only as the chrysalis is complete; this present world-age is perfect only as the preparatory form of a higher existence, into which it is to pass. Thus the human body, in which a thousand types rise to completion, is only a temporary acme, as it were, of nature—too highly organized to last longer than a moment. The type, indeed, is more permanent, but its realizations in individual forms are transient. Nature breaks into life, but the wave no sooner rises than it falls; our bodies are but the passing waves of nature's fulness of life, mere forms that come and go in endless succession. And these passing forms of embodiment are by no means flexible to all the necessities of the spirit which is in man. Though the best that nature can do apparently with existing materials, the body is not all that the soul requires for the full exercise of its own growing powers. Each sense seems to have been developed just far enough to make us wish it were better; to suggest to us the possibility of more glorious revelations if we were possessed of some finer sense, or some higher organ of perception. The limitations of that most marvellous mechanism, the brain; the frequent friction of the flesh and the spirit; the bondage of pain,—all show the incompleteness of the present physical basis of mind. Even the very perfection of the body, when considered as the end of nature's organization of existing elements, and compared with the possibilities of the life of the soul, compels us to cherish the hope that the process of God's creative work is not ended, its promise and potency not exhausted in the present visible system of things and our mortality, but that death and the resurrection need to be added for its completion.

Still other facts indicate the incompleteness of our present moral and mental faculties. The ideal of a human soul is risen with Christ, and waits for us in a higher kingdom. Our souls are as yet only begun. The foundations of moral being are laid in intelligence and will; the altar is raised in the sanctities of conscience; there seems also to be in the inmost soul a holy of holies, where no image can be found, no representation or definite conception of the Godhead, but where God is felt to be present, and the divine Shekinah is revealed. Nevertheless, though the human soul is the very temple of God, it is still an unfinished temple;—what mean these broken purposes, shafts uncrowned as yet with perfect capital? whither spring these airy instincts to heights unrealized? to what spaciousness of reason and loftiness of imagination shall this living temple not be carried before ever the design of its Divine Architect shall be finished in the perfection of a soul?

The social economy of this present world, also, manifests its own incompleteness. Society, human society, is only begun. It is at present but in part. That which is perfect has not yet come. Its best forms are typical of better, in which they shall pass in fulfilment away. Jesus interpreted our human affections, and the ties of nature, as types and prophecies of a higher order of existence, the perfect society, in which they shall be fulfilled; for he answered the Sadducee's question by the assertion that in heaven "they neither marry nor are given in marriage"—that which is preparatory and natural falls of itself away; "but they are as the angels of God in heaven"—that which is perfect, and the conservation of all that natural affection strove to attain, shall be the heavenly state. The lower and former order of society, so he seems to teach, shall not return; but its real worth shall be conserved, its treasure preserved, in the higher order of the kingdom of heaven. Natural ties are as the sheath in which the grain ripens; and though the sheath be cast away, the grain shall be gathered into the heavenly garners.

If, now, we look more closely at these evidences of an unfinished world and our hope of its completion, it will be well to confine our search to two main questions, or leading lines of examination. These two determinative questions it remains for us, therefore, to follow out so far as we possibly can, by the aid of whatever scientific probabilities we may gather, and in the light of revelation. They may be stated as follows: Are there evidences, growing rather than diminishing with the advance of knowledge, that this present visible system of nature is not the only order, or final form of the creation? and, secondly, Are there evidences, gaining or losing in force with the advance of science, that our present embodiment is not our final mode of existence, but that it is to be made perfect in some process of resurrection?

The preceding chapters, so far as they have shown reasons for belief in a supernatural order of creation and history culminating in Christ, contain an answer to the first of these questions. But we have to bring forward, at this point, cumulative proofs, and evidences from other quarters, which we have not yet taken sufficiently into the account.

The authors of the "Unseen Universe"—a suggestive book, which shows, at least, how the scientific imagination may look as easily up into the heavens as down into the dust— quote a remarkable passage from Dr. Young's

"Natural Philosophy," in which he expresses this opinion: "Nor is there anything in the unprejudiced study of physical philosophy that can induce us to doubt the existence of immaterial substance; on the contrary, we see analogies that lead us almost directly to such an opinion." "We know not," he adds, "but that thousands of spiritual worlds may exist unseen forever by human eyes; nor have we any reason to suppose that even the presence of matter in a given spot necessarily excludes these existences from it." There may be worlds "pervading each other, unseen and unknown, in the same space; and others again to which space may not be a necessary mode of existence." Modern science has verified Dr. Young's suggestion of the wave-theory of light; is it verifying his suggestion, also, of an unseen universe? The inquiry leads along hazardous heights. It tempts to fascinating, but dangerous speculations. Along the very horizons of knowledge clouds may easily be mistaken for realities. But, without venturing too far, we may possibly find footing in positive facts, where we may look up and gain larger views of this universe and its destinies than the materialist has dreamed of in his philosophy.

Let us be cautious, however, at the very start. We should not gain much for the hope of immortality by admitting simply the possibility of worlds within worlds of similar constituent elements, of more ethereal matter of the same atomic constitution. Nothing under the laws of ordinary matter, however ethereal, can be of itself immortal, or a permanent organization. Matter is a flowing stream; only its wave-forms remain. A spirit, if materialized of any matter of which our senses can take cognizance, would be liable to changes of temperature and dissolution; and would not necessarily be freed from the ills of mortality. It would not be unclothed of mortality. To prove a more ethereal sphere of existence, but still like this material world in its physical constitution, would not prove the existence of a world where death may not invade. Death reigns so far as we can see. Any matter of molecular constitution is subject to dissolution. But Dr. Young's suggestion may be put in a different way. It is conceivable that there may be a sphere of life, an order of existence, still material as distinct from the purely spiritual, and yet possessed of some specific property which distinguishes it from the matter of atomic constitution, of which our senses alone can take cognizance; there may be supersensible, yet not purely immaterial existences. Certain phenomena of the visible universe suggest the supposition of an unseen universe related to the present, yet of a different kind or order, out of which came the things which appear, and into which they shall be dissolved, enriching it as they pass into it—the new heavens and the new earth of revelation. Certain phenomena, I say, suggest and lend probability to the supposition that there is a larger, better half of the universe than as yet appears; they do not, however, demonstrate its existence, for physical science never can prove the supersensible. One species or type of existence, if taken by itself, does not furnish the positive proof that another species has existed before it, or that a higher type is to come after it; although the embryology, the growth, and the peculiarities of a particular species when matured, may suggest to the scientific eye the previous existence of lower forms of life, and be a prophecy, also, of higher types to follow. We know that this is true with regard to the typical forms up to man, for we now have the record of the succession of species open before us. But if we should take any type by itself, and reason from it alone, we should not have a positive science, but only rational conjecture and hope of what must have gone before, and might come after it. Similarly we have made known to us in this material universe only one general form or type of what may be a vast evolution, and we cannot prove absolutely from a single form of creation—the only one known to us—what was before it, or what new and higher orders of existence may have dominion after this world-age shall be over. We may find, however, in its structure and development, reasons enough for a rational belief and expectation of something still human, but diviner, to come. We possess, moreover, in our own spiritual consciousness an energy, as positive as any material force, by means of which the natural probabilities of things may be converted into living, working faiths. Faith, indeed, is the act which brings to the suggestions of nature, and the probabilities of the understanding, the affirmative power of the spirit within man. Faith is the spirit within us, saying, "It is," to the reason's intimations of immortality. Faith is thus a rational act; yet, at the same time, it is more than reasoning, for it is the act of the soul affirming itself; it is the positive exercise of our inner spiritual energy in the conversion of the suggestions of the senses, or the probabilities of the understanding, into the beliefs by which we live and die. But this spiritual energy may differ in different persons; this self-affirmative force of the soul may vary widely with opposite temperaments; it may have been developed or repressed by lifelong habits, or education. Soul-energy may be left latent for years, or it may be developed by exercise. We can bring forward, therefore, the arguments for our belief; but something besides reasoning is necessary to produce faith. Our reasonings as to the unseen universe may be cumulative in their force; but faith in immortality and heaven requires of every soul the exercise upon the arguments, in view of the evidences, of its own spiritual energy and power.

With these preliminary cautions we address ourselves to the present state of the evidence for belief in some supersensible order of existence, or the unseen universe.*

1. It becomes more probable, as our knowledge of physics deepens, that the present visible universe had its origin from a different order of things. Science has pressed nature to yield the secret of matter until the last hiding-place of the molecule is no larger than the one-five-hundred-millionth of an inch. And theory goes closer still to the ultimate nature of matter. There are some observed peculiarities of the conduct of the infinitesimal atoms from which the scientific

---

* In some of the reasonings which follow I would acknowledge again my indebtedness to Profs. Stewart and Tait, though their conception of the "Unseen Universe" seems to me to need some modification.

imagination proceeds to form a theory of their nature and origin. These infinitesimals of which the worlds are made were compared by Sir John Herschel to manufactured articles on account of their uniformity. The fact, that is, that certain things exist in great numbers, and all in equal quantities, or in exact and constant ratios, would indicate that they were manufactured; as the regularity in size of the pins in a paper, for example, shows that they have been made. Prof. Maxwell, following out Herschel's reasoning, concludes that " the formation of the molecule is, therefore, an event not belonging to the order of nature in which we live." * The very atoms, then, so we are assured by high scientific authority, come from beyond the limits of what we call nature, and have their origin in some other and older element. At this point theory takes up the facts, and suggests a possible conception of that other, more ancient state from which the present constitution of the world was received. Sir Wm. Thomson, availing himself of Helmholtz's researches into the nature of a perfect fluid, supposes that each atom is a vortex-ring. It is a ring formed by motion in some pre-existing perfect fluid.

This ingenious theory accounts for much,

---

* See Article Atom, Enc. Brit.

and is perhaps contradicted by nothing. But our concern with it now is simply this, that the latest and most plausible scientific speculation as to the ultimate constitution of matter, and the nature of the law of gravitation, only confirms the impression which common people find left upon the very face of things, that the world is made; that the creation, at least in the form in which we now have it, has not existed always, but has come forth from something different from itself; that this terrestrial system, therefore, is but a part, the present, visible part of the whole work of God. One conclusion towards which physical science in its quest for the origin of things, in its researches into the ultimate constitution of matter, is borne with increasing probability, according to Profs. Stewart and Tait, is this: " The visible universe cannot comprehend the whole works of God. . . . Perhaps, indeed, it forms only an infinitesimal portion of that stupendous whole which is alone entitled to be called THE UNIVERSE." *

2. Another suggestion of an unseen universe different from the present material system, yet not without some relation to it, arises from the apparent waste in the present economy of things. We do not refer simply

---

* Unseen Universe, p. 66, 1st Edition.

to the apparent waste of moral and spiritual forces, from which we reason instinctively to the existence of some higher realm of being, in which the earthly loss is made heavenly gain; but also we refer to the difficulty which scientific men meet in thinking out their leading principle of the conservation of energy, to avoid which some of them are inclined to open a speculation concerning the existence of another medium, or mode, of existence, different from ordinary matter, yet sustaining some relation to this material system. We shall consider presently whether chemical changes are sufficient to account for all the energy which disappears at death. Life, at least, is not a reversible process, and we have no mechanical equivalent for it—it goes out, but into what does it go? But, besides that, there are other losses of energy to be made good. The waste of the forces of the solar system nonplusses our science of the conservation of energy, unless it calls to its aid an hypothesis which, to say the least, introduces the conception of something very different from the kind of matter which manifests itself to the senses. "That the great machine for the dissipation of energy," remarks Principal Dawson,* "in which we exist and which we

---

* Origin of the World, p. 11.

call the universe, must have a correlative and complement in the unseen, is a conclusion now forced upon physicists by the necessities of the doctrine of the conservation of force. In short, it seems that, unless we admit this conclusion, we cannot believe in the possible existence of the material universe itself, and must sink into nihilism." The sun is daily squandering his resources of light and heat in space, and at his present prodigal rate will eventually become a bankrupt. What becomes of all but a tithe of this waste of his substance we do not know. It is supposed, also, that the ethereal something absorbs a certain portion of the starlight. But to what further uses, through that mysterious ethereal medium, are the absorbed radiant energies of the sidereal system put? Science forbids us to suppose that they can be lost; not a solitary wandering sunbeam can be lost out of existence in empty space. The ether conserves, or something transfers, and puts to some further use, everything apparently wasted by our slowly dissolving system of worlds. All will be born again in some future evolution. It is not surprising, therefore, that trained and eminent scientists are constrained to hazard the conjecture that the ether—that unknown yet everywhere present something—may be the connecting link, the vibrating medium, between our present system and some other as yet unrevealed mode or order of existence.* If, however, with Clerk-Maxwell, we are disposed to regard their suggestion of possible remoter uses of the ethereal medium as " far transcending the limits of physical speculation," we have, at any rate, in the very existence of the ether an intimation to the senses of the possibility of other forms of material existence than the kind of matter with which we are conversant. If physical science is compelled to admit the presence of matter which is not molecular; if what Maxwell calls the largest body we know is unlike anything we know, homogeneous, continuous, inconceivable,† surely natural science is estopped from gainsaying any suggestions, or intimations, which may come to us from any quarter, of super-physical modes or spheres of existence.

But, not to insist further upon these scientific speculations, we take up another application of the principle of the conservation of energy which seems legitimately and necessarily to lead us out again to the conception of a larger outlying universe in which the things that are seen have their existence. The scientific basis of this conclusion is thus suc-

---

* Unseen Universe, p. 158.
† See Article Atom, Enc. Brit.

cinctly stated by Prof. Le Conte:* "Evidently, therefore, in the universe, taken as a whole, evolution of one part must be at the expense of some other part. The evolution or development of the whole cosmos—of the whole universe of matter—as a unit, by forces within itself, according to the doctrine of the conservation of force, is inconceivable. If there be any such evolution at all comparable with any known form of evolution, it can only take place by a constant increase of the whole sum of energy, *i. e.*, by a constant influx of divine energy, for the same quantity of matter in a higher condition must embody a greater amount of energy." So far, then, as we have reason for believing that evolution is not an everlasting see-saw; so far as we are warranted in cherishing faith in a law of progress working out ever larger good, we are compelled scientifically to suppose the influx of higher energies into this material part of the cosmos. If there is going on a really progressive development of the creation; if the last state of nature is to be better than her first—then we must suppose that influences above nature, the powers of the world to come, do work within nature, and are hastening the coming of the day when former things shall

---

* Int. Scien. Series, Cons of Energy, p. 199.

pass away, and that which remains shall be more glorious. But this higher energy, which is bearing nature on to diviner issues, we may either conceive of as the direct action of the Spirit of God upon this material system, or we may suppose, also, that spiritual and divine forces work down upon the natural through some subtler medium, through the orderly processes and laws of some spiritual realm, which was created in such relations to this present visible world, as to permit action and reaction between the two. Prof. Tait says that the ultimate structure of matter should be considered " as a cage ; " it is open as wicker-work ; the molecule is not a close corporation. This material system in the midst of a larger spiritual universe may be conceived of as like a veil floating in the air, taking the motions of its currents, revealing in the very wavings of its folds the breath of the breeze upon it ; yet not a film of it broken, its texture nowhere torn, by the invisible element all the while playing in and out among its many threads. But, whatever may be the mode of the influx of energies from without, our present point is, that scientifically we must suppose something without and above nature, if we believe in a really progressive evolution, and expect that the end of God's ways in the creation shall be more glorious than the beginning.

3. Additional evidence in favor of the view that the visible worlds constitute only a part of the whole universe is derived from the probable destiny of the present material system. It is now the prophecy of science that the creation, in its present form, is not everlasting. La Place's famous demonstration of the stability of the solar system, even if free from mathematical errors, ignores entirely the physical instability of the sun and the planets. Slowly, yet surely, our system is losing its energy; it has passed its spring-time of growth; it is fully formed; its natural force is abating; the end, so Herbert Spencer says, is universal death.* Heat, which has been called the great communist, is expected at last to reduce all things to a dead and motionless uniformity. In available energy, at least, our physicists are quite at one in supposing the present universe shall come to an end. The indestructibility of the matter of our system cannot be proved, and if we suppose that the pre-existing fluid, from which Sir Wm. Thomson derives the atoms, is not in every respect a perfect fluid, then the very atoms must at last vanish away. The universe, it is predicted, †
" shall bury its dead out of sight." This whole

---

* First Principles, p. 473.
† Unseen Universe, p. 119.

system of worlds has been conceived of as like a ring of smoke,* or a wreath of cloud, which one moment is developed out of the viewless air, and another moment disappears again into the invisible element from which it came. As the atmosphere holds the clouds which come and go, so the larger universe contains the finite and passing worlds; the things which are unseen are before and after the things which are seen, for they are eternal. This world-age, the present creation, is as a vapor that passeth away.

We approach another still more mysterious indication of a realm of supersensible force, related to this present system, yet not identical with it. I refer to the phenomena of life. In considering (so far as our argument requires) this greatly vexed and still undetermined question, with regard to which scientific authorities are by no means agreed, we need, at the outset, to distinguish carefully things that differ, and throughout to discriminate between the results of scientific observation, and the affirmations of our reason when we take up those results in our whole thinking. We begin, then, with the generally admitted facts.

These are (1) certain peculiar phenomena

---

* Unseen Universe, 118.

of vitality. Minute particles of apparently structureless matter move, we know not why, and reproduce themselves, we cannot tell how; mysteriously transform nutritive matter into new combinations, build up the most diversified structures, and show, in short, the great marvel of growth. The peculiar phenomena manifest in living cells and their products, constitute a specific science. (2) The correlation of vital energy with other forces is admitted on all hands. The most pronounced believer in vital force does not deny that life is bound up with physical and chemical forces. It enters with its energy, according to his belief, to do special work in the established system of things. We can detect, and can admit, no break between the chemistry and the vitality of a living cell. (3) The analogy of the physical sciences might lead us to suppose that life, also, is a force to be placed in the same order or category as light, or electricity, or any chemical force.

But (4) it is generally admitted that no experiments have enabled us positively to put all vital phenomena into this general category of physical or chemical phenomena. Chemical combinations of a high degree of complexity form the material which manifests vitality; and physical changes are observed to take place in the formation of living cells. But the chemical synthesis for life certainly has not been discovered. Mr. Lewes replies to Dr. Beal's assertion of vital force, that it is not scientific to base a positive conclusion upon our ignorance, and that the special synthesis of the inorganic elements in the living cell may yet be discovered. That we must grant, Mr. Lewes, is possible; but we certainly have as yet no physical explanation of the mystery of life, and (5) the advance of science renders it less, rather than more, probable that we ever can find one. Some scientists anticipate, it is true, the final resolution of life into its chemical equivalents, but science, with all its subtle researches, is still no nearer the secret of life than is the child who wonders what made the flower grow which he holds in his hand. There are certain residual phenomena of life which defy analysis, elude the microscope, and are utterly beyond our chemistry. We cannot so arrange the inorganic elements, under any known conditions, that life shall spring up, and manifest its peculiar energy, according to laws capable of demonstration; as, for example, we may set existing forces at work in producing crystals. The origin of life is beyond all science; as Lotze, who has argued with great acumen against the supposition of a special vital force, admits: "Only its preservation," he says, "do we believe is committed to the connection of the course of nature without the interposition of new powers."* Continued and determined assaults have not succeeded in breaking down the law that life always comes from life. We are compelled, then, to look away from this earth for the origin of it; for the elements of which this world is formed were once in conditions which precluded the existence of any germs of life like that with which the earth now teems. Unless, therefore, we suppose that in some distant age the earth possessed powers of germination unlike any observable under the present system of nature (and this supposition itself assumes the extra-physical, if not the supernatural), we are obliged to seek elsewhere for the source of life. Accordingly, very much as theologians have sometimes attempted to account for the origin of evil by pushing the difficulty back into some pre-existing world, so scientists have suggested that some primordial germ of life may have been wafted from other worlds to the fruitful soil of this earth. But this gratuitous supposition only transfers the problem of life to other worlds; it brings us no nearer the solution of its mystery. Whence came that primordial germ? Nothing from all known causes can

---

* Mikrokosmus, i., s. 83.

rise up and say, "I am the father of life!" Follow that germ back from planet to planet, away from star to star, and still each orb in turn must answer, "I am but as the common earth; I hold not the secret of life!" Trace life to the outmost limits of this material system, down to the last centre of the least living cell, and still we find it to be without father, or mother, or beginning of days.

Equally impossible is it for us to follow life through the changes which occur at death. The end, as the beginning, of life passes knowledge. The changes in the body which manifest themselves to our senses are physical changes which result from death. "What is it that is gone," asks Prof. Le Conte,* "and whither is it gone? There is something here which science cannot yet understand." The process of life is not a reversible one; we cannot, that is, transfer its energy backwards and forwards, as we can heat or electricity, from one form of force to another. In this respect there is something in life which takes it out of any known correlation of forces.

What conclusion, then, are we warranted in drawing from the distinctive facts of vital phenomena? We infer, Dr. Beale and the vitalists would say, a special vital force as

---

* Conservation of Energy, p. 201.

their cause. But we should gain little, if anything, for a spiritual philosophy by that inference, and we transcend the limits of positive science, at least, when we draw it. For, if there is a special vital force, it must either be a supersensible or extra-physical force—in which case it cannot be a matter of scientific determination—or else it must be a peculiar, as yet undiscovered, physical force, in which case it would prove nothing for the believer in spirit. So far as it can be observed, life is a physical process, and belongs to the present world. Spiritualists have no reason or right to dispute biologists who treat vital phenomena as they do all other phenomena, which can come within the field of their science, as belonging to the present world, as facts of the present system of nature. Spiritual philosophy has really no more to do with the question as to a special vital force, or with the physical definition of life, than it has to do with the properties of magnetism, or any other force capable of demonstrating itself to the senses.

What, then, is the real, undeniable, spiritual significance of life? We find the evidence of something supersensible in life, not when we look merely at vital movements through the microscope, but when we view the mystery of life in the world without us, through our own consciousness of life, and seek for a rational interpretation of its phenomena. The final judgment as to what life means, is to be determined in a higher court than that of biological science.* There are residual facts, and admitted peculiarities of life, which biology cannot explain, which would remain after any supposable chemical analysis of vitality, which, in the light of our own spiritual consciousness, are suggestive of something more than the eye can see in them, and which render belief in the origin of life from without and above nature a rational faith. And this evidence for the unseen, or the spiritual significance of life, remains much the same, whether we look upon life broadly, as it is manifest to the untaught eye in nature, or whether we pursue it into the living centre of a microscopical cell.

---

* The phenomena of life belong to physical science; the question as to the cause of life, or the interpretation of the phenomena of life, is a problem of metaphysics. Thus it is noticeable that our biologists, while agreeing substantially as to the phenomena of life, cannot unite in any definition of life. Is not the reason simply this, that the definition of life involves ideas of nature, and cause, and end, or a philosophy of life—which they would exclude from the science of biology? That science can only describe vital phenomena and their correlations; but to define life—to say what it is and means—is to go beyond physics, and to seek for a metaphysical conception of it. " It is impossible to adequately define life without taking into our definition the idea of 'an end' in the orderly changes which it presents,"— a just criticism on attempted definitions of life by Mivart, Con. Rev., 1879, p. 707.

There is no argument which a spiritual philosophy may draw legitimately from the great wonderful fact of life on earth, which may not be as well drawn wherever science may be compelled to close the microscope, and give up her search for its ultimate chemical correlations. For it is not merely the so-called vital phenomena themselves which determine the spiritual inference from the existence of life, but rather that which we do *not* see in the movements of living matter—that which is more than physical in them—their predetermined collocation, their intelligent combination, the manner in which physical machinery is worked for the special designs of life. The nature and combinations of the forces employed, science may determine if she can; the *direction* of the forces is our problem. Common forces, if you please, are here combined and worked for uncommon ends. Elemental powers, if you will call them so, are here bound under a special law which determines the descent of life. Physical energies—if such they prove— are here grasped by some higher law, which compels them to fashion out of ordinary materials extraordinary products—each product, too, according to its own type or design. There must be something without the machine which so arranges its shuttles, and orders its motions, as to produce out of similar materials the most variegated designs, each perfect after its kind. In this intelligent co-ordination, in this unity of operations according to one and the self-same spirit, lies the real mystery of life and its extra-physical significance.* Revelation does not close the microscope at any fraction of the inch, and say, "That last visible movement of a dot of matter is the action of an extra-physical force!" But Moses made no mistake when he taught that God was the author of life; for all the researches of science do not yield any material explanation of it, and leave uncontradicted our rational and spiritual understanding of its origin, meaning, and destiny. Biology makes more and more probable the inability of the senses to deny the evidence of the spirit within man; but the final interpretation of nature must always come from within our own self-consciousness. To the brain of a dog, nature nowhere could be suggestive of spiritual reality. If dogs reason at all, they must of

---

* In an address before the British Association, which I have read since the above was in type, Professor Altmau argues that "life is a property of protoplasm," and that there must be "much complexity" hidden deep within the molecular constitution of protoplasm; "while in all this," he says, "there must be an adaptiveness to purpose as great as any claimed for the most complicated organism." So, in the view taken above, the hidden molecular constitution of the matter of life is regarded as a proper problem of science; but the "adaptiveness to purpose" is unmistakable evidence of some spiritual energy in life.

necessity be positivists. For they have in their own sense of existence no higher principle of interpretation, and therefore dogs, if reasoning machines, as some think, must always be positivists—never idealists. But man brings in his own spirit an ideal light to nature; and our own self-consciousness furnishes the key which unlocks the diviner meanings of creation. So then, we conclude, that life is another evidence to human reason of a higher order or realm of supersensible force. Life is the constant mode of some extra-physical law, one established method of divine energy. We have in life the supersensible in correlation with the sensible. " Life "—so say the authors of the " Unseen Universe "— "is a peculiarity of structure extending to the unseen." And, if we may trust the analogy of nature, this directing energy in life from beyond visible nature, this influence sent from God to call matter for a season to nobler uses, shall not be lost with the falling away of the present conditions of its activity, but shall enter into other correlations than with the matter of this earth, and shall be conserved in other forms of existence. As it came from beyond the visible creation (whether directly from the hand of God, or mediately through some series of higher causes, it is immaterial to our argument to determine), so it passes into, and shall be manifested in, realms of being which shall remain when present things shall have passed away.

To prevent our meaning from being misunderstood, and our reasoning turned against itself, as though we had proved too much, I add the remark that the necessary conservation of life in a world to come does not of itself prove the continued individual existence after death of any living creature; for other conditions may be requisite for the development of personal immortality—conditions of rational and moral consciousness which would seem to have been reached not lower down in the scale of animate existence than the soul of man. But our argument from life goes to this extent, that life is a fact of extra-physical significance, and that it leads reason out again to the borders of a realm of spiritual forces, and to possibilities of being which transcend our present experience. Not otherwise, or by supposing less than this, can we render to ourselves any rational interpretation of the origin, conservation, and outcome, of life.

We reach by still another line of reasoning the same conclusion when we follow out the most probable theories concerning the nature of the soul. If we knew what life and soul really are, we might almost know what the essential nature of God himself is. But our proximate knowledge of life and mind, the further inward we are able to pursue it, leaves reason nearer God. Already the effort to search through nature, and in the hidden recesses of the brain for the cause of life and mind, has hurried modern science out of the jungle of gross materialism. There are few scientific leaders at the present day who would not resent the imputation of holding what is commonly understood as materialism. Reckless writers, in the first excitement of a new science, aimed to transfix the mind itself, from whose movements the metaphysicians and theologians draw their divinations, as it is said a famous Jewish archer shot at the bird from which the soothsayers were drawing their auguries. But it was idle for Vogt, or Büchner, to dream of reaching with such shafts the empyrean of Thought, and of bringing genius down to the dust. Science has no physical principle by means of which it can transfix spirit. We may regard, then, as virtually out of the field the reckless materialism which reduces all the higher mental phenomena to a mass of quivering brains. But what Prof. Bain characterizes as "a guarded or qualified materialism " * has taken its place. The present fashion in many quarters is to

---

* Mind and Body, p. 140.

rule out all metaphysical ideas, and to substitute everywhere in scientific thinking physical formulas for the spiritual entities of the philosophers. Great pains have been taken in the invention and perfecting of a suitable physical symbol for the mind. A formula which neither affirms nor denies its immaterial essence, but by which it may be represented as a physical quantity in the scientific equation of things, has lately been elaborated. Prof. Bain, accordingly, writes of "one substance with two sets of properties, two sides, the physical and the mental—*a double-faced unity.*"* Mr. Lewes † represents these two aspects of life as like the convex and concave sides of one identical curve—though he fails to inform us what is curved, or what substance possesses these contrasted properties. This new positive philosophy of mind escapes the charge of grossly confounding mental and physical processes, and conveniently faces both ways; but Lotze justly characterizes it as a fruitless hypothesis, for it explains nothing—not even, as we may add, itself. When we think it logically out, it leaves us no better off than we were before. For either these opposite properties, the mental and the physi-

---

* Mind and Body, p. 196.
† Physical Basis, p. 377.

14*

cal, must be properties the one of the other—the mind a function of the brain, or the brain of the mind—which would be the old materialism, or idealism, over again; or else these properties must inhere in some third something, which would launch us again into metaphysics; or else we must try and conceive of nothing with two sides to it—a feat which might task the power even of a Hegelian. In fact, this scientific formula for the soul only substitutes one metaphysical idea for another. Our present purpose, however, is not to show the insufficiency of this "guarded materialism," but rather to avail ourselves of whatever new light mental physiology may be able to throw across the old problem of the nature of the soul.* Possibly from these modern studies of mind and brain a modified immaterialism may be produced, which we may set over against the qualified materialism of Mr. Bain as "the growing opinion."

The one great result, which the physiologists assure us their experiments have given them every reason to believe, is the fact of an unbroken material succession coinciding with all

---

* For a searching exposure of the manifold insufficiency of any materialistic, or semi-materialistic explanation of mind, and its failure in particular to explain the unity of consciousness, the act of comparison, and the method of memory, I would refer to Lotze's Microcosm, Vol. i., Books 2 and 3.

our mental operations.* Molecular changes in the cells of the brain uniformly accompany modifications of consciousness. The mental and the physical are correlated in and through the brain.

It cannot be shown, indeed, that vibrations of the cells of the brain and conscious perceptions, excitations of the centres of sensation and reactions of will, are coincident *in point of time;* on the contrary, the experiments of physiologists have proved that there is a measurable interval of time between the moment when an impression made upon a nerve of sense, as the ear or eye, reaches the brain, and the moment when the mind reacts upon it, through attention and will.† The two processes, therefore, the mental and the physical, though related, cannot be proved to be identical. Neither can it be shown that they are coextensive, or that the one is the quantitative equivalent of the whole of the other. On the contrary, Prof. Ferrier asserts that " the physiological activity of the brain is not, however,

---

* Bain: Mind and Body. Ferrier: Functions of the Brain, p. 255 seq.

† Wundt—Grundzüge der phys. Psychologie, pp. 730 ff.—gives the results of series of experiments to determine this "*psychophysical*" interval. It is estimated by Helmholtz (Ulrici: Gott u. die Natur, i. s. 279) as from one-tenth to one-twentieth of a second. It varies, however, under different conditions of expectancy, and may be reduced to zero by anticipation, as is the case of attention to a regularly recurring sound.

altogether coextensive with its psychological functions."* The completeness of consciousness, and the power to carry on all mental operations, according to the same authority, are not destroyed by the loss of one hemisphere of the brain. Neither can it be shown that mental phenomena are in any way necessary to the continuity of nerve-circuits, or neural processes. The physiological action, that is, might pass through a complete round, along the nerve-circuits, without the necessary rise of consciousness. " Consciousness," says Prof. Ferrier,† " is not necessarily a concomitant of reflex action." It is not necessary to any nerve-current, for the completion of its own proper action. The law of the conservation of physical energy does not require anywhere in the nervous organization the intervention of mind. Thought is not needed in order to complete any physical circuit. The origin of mind is not demanded in a continuous, physical evolution,—an important consideration which the materialists overlook.‡

---

* Functions of the Brain, p. 257.
† Ibid., p. 17.
‡ Mr. Lewes labored against the weight of the received theories of reflex action in his effort to show that the lower nerve-centres possess sensibility; still more difficult would it be to prove that consciousness is a *necessary* product of the nervous organism, or a factor essential to neural processes. But so long as consciousness is only an *incidental* result of physiological processes, so long as sensibility and neurility, consciousness, and

While enough, therefore, remains on strictly physiological grounds to show the impossibility of identifying mental operations with nerve-processes, the correlation and continuity of the two is, nevertheless, a demonstrated fact. Physiology knows nothing of the force which plays along the nerve-arcs, nor of the mode in which excitements of nerve-centres and thoughts are related; but it does know that the material circuit is unbroken, and that the two processes are correlated according to some invariable law. How, then, we ask, should this fact lead us to qualify our immaterialism? We may derive, from a suggestion of the German physiologist, Wundt, a useful hint in this direction. We need to find a conception of the soul which shall leave room for any possible results of physiological researches, while it shall remain true to the immaterial consciousness of man. Wundt, in the passage to which I refer,* admits the clear testimony of consciousness that the soul is a unity which materialism utterly fails to under-

---

complex nerve-activity, cannot be shown to be *necessarily* related and convertible, in one continuous, physical process, it is idle to talk of the "fiction of mind." Since the above was written I have noticed the significant admission, in an article by Prof. Tyndall on "Virchow and Evolution," that "the physical processes are complete in themselves, and would go on just as they do, if consciousness were not at all implicated."

* Grundzüge, p. 862.

stand, and the knowledge of which, he says, stands firmer than the certainty of the outer world. But he raises the inquiry whether the unity of the conscious self necessarily implies that the soul is a simple substance, as is usually supposed; and he presumes rather that the soul is "the ordered unity of many elements." Now, however that may be, at least we would say, one of the very elementary powers of which the soul consists may be its capacity of embodiment. One of the rudimentary necessities of mind may be a certain organization of matter, which is reached first in the human brain. The physical life may be one element essential to the existence, or the completion, of a soul. It may be the very nature of a created soul to strike its root down deep into matter, and to take up material forces into its own life, while it rises itself into a higher element, and derives its transforming power from the breath of the Spirit of God, and has its ultimate being above the earth. We need simply to enlarge, or to modify, our conception of soul so as to take into the idea of it its physical root, as well as its immaterial life and its spiritual flower. Indeed, it is not true that we are ever conscious of soul *and* body, but of soul *in* body, and body in relation to soul. In the nature of things, so far as our consciousness can disclose it, mind is made elementarily for matter, and matter is made ultimately for mind. Soul is made to come into full conscious existence as embodied. And so, on the other hand, matter was made with a long look forward towards mind; and the material creation reaches its final development only when at last, through the human brain, it vibrates in perfect response to mind. Organic life all the way up is a growing prophecy of soul.* The believer at least in the creative Spirit of God is the very last person who needs to deny that there is a natural and necessary relation between matter and a created soul. He may hold to the difference in kind between things spiritual and things material, which we experience all around our consciousness, without supposing any real breach of continuity in the growth and adaptations of that great whole of creation of which mind and matter, body and soul, are alike original and divine parts. The embodied soul appears to him as the natural, predetermined unity of two great processes of evolution—the material and the spiritual—both of which come from the living God. The conscious soul is the mirror of all the world before it, and the reflection gleams in

---

* See Rothe, The. Ethik, vol. 1, pp. 303 ff., for a speculative, but suggestive, development of this subject.

it of a higher world beyond. The besouled body is the goal of one world-age, as the embodied soul may be the beginning of the power of the world to come. And, if we begin with this fundamental assumption that the soul in its very make, or elementary nature, needs some body for its own birth into conscious existence, and that body needs some soul for its own highest organization; then we are already, at the start, beyond the old dualism of Descartes and Leibnitz, and we need not suppose any miraculous assistance or mechanical harmony, like that of two clocks regulated to keep time together, in order to maintain our belief in the union of an immaterial spirit and a mortal body. There is, indeed, a pre-established harmony between the two; but it is not the harmony of a miracle, or of a mechanical adjustment, but of two natures and growths from the same spiritual and divine source.

We shall show in another chapter how these qualifications of immaterialism affect the belief in immortality. If, however, we press our questionings beyond the mere fact of the natural and necessary relation of mind and body, and seek to gain some definite conception of the mode of their adaptation, we can only hope, at best, to form some notion which may be useful simply as a tentative theory or scientific imagination. Now that the older and once favorite hypothesis that some one point or atom in the brain is the seat of the soul, has been exploded by recent physiology, two suppositions have been proposed in its stead. The one is put forward by Lotze, who supposes that the mind is so made as to affect, and be affected by, a particular kind of organized matter; and, wherever that matter for mind exists (whether all in one place, or at intervals), there the soul is and acts. This matter for mind Lotze, however, thinks is confined within certain limits in the brain. The fact of the relation and interaction between the two he regards as no more, and no less, mysterious and inexplicable, than the fact of the action between any two particles of matter, or between two wheels. No action or relation, he holds, can be understood without the belief in the one spiritual ground of the universe, the One in whom all things have their being.

The other view, which rises perhaps to the dignity of a scientific imagination of the soul, is that propounded by Prof. Ulrici, starting from the maxim, " No force without stuff." Ulrici works out with ingenious plausibility the supposition of a spiritual body, or soul-substance. The soul is a continuous, non-atomic body, or fluid, which has its own centre of energy, and is circumscribed by the nervous organism of the body. We are not anxious to adopt, or to defend, either of these ideas of the nature of the soul in its relation to the body; we mention them simply to show how any speculations, which do not beg the whole question of mind, and which possess the slightest degree of plausibility, carry thought out into the realm of supersensible realities.

Having thus brought before us modern ideas and tendencies with regard to the nature of the soul, we are now prepared to see how the only tenable conclusions from these discussions lend additional confirmation to our belief in the unseen universe. Whether we refuse to be led one step beyond the pure and uncompromising immaterialism of Descartes, " I think, therefore I am;" or whether we seek to qualify and modify our spiritualism by the use of physiological methods; we are conducted, upon any theory or imagination which does not confound all distinctions, far beyond the confines of sensible nature, and are compelled to believe that as besouled bodies we are not only born into this material sphere where death reigns, but also have our birthright in a different kingdom, and larger domain of life, to whose order of forces and laws we are now in our higher nature subjected, and which we know in part. The phenomena of mind, and the phenomena of life, open avenues out into dim and distant vistas of existence. As within the limits of our senses we discover element suffused upon element, and life rising out of life, so our own spiritual nature and thoughts are the evidences of things unseen, the intimations to us of possibilities of being beyond what now appears,—as an apostle believed that our world is surrounded by realms rising above realms of principalities, and powers, and thrones, and dominions.

These suggestions and probabilities of nature are cumulative in their force. We may be mistaken in particular facts or reasonings from nature ; but we can hardly be mistaken in the impression of the whole. Many signs in the make of things conspire to point us to something beyond the limits of the present world. Nature seems, according to all appearances, to be but a part of one stupendous whole. And this first impression of nature upon us, we say, is not contradicted, but rather confirmed, by all our subsequent knowledge of the present visible system of the creation.

If we turn now from nature to the Bible, we shall find that the conception which has been growing upon us of an unseen universe of a different constitution from the present world—celestial, not terrestrial—yet in some way connected with this present world, and in its final form the glorified consummation of all God's creative processes, is the express truth of revelation. This conception, which we have seen to be not contrary to the course of nature, or unscientific, is held up before us by revelation, yet it is not fixed for us in any one definite picture or determinate idea; the Bible leaves us as it were gazing into a glowing sky at the close of the long day of this world's history, but if we attempt to fix in the eye its changing hues, or to make a picture of it, the vision passes from us. While pictorial representations of heaven are usually unscriptural and hurtful, there are, however, certain general conceptions contained in the Bible with regard to the final completion of our unfinished world, and broken lives, which we may happily compare with the suggestions of nature already noticed. Rejecting, without further discussion, extreme materialistic, and purely idealistic views of the future state, as these are thrown out by the course of the general historical tendency of biblical interpretation, we derive from revelation the following particulars: 1. There is, according to the Bible, a realm or order of existence which existed before and shall remain after the things that are seen. At the beginning of this present world-age there was another, older order of existence than our system of suns and stars.* Many scriptures have familiarized us with the idea that the present material system shall finally be dissolved. As a richly jewelled robe this starry space shall be folded up and it shall be changed. Besides direct assertions of impending dissolution, and the vivid metaphors of universal change to be found in the New Testament, it is expressly said that several elements which enter into the very structure of the world, and are necessary to its continuance, shall pass away. " There was no more sea." Looking out from Patmos' lonely cliff, St. John saw before him the boundless sea—the sepulchre of fleets—the oblivion of the pride of kings—the devouring sea—from the days of old the restless, ever-hungry sea; and the sea, spreading its waste of changing waters around the whole horizon of the revelator, became to him the one great emblem of mutability, the image of this passing world-age; and he saw "a new heaven and a new earth, and there was no more sea;" the whole changing world is passed away. St. John saw also the stars rising from the changeful sea, and sinking into its insatiable depths; the stars of heaven, as they rose

---

* Gen. i. contains no account of the creation of the angels; compare Job xxxviii. 7 ; also Heb. xi. 3.

and fell, marking succession and time; and in the spirit the revelator saw above the sea, and from beyond the stars, another vision of exceeding glory; for he saw an angel standing upon the sea, and upon the earth, who "lifted up his hand to heaven, and sware by Him that liveth forever and ever, who created heaven and the things that therein are, and the earth and the things that therein are, and the sea and the things that are therein, that there should be time no longer." Time itself shall pass away with the restless sea, and the rising and the setting of the stars, marking the change of night and day; and eternity shall take the place of the succession of events in time. What the order of eternity, into which our world-age shall be dissolved, is like, we cannot tell; we gain, perhaps, the only possible suggestion of it, not when we add years to years interminably, but when we lose all sense of time in thinking; when events lie in memory or imagination like a picture before us—translated, as it were, out of time—and in one mental vision we see them as a continuous whole.* Inconceivable as the eternity around

---

* In the discussions of eternal life and death it is too often forgotten that the word eternal is the unknown quantity of revelation, transcending present experience, and not to be represented by heaps of ages, or to be defined as endless. It is the timeless state.

time may seem, the Bible teaches that there is another order of existence which is not temporal, and into which the heavens and the earth and all things therein shall pass away.

2. Another clear teaching of revelation is that this unseen world is not a shadowy or unsubstantial existence. On the contrary, in comparison with its reality, the visible world is the shadow; and in comparison with its activities this present life is as a sleep and a dream. The New Testament revelation of the other world brings to the front the conception of fulness of life. When the heroes were slain upon the plains of Troy, Homer says their souls were dispatched to the shades, but they themselves were left a prey to dogs and birds. Christianity has reversed the language of the ancient bard, and one of its poets sings:

> "I looked behind to find my past,
> And lo, it had gone before."

Achilles regards the life of the merest drudge on earth as better than the best of the unsubstantial glories of Elysium. The Christian hero is willing to live, but he desires to depart to be with Christ, which is far better. Though the Bible represents the realm of the invisible, into which the dying awake, as not material in the same manner as the visible heavens and this earth are material—as of a celestial and not terrestrial structure—it is too plain to need proof that the Bible holds out the hope of an existence which shall not be wholly immaterial, or without some form of embodiment.

3. This other world has some connection, or correlations, with this present world. This unseen realm of existence is as the other hemisphere of the whole universe, which is the one creation of the living God. At some points its laws are made continuous with present physical laws, and in some ways the powers of the world to come act, and are acted upon by the forces of the present world. The Bible reveals the existence of a vital relationship between our life here and in the unseen kingdom of God. And, according to the Scriptures, the two parts of the universe, the higher and the lower realms, are "at sundry times and in divers manners" made to touch each other. There have been historical actions and reactions, so the Bible teaches, between the two. Christ, in his sinless humanity, was conscious of the meeting in his own person of both worlds—the natural and the supernatural—and his life was the harmony of two lives—the earthly and the heavenly.* The miracles of the Bible may be regarded in this light as

---

* John iii. 13.

the descent of the higher energy which sets the lower forces quivering in unwonted ways; and the higher works upon the lower at points where the two are made capable of contact and influence, so that energy may be transmitted from above for the working out of operations beyond nature, and yet the lower remain unshattered. A miracle is not a sudden blow struck in the face of nature, but a use of nature, according to its inherent capacities of service, by higher powers. At some point the elastic net-work of material forces yields, without breaking, to pressure from the element without in which it has its being; and we who dwell within the sphere of nature, and can therefore see only the side which is moved, or pressed in, call it a miracle;—its own laws of contraction or expansion we know could not produce that special motion; but the miraculous in nature was not miraculous to Jesus, who knew that there are two sides, the one answering to the other, a visible and an invisible half, of the one great whole of God's universe. A miracle would be an impossibility only in a cast-iron universe; but we know that this material system is not a ...rd, dead, brazen sphere, but instinct with life, and vibrating to a thousand influences; and forces which we can hardly name, still less, follow and understand, play in and out among its threads. For aught we know an ultimate law of matter may be the power to receive the impression of a spiritual force; and the first principle of motion may be the impulse of a divine will. The Bible has no trouble with miracles, for prophets and apostles believe in both spheres, and their natural correlation— the celestial and the terrestrial. Perhaps all we need do to escape from scientific scruples with regard to the possibility of the miraculous, is simply to enlarge our conception of nature until it shall include the whole of things. A miracle, then, would be no breach of the law of continuity. It might be defined as the natural conservation of a supernatural force, and that in accordance with the whole nature of things. To one taking into his philosophy both elements, both spheres of force, a miracle ceases to be miraculous, and would seem no more incredible than would be the shaking of a tree-top in a breath of air from the sky, though the tree never could shake itself, and no hand is seen, stretched out from below, upon the bough. The breath of the spirit of God may bend and sway nature in manifold ways without uprooting it, or destroying its fibre and life. But if we do not believe in the powers of the air, of course we must deny, for scientific reasons, the testimony of our senses, and say, not a leaf has stirred, the tree-top was not shaken,—whenever we cannot see the hand reaching up from below.

But besides special impulses from without, or miracles, the biblical doctrine of providence implies, also, that there are regular and established means of communication between the two hemispheres of the one universe. God has provided regular lines for the passing to and fro of influences from both kingdoms. The spirit has not been imprisoned in matter, as a woman with her child, according to the old legend, was walled in by the masons of Magdeburg, who built up around her the walls of the city. Our souls, on the contrary, have air and life from the great unseen world without. The net-work of material forces, amid which our free-wills move, is made capable of conducting to us magnetic influences from the will of him who holds us, and the whole system of things, in his Almighty hand. The very system and order of nature render it the perfect instrument, responsive to his slightest touch. Were there not a natural order, no special providences would be conceivable. Providence is the intentional and intelligible use of a system of nature according to its capacities and powers. Hence the Bible, while nowhere denying second causes, often passes by them, and forgets the system in the presence of the power that uses it for his good purposes; as we hardly think of the instrument under the skilled player's hand, but give ourselves up to the enjoyment of his music. Prophets and apostles forget the keys, as they listen to the harmonies of providence. "What hath God wrought," is the exclamation of the Bible. So prayer is a regular or established mode of action between the two spheres according to the nature of the whole system of things. Prayer, in the biblical conception of it, is a power, a supernatural power, which escapes out of this material complex of causes, enters a higher sphere, reaches the throne upon which all things wait, returns through higher ministries to set in motion, or to direct, natural causes which else would have remained untouched. Yet nowhere on its ascent, or its descent, in going or returning, does prayer escape from the order and beyond the limits of the laws, which form the whole creation, and together work the perfect will of God. The biblical doctrine of prayer is simply the revelation of one established mode of action between earth and heaven; and our conception of nature, and doctrine of the conservation of force, ought to be large enough to include both halves of the universe, and to comprehend the continuous course of an effective prayer.

4. One other and culminating point of the

biblical revelation needs now to be stated. The whole process of creation shall reach its end, not in the perfection of either sphere alone—the earthly or the heavenly—but in the consummation of both in a more glorious state which shall remain. The end shall not be the new heavens, or the new earth, but the new heavens *and* the new earth. The consummation, in other words, shall be the result of the passing of both the heavenly and the earthly into a final reality in which the whole creation shall receive its glorious consummation. In the end all forces shall be conserved, and all things shall be fulfilled. Thus, the narrative of the transfiguration leads us to think of the dead as still looking forward to a kingdom which is to come; and another Scripture describes the angels as gazing into the mystery of redemption which is yet to be revealed; and Jesus himself is said henceforth to be expecting until he shall deliver his kingdom to the Father, that when the end comes God may be all in all. One passage from the Apostle Paul brings out in definite teaching the biblical hope of the final glorification of the creation. (Rom. viii. 21.) This whole visible creation, which has been made subject to vanity, that is, to frailty and transitoriness, and which, in its struggle of existence, groaneth and travaileth in pain together until now, awaits with earnest expectation its more glorious destiny, and it also shall pass into the liberty of the children of God. This world shall come to its fruition in the next. The perfection of the lower shall be a part of the perfection of the higher. Heaven shall be richer because the earth has been, and the earthly shall enter into the final glory of the heavenly. So the whole creation shall be finished. This material part of it shall be changed, but not lost. He by whom all things consist shall come in the last great day not to destroy, but to fulfil. All visible things, therefore, are types and symbols of the better things which shall be. Nature is one great metaphor of the world to come. Heaven and earth shall pass away, but flowers and fields, broad landscapes and the firmament of stars, the poetry of nature, shall not utterly vanish and be lost when the earth shall melt with fervent heat, and the heavens shall be rolled up as a scroll; for the material shall itself be glorified in the new creation, and the age-long process of creative wisdom and power, begun in the depths of the divine counsels, and continued in the growing wonder of God's manifold works, shall bear at last its perfect fruit in the kingdom which the Son shall deliver up to the Father when the end shall come and God shall be all in all.

The biblical teaching of the final completion of all things just stated includes the doctrine of the resurrection; and our review of the divine processes of self-impartation and self-revelation will not, therefore, be complete until we shall have brought into the light of the all-illumining idea of development the scriptural doctrine, also, of the resurrection.

We delay, however, for a moment to point out one useful result, which we have already gained at this point in the ascent of our argument. We have reached a position above one of the most chilling of those perplexities which are apt to rise in our minds, and to envelop in darkness our hope of immortality. A real difficulty to be overcome by our instinctive faith in immortality lies in the impossibility of finding any place within the bounds of space where we may suppose the scenes of the future life to be located. As an increasing knowledge of geography drove the Elysian fields, and the happy islands of the blessed, farther and farther away, until, when the globe had been circumnavigated, no place was left for the myths of the ancients; so modern astronomy seems to have banished the Christian's heaven from the skies, until at last no imaginable place for the resplendent city of the revelator seems to be left within the bounds of space. We still tell the child,

"Heaven is up in the sky." But the sky nowhere gives to our astronomy the faintest suggestion of a place for heaven. Swedenborg visited in the spirit certain planets known to the astronomy of his day, and had little difficulty in finding orbs upon which to domesticate his angelic acquaintances; but we now know enough of the constitution of those worlds to say that any life upon them like ours, or having any physical correspondence to our bodies, would be hardly endurable, and at all events must be transitory and corruptible. We discover, as we look away from this earth, what? An atmosphere extending for a few miles, and, by means of minute particles of common matter suspended in it, spreading over us the world's apparent ceiling of blue; then gradually growing colder, and losing its density, until the last filaments and fringes of it fly out into a medium still more ethereal. Along the pulsations of that ethereal something—what it is we know not—we look still farther and farther away, until, hanging suspended in space by forces whose nature we can only vaguely guess, some three hundred and sixty-one millions of miles from the earth, there appears another world, a mass of molten fluid, which is so hot as to emit a dull glow from its surface. Within the vast orbit of Jupiter it is difficult to imagine a place such as we hope for when we say to the child, "Heaven is up there!" Gases and heat, and molten fluid; but no paradise of green fields, and living waters, do we discover any signs of, from the sun to the planet which Swedenborg could people with beings having correspondences to ourselves. Give then imagination wings! We have messengers hastening to us from the farthest stars; but they bring no message of the heavenly city descending from God. We cannot with the ancients take refuge in our ignorance, nor hide the heaven of our hope in the mysteries of space. For we have learned the alphabet of these messengers from the stars. We can question them, and they all tell the same old story of the earth. The language of the heavens, which our science hears, declares the same perishable dust which we tread under foot. There is iron, and sodium, and heated hydrogen, and other earthly elements, to be found among the stars—nothing else. This visible universe is made throughout of the same perishable stuff; it is of one piece, and is growing old. There is no place for heaven in the skies! But faith, beset by the difficulties of our growing scientific knowledge of the physical structure of the sidereal system, may again take refuge in our ignorance, and ask: How do you know that some orb, though formed of common earthly elements, may not be fitted up and adorned by the hand of Omnipotence for the final abode of beatified spirits? But from this refuge in ignorance, advancing knowledge again drives faith. We know there is not a star at rest, not a sun that is not burning out, not a world that is not passing away. Change and dissolution are written on the face of the heavens, as well as on this earth. And we cannot conceive of an undying body composed of corruptible matter. The biblical conception of immortality is not the conception of a perpetual transference of life from one form of embodiment to another within a perishable creation. The doctrine of the endless transmigration of the energy of a soul is neither pleasing nor probable. We agree with the authors of the "Unseen Universe,"* so far as to dismiss the idea of a superior order of beings, connected with the present physical universe, as untenable. We give up immortality upon the present physical basis of life.

But what then? Have we given up the scriptural revelation of heaven? On the contrary, we have simply been looking for it in a wrong direction. As the microscope cannot find the secret of life, so the telescope cannot discover the land of the living. We have

---

* Page 151.

been searching for immortality in the wrong half of the universe, and with the wrong powers. We need to knock at doors which are closed to the approach of the senses, but which open to the thoughts of the spirit. We need to locate heaven without this material system which waxes old and shall perish. We must trust our intimations that the creation is more than appears, and that there is a larger realm of existence than the land in which we dwell. We must look for heaven—not anywhere under the stars—but in the other invisible hemisphere of the universe. It is not a part of the present visible creation, and shall not pass away with the dissolving worlds. Heaven with its abiding life is in the Unseen, out of which the worlds appeared, and into which all their glory shall depart. Heaven is the end of all the Creator's ways. It is, in its final and enduring perfection, the conclusion of the whole creation. "It doth not yet appear what we shall be." Thus we reach a point where faith may look into the future and wait in hope, undisturbed by any news science may bring from the stars, and untroubled by any difficulties in understanding where the living who are gone from us, are abiding. So the Bible reveals a celestial glory, which is more than the terrestrial, of a different order, and into whose higher realms of being, unrealized as yet, we and all things temporal are hastening. And so our latest physical speculations, call them flights of the scientific imagination if you please, sent out to search over the depths for the everlasting hills, bring back upon their wings the perfume of far-off lands, and some fresh signs of the rest that shall remain after the flood of the years shall have passed away.

CHAPTER VIII.

THE PROCESS OF THE RESURRECTION, AND THE END.

WE have to complete our review of old faiths in the new light of the scientific truth of development, by bringing under this modern method of thought that belief in the resurrection which lies at the foundation of historical Christianity, but with regard to which many believers at the present time have neither definite nor satisfactory ideas, and which, in the form in which it is popularly held, is often ridiculed by unbelievers as the reduction to the absurd of Christian faith.

The resurrection of Jesus was to the disciples both a fact and a revelation. The fact may not have been wholly a surprise to them; but the revelation was unexpected. They were not unfamiliar with the belief that the dead might be brought back to life by the power of God. As they remembered Jesus' miracles, and thought of his mystic words concerning the Son of man, they may have hoped that he would come forth on the third day from the grave, and return to his accustomed life, to walk with them again the familiar paths, and to tarry in the home at Bethany as the benignant friend of old. But they were amazed and affrighted at his appearance. Mary did not touch him; Thomas did not put his finger into the print of the nails; the beloved disciple leaned no more upon his bosom; a strange awe fell over them as he appeared in their midst when the doors were shut, and then vanished from their sight. Jesus did not rise, as they tell us Lazarus came forth— the manner of his appearance was a wonder and mystery to them. Jesus' resurrection, in short, was a revelation to the disciples of possibilities of spiritual life, which they had little dreamed of before.

The new revelation which took the disciples by surprise, we may not, however, forget, had a firm, historical basis in a new fact of their experience. We cannot cut the Gospels loose from their historical basis, and hope to retain long the ideal beauty and truth of Christianity. We cannot keep fresh long a flower broken from its stem; we must have the root implanted in the earth before we can have the fragrance in the air. Christianity, broken off from its historical growth, and uptorn from its firm basis in the historical facts of the Gospels, would be in our hands little better than a cut flower—it would soon fade and be thrown away for another. All that is ideal, beautiful, and refreshing in Christianity rests upon historical grounds, and is secured in the ineradicable truth of a divinely human history. Its preparatory law and morality were, as we have seen, worked out through the history of a chosen people. Its Gospel came through a Divine life with man. Its Christ was not first a dogma, but a fact. Its supreme faith is trust, not first in a truth, but in a Person— a real, yet ideal Person. Its transforming hope was gained, not by reasoning, but by the sight of an open tomb, and the appearance of the risen Friend.

Of the direct historical evidences of the fact of the resurrection little that is new remains to be said. The progress of critical inquiry, we may remark in passing, renders it apparent with increasing clearness that any attempt to destroy the historical genuineness of the New Testament narratives, and at the same time not to make the disciples spurious men, and to cast a dark shadow of reproach upon the sincerity of Jesus himself, is impossible. Enough of the New Testament writings, on the most unfavorable, credible hypothesis, must be admitted to have been started on their course of deceiving the world—if deception it be—before the beginning of the second century, to compel us to hold apostolic men responsible for the impression they have made upon the world. Critical ingenuity can hardly invent a way of avoiding the facts of the New Testament narratives without sooner or later running squarely against the moral character of the apostles. They had no business, so late in the day as the first century, to deceive themselves with an "execrable superstition," as the Roman historian calls Christianity; and still less to impose at the risk of their lives, and by the loss of all things, an immense practical deception upon mankind. If they have imposed upon us old wives' fables for facts, then Judas Iscariot really deserves the gratitude of the world, and the eleven were the real traitors to all that is sacred in humanity. It may be said that the Apostle Paul lived in a credulous age, but he had ample opportunity and time to investigate the facts reported among the disciples whom he persecuted; and all the prejudices of his education, and his own personal reputation were at stake, and would have compelled him, if he were a true man, to sift the evidence thoroughly, and to prevent a great religious fraud upon humanity. There is no reason or excuse for his becoming a victim to a deception. We gain nothing by transplanting the miraculous from the working of Jesus to the minds and the habits of the apostles. In its proper place the miraculous may be natural; but it is utterly unnatural and incredible when transferred to the conduct of common, sensible men like the disciples. Thus scepticism of historical Christianity has upon its hands a double difficulty. It must first prove that the disciples acted unnaturally, and then it must disprove their moral sense, which belies the alleged untruthfulness of their conduct.

But, not to delay longer with the direct historical evidences, upon which so much has recently been written, we would notice the large amount of indirect historical testimony, of cumulative, circumstantial evidence, which cannot easily be set aside. Something happened in Judea which has changed the world. Something happened on the morning of the third day which has made it a new world for mankind. Something took place which changed this earth, and the whole aspect of life and death, to the eyes of the disciples. Something occurred which turned mourning into joy, despair into courage, darkness into day. All things were become new to them;— over hillside and valley, along the way to Emmaus, over the beach of Galilee, and the slopes of Olivet, a new, unearthly light was shed, and the earth lay before them transfigured with a new hope, and the brightest spots in it were those where but yesterday the deepest shadows rested—its places of burial. Something happened upon the morning of the third day which changed the most sacred associations of a large company of men, and the religious habits which had grown with their growth from childhood.

A wonderful revolution was wrought in the transference of the sanctity of their Sabbath to the Lord's day. The Christian Sunday is still the great circumstantial proof of the resurrection upon the first day of the week. What teaching could change our day of worship, a day hallowed from childhood, and made sacred by the traditions of our fathers? Yet something happened in Judea on that first day of the week which naturally, spontaneously, without conflict, and without discussion, so readily that hardly a trace remains of the process by which it was accomplished, did change the whole religious habit and the most sacred associations of Jews exceedingly tenacious of the old traditions. There is nothing accidental in history—the light which put the glory of the Sabbath into the shade was the glory of the risen Lord.

Something happened then and there which has changed this world to all succeeding generations. Something wonderful and re-creative in its power took place upon that Easter morning, the enduring results of which are

Christian homes and morals, Christian society and culture, Christian laws and liberties. When one stands by the ocean, and watches the great waves charging against the rocks, he knows that somewhere far out at sea the winds must have descended, and swept over the depths, though not a breath of air may be astir in the tree-top overhanging the cliff. So in human history every mighty movement which breaks upon our shores must have had a cause, far away perhaps, whose effects we see. If, while we are watching the waves, a log-book should be washed ashore, and we should read from it an account of the descent of a mighty wind upon the face of the deep, then we should know for a certainty, though it might be calm within our horizon, that there had been a storm at sea. Floated down upon this mighty tide of Christian history, we find the records written by men who lived when the power of God swept over human society, and stirred it to its depths—this is the direct evidence,—and we have, also, the movements of thought and life still breaking upon our shores—we have the great tide, and the waves themselves—as the present evidence of the descent of a higher power somewhere in human history. Deny the records; say they were thrown into the history as a hoax; but you are met by the advancing wave, and that is no deception! Deny the Gospels; but the history itself confronts us; is its own evidence; tells its own story of something supernatural, of the moving upon the hopeless waste of the Spirit of God. Something happened over eighteen centuries ago in Judea, on the morning of the third day, which has changed the whole current and flow of history;—men's lives, their homes, the rights of children, the lot of slaves, the position of woman, the whole order of society, all things human are taken up into, and swept along by, a new, resistless movement, which still bears upon the crest of its advancing wave the hope of the world's future.

Doubt, however, of the fact of Jesus' resurrection does not usually spring in the first instance from the discovery of defects in the historical evidence, direct or circumstantial, but from the fact that it lies beyond our experience, and from the difficulty of conceiving of it. We turn then to the revelation of the nature of the resurrection made by the appearances of Jesus to the disciples. Our final question shapes itself accordingly, after this manner:—Is the Christian doctrine of the resurrection, as that doctrine was revealed and illustrated in the resurrection of Jesus, in accordance, or not, with all that we have already observed and can know of the processes by which God is working out the purposes of creative love, and, therefore, in the truest and broadest sense, most natural and credible?

First, then, we have to follow the resurrection of Jesus as it took place before the disciples. He lay until the morning of the third day in the sepulchre, long enough to give the body over to the ordinary course of nature. But God did not suffer his Holy One to see corruption. Miraculously and, as we believe, for our sakes, the process of the resurrection with Jesus was shortened, or rendered exceptional in its mode, and made to take place partly in a visible manner before the disciples. The stone was rolled away, and Jesus rises, but no more as a mortal belonging still wholly to this world. He has not come back to life, like Lazarus, to be borne some day a second time to his burial. Already when he leaves the tomb he belongs partly to the other world, to the Unseen Universe. He appears first to Mary. She thought him to be the gardener—his appearance was at the first glance like that of a mortal man;—the next moment, as is to be inferred from the best interpretation of Jesus' answer,* she sees something unearthly in his appearance, and takes him to be a spirit. Jesus, having just left the

---

* See Meyer Com., in loco.

sepulchre, begins already to be transformed. He is of this world still, yet not wholly of this world. There is something about him as he appears and disappears which impresses the disciples with a new sense of his superhuman nature. He is the same Jesus, yet not the same. The semblance of something different, something more celestial and divine, shines from his face, and at times they take him to be a spirit. He appears on several occasions while the marvellous transformation is taking place. One who doubted, sees the marks of the nails; but something prevents him from reaching forth his hand and touching his side. Jesus moves, as it would seem, along the borders of two worlds, now becoming visible, now vanishing from sight, partly under the laws still of the lower kingdom, partly possessing already the liberty of the higher life. There are indications, also, or hints, that, as the time of his final disappearance into the Unseen drew near, he belonged less and less to the earthly, and more and more was transformed into the glory of the celestial. Thus, upon one of his first appearances he asked, "Have ye here any meat?" and he ate with the eleven; but later he gave to the disciples bread, and the fish which he took from the fire of coals; but it is not said that he partook of them himself. And when the disciples, through the morning mists, saw One standing on the beach of the sea of Galilee, it was not first Peter's eagle eye, but John's intuition of love which assured them, "It is the Lord." Was it more difficult for the disciples to recognize the man Jesus, the old time Friend, in his successive appearances? In a still later manifestation of himself on the mountain which he had appointed in Galilee, we read, "They worshiped him; but some doubted." Already was He so far exalted, so distant from the touch of the disciples, of appearance so spiritual, and transcendent, that some could doubt, while others worshiped?* Very significant in this respect are the brief narratives of the Ascension, in which after forty days his resurrection was completed. He leads the disciples out to Bethany;—the narrative relates no simple human word or friendly incident such as at other times had made the way to Bethany sacred to the memory of the man Jesus;—He speaks now of the great things of his kingdom, and his Gospel for the whole world. Jesus is now a superior Being, almost supersensible, a heavenly Pres-

---

* Meyer (Com. in loco) supposes as the reason for the doubt "an alteration in his bodily appearance," "a mysterious change of his whole appearance, a middle condition between the bodily nature as it was before, and the glorification which took place at the moment of the ascension."

ence for the last time visible to mortal sense; and, "It came to pass while he blessed them"—speaking not now words of human sympathy as before the crucifixion, but as a Divine Friend, with a more than human accent, blessing them—"he was parted from them and carried up into heaven!" The transformation is over. The resurrection is finished in the ascension. The dust is committed to dust; the perishable is laid aside; the flesh which in him saw no corruption, but which cannot enter into the kingdom of heaven, is given up to the elements of nature—the last particle of earthliness left to this world's gravitation—as he ascends, vanishing forever from sight as the glory of the celestial is given him;—and the disciples return to their homes knowing that he who had left the tomb and appeared to them as the same Jesus, yet changed, is now parted from them, and, like a cloud vanishing in the evening light, he had been received from their sight.

The resurrection of Jesus, then, was the divinely appointed process by which his holy life changed the terrestrial for the celestial, and, in an exceptional manner, without undergoing the process of corruption, passed from the seen to the Unseen. It was a new revelation of the possibilities of spiritual and glorified embodiment. And the miraculous element of it was not so much the fact that he rose from the dead (for that we hold to be a part of the appointed order of nature), but the manner in which his resurrection was accomplished, and made a representation to man of the great divine law of the resurrection. It was a miraculous representation, a divine illustration, a picturing before the eyes of disciples, of the general resurrection. It was an illustration which no man could invent, but which it has pleased God to give, of the end of mortality, and the final transformation into the spiritual body. Nothing else adequately illustrates the resurrection but this great historical object-lesson, as it were, and foreshadowing of it, which the disciples beheld who found the tomb empty and saw Jesus appear and disappear, and at last ascend into heaven. As nothing else, the transformation of Jesus from this material body into the spiritual, his passage through the grave, and partly within sight of the disciples, into the glory that excelleth, brings life and immortality to light. For, observe further how the revelation of the resurrection, made through Jesus' appearance and final parting from the disciples, entered into the apostolic doctrine, and became the hope which has been cherished ever since in the heart of the Church.

Without burdening our pages with critical

discussions of particular texts, we may specify the following elementary truths, or essential parts, of the doctrine of the resurrection, which the apostles gained from their experience of the risen Lord.

In the great resurrection chapter, the Apostle to the Corinthians has made the discovery that the resurrection is not unnatural, but in accordance with the very intention of the creation. It is a moment, or part, of that grand order, and comprehensive process, by which the earthly order shall pass into the heavenly, and the whole creation be redeemed from the bondage of corruption. There are two orders, the natural and the spiritual; they are not unrelated; there is a divinely appointed succession, or progress, from the one to the other; and death and the resurrection have their place and purpose in the whole divine economy whose end is eternal life. The chosen metaphor for the marvellous change and perfection of the earthly is the growth of the seed into the green blade and the full-grown ear. It is important not to lose this primary truth of the scriptural doctrine that the resurrection is according to law. It is prepared for in the very make of the creation, in the whole order of things. No green blade from the buried seed, no ripened grain in the ear, is more natural.

Two elements of this most natural process of resurrection are brought out into light, and upon these two elementary truths the whole emphasis of the apostolic doctrine is made to rest.

1. The first truth is that our present embodiment has some real relation to, some preparatory significance for, our future embodiment. The one is the first step in a process of embodiment which shall be completed in the other. The future life shall conserve and carry out the present life, not only mentally and spiritually, but also physically, or as an embodied life. The spiritual body shall be the end of God's way through nature to a glorified creation. The present body, therefore, has value in this preparative dispensation of nature. It is not to be despised. It has worth in God's plan, and exists now for the sake of the higher order, for the glory of the celestial which shall be. Its lifelong history, its birth, its growth, its training, its sufferings, its death, all are not causeless, nor out of the divine order; but they have, as everything earthly has, a preparatory and prophetic worth; and they are now for the perfect life which shall be, when the whole creation shall be redeemed. This truth of the physical conservation of life in the world to come, and the organic relation of the body which now is to the body which shall be, is plainly taught in the apostolic lan-

guage concerning the resurrection. The revelation of Jesus' resurrection was to the disciples the pledge of full, rounded, complete personal existence after death. The next life is, in every thread of it, continuous with this; and the whole life passes on into the glory of the celestial.

2. The other truth concerning the resurrection body, which the Sadducees never understood, but which the apostle who preached Jesus and the resurrection has learned as a first truth of his hope, is this. The body which shall be is not fashioned of matter of the same kind as these earthly bodies. It is not to be woven of perishable stuff. It is not of the earth earthy. Flesh and blood, Paul says expressly, cannot inherit the kingdom of God. The Lord who left the tomb entered heaven in the glory of the celestial body. We shall be changed. There is a real connection, or some correlation, between the present and the future embodiment, but not identity of substance. The life, the principle of life, the individuality of it, shall remain unbroken; but the matter of life, as the physiologists say, shall be changed. We commit dust to dust. The earthliness in which the seed is buried does not appear in the flower. The glory of the terrestrial is one, the glory of the celestial is another. There is in the soul the necessity

for embodiment. The Creator has linked its life with the elements of his creation. We shall be clothed upon, says the apostle; we shall not be found naked. The soul, in the final redemption of the creation, shall assimilate for its form and beauty the matter of the unseen universe; and possibly, we may already have connected with this mortality the rudiments, the forming principle or germ, of this future embodiment. Certain passages of the Scriptures seem to indicate that the conditions for the full development of the spiritual body shall be given only when the whole visible economy shall pass in fulfilment away; that the saints wait in blissful expectancy, until the consummation of this world-age, for the highest possible perfection of heavenly life; that the harvest is the end of the world. But here we look into the distant horizons of revelation, and the light is too diffused along the far horizon for distinct vision. The two points already indicated are, however, brought within our reach by the representation of the resurrection made by the risen and ascended Lord; and, as we have seen, they were firmly grasped in the apostolic doctrine. Upon these two points, therefore—the connection and the difference of substance between the present and the future embodiment—our whole statement of the doctrine should be made to depend. If between these two fixed points, which are lifted up into the light by revelation, we stretch all our theories; if around them all our imaginations of the future life gather, we shall not find the substance of the hope of the resurrection floating off into the empty air, nor, on the other hand, shall we see the doctrine lowered and dragged amid the grossest conceptions, until torn to shreds upon the hard edges of scientific facts. A life in all essential energies continuous with the present, yet transformed, and passing into a higher order,—that is the essence of the hope for which the biblical doctrine of the resurrection of the dead still stands as the faith of the Church of the risen Lord. This mysterious cord of life, whose beginnings reach beyond our sight until it is bound to the throne of the living God; this marvellously braided cord of life, plaited of many threads—matter, mind, spirit, fibres of nerve, and lines of sensation too subtle to be unraveled, being all bound up together in it— a life here often strangely knotted and tangled; —this wonderfully woven life of ours shall not be broken by death in a single strand of it; it shall run on and on, an unbroken life, upheld by the will of the Eternal. Death cannot break it, but it shall change it. It shall draw from it all perishable dross. While the life remains the same, some elements of which its strands are woven shall be changed;—instead of the silver cord shall be the thread of gold; for the corruptible shall be the incorruptible; and there shall be no more entanglement and imperfection, no more strain upon any strand of it; the flesh shall not chafe against the spirit, nor the spirit against the flesh,—but there shall be at last the one perfectly accorded, incorruptible, and beautiful life.

Is it necessary for any one at this late day to spend time in clearing the simplicity of the biblical doctrine of the resurrection of the dead from the cumbersome additions of the traditional teaching of the resurrection of the flesh? In this doctrine, as in others, the work of restoration has been for some time going on even under the most cautious orthodox hands;—after tearing away the elaborate reconstructions and "improvements" of later styles of theological architecture, after removing the colors laid upon colors with which clumsy hands have sought to retouch and to preserve the divine original, we are beginning to see come forth again the simple naturalness and the inimitable beauty of the Gospel of Jesus and his disciples. In an article, however, in Smith's Bible Dictionary—upon whose authority our clergy and intelligent laity justly lean as a work well up to the demands of sober modern scholarship—we notice, to our surprise, that the simple essentials of the apostolic doctrine of the resurrection are still burdened with reasonings concerning the possibilities of the resurrection of these same bodies, which remind one of the ingenious speculations of Athenagoras of old, who with equal subtlety endeavored to show how mortal flesh can be preserved for immortal uses. It should teach us caution in our approach to this glorious mystery of revelation, that our familiar traditional phrases, "resurrection of the body," "resurrection of the flesh," are not the biblical expressions, "the resurrection of the dead," or "the resurrection from the dead." The heavenly light entered an atmosphere heavy with earthly emanations, and in the lingering Judaism of the early Church many a truth was broken and refracted. So it happened with the pure hope of the second coming, or presence, of Christ; and the revelation of the last things, in the same gross atmosphere, could hardly escape distortion and corruption. The wonder is that the light of the Gospel shone so brightly and so clearly as it did over the troubled horizon of the second century, down through an age when all the winds of agitation seemed to be let loose, and mists and clouds and currents from every quarter of the known world seemed to meet and gather. It is not surprising, therefore, that an expression which never fell from the tongue of the inspired preacher of the resurrection should have trembled upon the lips of early confessors and martyrs, and have become a part of one of the most ancient creeds of the church.*

The needless burdening of the apostolic teaching with the conception of the literal resurrection of the flesh was not left without opposition in the early Church. Origen called it the foolishness of beggarly minds.† In seeking, however, to avoid the unapostolic blunder of preaching the literal resurrection of the flesh, Origen and the Alexandrian school hardly escaped the opposite danger of an allegorizing and idealistic interpretation. The materialistic view of the resurrection became the prevalent scholastic view, and still lingers, as we have just observed—really cast out, but not yet laid—in modern theology. Our science leaves us no tenable support for it. Any proper physiological conception of the human body precludes it. For the matter

---

* The phrase σαρκός ἀνάστασιν occurs in what is now thought to be the original of the "Old Roman Creed," and to have been in use at Rome prior to A. D. 140. The necessity of meeting decisively the Gnostic Docetism and contempt of the body may have been the occasion for the substitution of this phrase for the New Testament forms; one extreme in theology thus giving birth to another.

† Op. II. 532-36.

of life is always changing. The form only is identical, not the flesh. Lotze's apt comparison of the body to a ripple around some hidden stone in a stream is physiologically true. We see day after day the same ripple on the stream, the same wave-form, produced by the same cause, but the drops of the water are always changing;—matter is in perpetual flux; the stream of existence is ever flowing by; our bodies are but momentary forms, never the same, two successive seasons, and destined soon to pass away. Nor does the hypothesis of some single, indestructible, material germ of the immaterial body escape the scientific reduction to the absurd. Descartes thought he had found the material centre of the soul. But modern physiology has dissipated the dream of some central atom through which mind is united to matter, and which may be supposed to remain after death, and the dissolution of the body, as the indestructible germ, the earthly nucleus, of the spiritual body. The more thoroughly the convolutions of the brain are explored, the more obvious does it become that there is no physical centre of soul-life; no one spot to which all lines and fibres of its marvelous network of nerves converge. The brain, physiologically examined, has not proved to be like the Hebrew Temple, provided with an inner chamber, a mysterious holy place, for the dwelling-place of the unseen spirit that is in man. Matter, so far as we can have any knowledge of it, nowhere, at no one point, at no single moment of its perpetual motion, becomes the inalienable personal property of man. Like the woman mentioned in the Bible who had had seven husbands, so, it has been said, the same matter may belong in succession to several lives, for they all had it; and, like the Sadducees, we greatly err if we do not know Jesus' own Scripture that in the resurrection we shall be as the angels of God. The power of God, which in the larger course of nature may have already provided for the new heaven and the new earth, and the change of this mortality into the glory of the celestial, does not need for our future embodiment, to work a miracle against the constitution of this lower half, and temporary order, of nature. We need to have no atom laid aside and held fast for our use in the higher sphere;—let nature flow on in us and through us, from generation to generation, until this world-age shall be over. Why should God lock up in the perishable earth a single particle of dust for our immortal inheritance? It is enough that he has so connected the mortal and the immortal, and created the two kinds of existence in such organic relationship, that the natural is the preparation for the spiritual;

that the image of the heavenly which we shall bear is the fulfilment of the earthy which we shall lay aside; that in some natural way, according, that is, to the whole nature of things, though beyond our knowledge—for we know now only in part, only the half of the nature of things—the body which shall be, shall conserve and glorify the forces, and individuality, and form, of the body which now is. The person shall rise from the dead.

We should notice in passing that this view is to be distinguished from the Swedenborgian conception of the loosening and escape, at death, of the spiritual body. The spiritual beings of Swedenborg's philosophy still belong to this present visible universe; the spiritual body, in the Swedenborgian conception of it, is only a finer efflorescence of matter, and heaven corresponds to earth. The biblical revelation seems to us, on the contrary, to prophesy a great advance to a higher order, and to inspire the hope of a final transformation of nature, and a change into a new type or mode of existence, whose advent shall complete the whole evolution of love's creative and self-imparting purpose. The earthly and the mortal are the heralds and emblems, but not the correspondences, of that which is to be revealed; and, like the apostle of old, we know not what we shall be. Our resurrection shall not be, as we read the signs of it, simply a setting free from the bonds of the flesh of a finer spiritualized form, which belongs still to the present economy of nature; but it shall be, so far as we are able to throw over our conception the lines of a definition, the assimilation by the living energy or soul of these bodies (by that nature-side of us which makes some embodiment of the spirit a necessity of the creature) of the material of the unseen universe. The resurrection, to speak of it after the latest scientific fashion of speech, may be the continuation after death of that process of differentiation and integration which we observe going on up to the death of man. It may be, that is, a further differentiation, or separation of the organic principle, the soul-life, from gross corruptible matter; and also a further and final integration, the formation of a new and higher mode of existence, the gathering, around the vitalizing principle, of the materials of a more spiritual body from the heavenly places.

We do not say that that process may not even now be going on. We do not deny that the spiritual body may be embryonic, or rudimentary, in the physical basis of this present life. We do not say when the process of its formation shall be completed. We do not know. Revelation does not yield distinct outlines along these horizons. We look, and wonder, and wait. We may only say that certain Scriptures seem to imply that the termination of the whole present course of nature, and the beginning of the new course, shall be necessary, before all the conditions for this full, final, and perfect spiritual embodiment shall be furnished. The end of this world-age may be an object of joyous anticipation to all the saints who are with the Lord, expecting; and the end of the world may add something to the blessedness of all the generations who have left it. It was but forty days between Jesus' resurrection and its completion in his ascension. But he was the firstfruits of the resurrection. The period of transformation, the interval of happy expectancy may, in our case, extend from the day of our death to the hour when the last trump shall sound, and there shall be a general resurrection,—the final embodiment of all souls according to the deeds done in the body—the ascension of all the redeemed into the glory of the spiritual heavens and the joy of their Lord.

We have given, thus, what seem to us to be the essential truths for which the scriptural doctrine of the resurrection stands; truths which were miraculously represented in the appearance of Jesus after death, and his final parting from his disciples. We have distinguished this view from fanciful speculations concerning a present spiritual body, and indicated that it is not inconsistent with those passages of Scripture which seem to teach a general resurrection at the end of the world, at the harvest of this whole course of nature. It remains for us now to turn again to our scientific questionings, and to ask whether under the light of the idea of development this simple biblical doctrine of the resurrection can be put to confusion.

We hold that there is no analogy of nature against it; but that, on the contrary, it is a conceivable and fitting termination of the whole course of nature, and a possible and worthy end of the whole struggle and ascent of life; that it is the natural fulfilment of the moral purpose which runs through the present evolution of nature, and the normal and only perfect conclusion of creative love. Our future and final embodiment is not the manufacture of a moment; for God works, as we have seen, through age-long processes, and the final and glorious embodiment, likewise, we expect as the consummation of a great course of nature, and as the final result of this world-age. What that resurrection body shall be, must be made known to us now, if at all, through revelation; but, while science can never demonstrate the unseen and the eternal, there is nothing in our positive science which need prevent us from listening on this subject to the hope of revelation, or from carrying out in a belief in the resurrection our moral interpretation of the course of nature. On the contrary, the biblical teaching affords with regard to the future life the simplest, most connected, and intelligible reading of many phenomena of this present life which are hieroglyphics to the science of the senses. Revelation indicates *future* correlations and conservations of existing forces, which we now know in part, but which we are not yet able to comprehend in a perfect science of life. The biblical doctrine of the future state is the logical conclusion of tendencies and laws whose operation within the limits of this present life is a matter of positive knowledge.

As we have already seen, it is not unscientific to assume that matter in its make and form is only a passing mode or transient stage of a process of evolution which is older than all visible worlds, and which has in it the promise and the potency of new and still more glorious creations. It is not unscientific to suppose that the law of continuity obtains not only within the limits of the present system of things, but also beyond them; that what we call nature is but a half truth, a part of the thought of the Eternal; and that when infinite Love shall have finished its perfect work nothing shall be wasted, and that which remains shall be more glorious than that which passes away.

From what we have learned and suspected, also, of the natural relation of soul and body, the prospect of immortality through a higher embodiment would seem to be but the continuation of a course of nature already begun. We have regarded the wonder of the human brain as the end of one course of evolution in the gain of the first possible physical basis for a created soul. We have every reason to believe that it marks the first step, the beginning, of self-conscious, thoughtful life; we have no reason to imagine that the first step is the last, the beginning the end of spiritual existence. Rather the progress of nature up to the human brain leaves us no reason to limit the process of organization of matter for mind at the point of sight. The brain may be only the embyronic condition of the matter of mind. Indeed, in the present union of mind and body the process already has gone beyond our sight, and no microscope can show us where the matter upon which mind rests first begins. The physical basis of our present life of thought defies analysis—no science can lay it bare. But if mind, a spiritual force, can in any way enter into living relation with matter so gross and palpable as a convolution of nerve cells, much more might it enter into possession and enjoyment of matter of a still finer sublimation, and of a more ethereal constitution. If even in the dull brain there can be laid up the materials of an organic memory, much more in a spiritual body might mind make itself master of all things. We cannot be stopped short in this inference by the assumption which Mr. Lewes says biology makes, that there is one matter everywhere the same;* for, as we have already noticed, physical science is compelled to admit the existence of at least one kind of ethereal matter of a different constitution from ordinary matter. We are not obliged to adopt the conjecture that the ether is not a mere medium, but a medium *plus* the invisible order of things; † nor need we entertain the kindred supposition of Isaac Taylor,‡ that "there is about us a fluid, the counterpart of the ether," with which mind may be amalgamated. We need cherish no imagination whatsoever of the nature of spiritual body; we need simply admit the perfectly scientific possibility of a higher and better organization of some kind of matter for mind, as the future physical

---

* Physical Basis, p. 4.
† Unseen Universe, p. 198.
‡ Physical Theory, p. 219.

basis of immortal life. We reason, then, from the way the Creator has taken up to the brain of man, to the way he will take beyond this present mortal body. The same divine operation which in the human body has fashioned a material organism for the free play of conscious thought, can work that process of organization out to perfection. The very momentum of life must carry it through death. As we know that a train which comes within our view, and the next moment swiftly passes out of our sight, must be hurried on by its own motion, and, though disappearing, does not come to a sudden stop; so we reason from the momentum of present thought and purpose to a future existence, and believe that the life goes still farther on in the world beyond our sight. It is contrary to experience to suppose a sudden stop at death. It is not the way of the Creator up to man to bring his growing work to an end in one fearful crash and destruction. Therefore we say, as he is a faithful Creator, as the whole course of creation thus far is not one stupendous lie, death does not end all. We shall put off this mortality to be clothed upon with immortality. First the natural, afterwards that which is spiritual.

These special probabilities of immortality through the resurrection of the dead, gain additional strength and consistency when we take them up and weave them together, with all our previous reasonings, into the whole woof and substance of our Christian thinking. The Christian evidences are so complementary, and mutually confirmatory, that we cannot do them justice by treating them as though they were detached threads. We have to pursue continuous divine processes; we have to interpret a development of nature, a course of history, a progressive revelation, an increasing purpose running through all towards one "far off, divine event." He who can follow with the spiritual understanding the paths of a Diviner Presence than eye hath seen along the ways of nature and through history, will find that he is ever "stepping westward," and with a glowing sky to lead him on. History, the echo of humanity's low voice, will give him hopeful greeting,—

> "A sound
> Of something without place or bound,"—

and, as he gazes into the vistas of light beyond light of futurity, he will feel as the poet, looking into the evening sky, while walking in the highlands, felt:

> "The echo of the voice inwrought,
>   A human sweetness with the thought
>   Of travelling through the world that lay
>   Before me in my endless way."

We cannot refrain from drawing the contrast between the vision of life in worlds to come which inspired the great apostle who preached the hope of the resurrection at Athens, and the outlook into the dim, uncertain future permitted to the great philosopher who in our times has built again the altar to the Unknown God. "Evolution," says Mr. Herbert Spencer, "has an impassable limit." *
"A universe of extinct suns round which circle planets devoid of life," is the "proximate end of the processes everywhere going on." †
"Universal death" is the end which the evolutionist must contemplate as the last state of a worn-out creation. "Universal death" is the inevitable close of evolution, and that fatal end "may continue indefinitely." But the evolutionist recoils from his own conclusion, and flies for refuge to the mystery of the Unknown. The end may be only proximate, the tragic death of nature only another birth. That the law which has developed from nebulous beginnings and primordial worlds these starry constellations, and habitable worlds, and life's rich and infinite variety, should prove after all to be only a law of death—death playing at life—that it should build only to destroy, and find the goal of all its mighty working only

---
* First Prin., p. 440.
† Ibid., p. 472.

in reducing all its works to chaos and night—this seems even to the sternest of evolutionists almost too great a tax upon the faith of the human heart. He admits that the evolution which his thought has followed to universal death may be only relative,—as we suppose that visible nature is itself only part of the whole stupendous process of creative power. He admits that things seem to point to another future, and that, "on carrying the argument still further, we are led to infer a subsequent Universal Life." * This "possible hypothesis" of the great philosopher of the Unknown we may at least claim as a scientific permission for preaching the hope of the great apostle of the revealed mystery of the ages. Herbert Spencer, having by most laborious toil gained the summit of this nineteenth century wisdom, looks about him to see a rayless horizon and the approach of universal night. Yet beyond that horizon may lie, he thinks, the possibility of another dawn. The Christian revelator, likewise, sees the night coming, but also the day. The possibility of science is his sure hope of that which lies beyond time, and which transcends knowledge. He, too, sees the cloud and the darkness; but he has a larger vision of the spirit, and is assured that

---

* Ibid., p. 483.

the cloud is of the moment, and the sunshine is eternal. "There shall be no night there." Death, he believes, is a moment and part of the larger process of life, and the passing away of the earth and the heavens—the tragic end of the creation in universal death, which our very science must foretell—is but a moment and part, likewise, of that divine work and order through which the natural shall bring in the spiritual, the glory of the terrestrial be transformed into the glory of the celestial, and perfect love, having given of itself to the uttermost, shall reach at length the end of all its ways from the beginning in that great city, the holy city, descending out of heaven from God, having the glory of God.

It remains for us now to gather up in one general conclusion the separate lines of our reasoning. We began by accepting loyally the results of scientific research into the present constitution of things. We trust our senses, and the logic of the senses, just so far as the human understanding can work out a positive science. We admit that the course of visible nature can be best summed up in some general law of evolution. We do not question, and have no moral interest in questioning, a physical evolution, and a mechanism coextensive with the bounds of nature, so far as by such conceptions the sum total of our scientific knowledge can be at present expressed to the best advantage. But ours is by birthright the duty, also, of subjecting visible nature to the interpretation of the spirit, and of reading the formulas of things in the light of our own moral ideas. The science whose source is within us, can never yield to any sciences whose sources are in the world without us. Perfect knowledge must be the harmony of both. Our objection to evolution is not that it may not be true; but that, if proved true, it is only a half-truth. We dare not put a part for the whole; we refuse to measure the possibilities of the universe by the diameter of the little circle of our knowledge. Besides the curve of the earth which we can measure, there is the immeasurable sweep of the sky above us. A philosophy worthy of the name must admit both sciences—the science of the natural, and the science of the spiritual which transcends nature,—or its conclusions will be only half-truths. Physical evolution finds its complement only in a higher truth. The one thought of the Creator is expressed in two parts of speech, a noun and a verb; matter and mind, body and soul, nature and the supernatural, are the two parts, the noun and the verb, of the one creative word. But the prevalent evolutionary philosophy is a grammar simply of the noun to the neglect of the verb.

It is a science only of one part of the creative speech; it goes off exultingly with the substantive, and leaves metaphysics to learn, if it can, what is really affirmed of it. It takes nature as the only part of the divine speech worth knowing, and separates it from all the affirmations of our consciousness. But we cannot so easily and so arbitrarily construe the Creator's thought. It may be difficult to see how in some points the noun and the verb agree; how together they make one intelligible meaning; but no difficulty in our earthly grammar can warrant us in giving up one iota of the sentence set before us for our study; and if we should, it would be easier to sacrifice matter to spirit, than spirit to matter. But we hold fast to both noun and verb; to the great generic substantive without us—the world that is made, and which stands for something; and also to that which is affirmed within us—thought, will, love.

Wherever mechanism can be found, even within the domain of life, we are ready to receive the proofs of it.* But mechanism explains nothing, not even its own motion. We have given in the preceding chapters evidences

---

* The burden of proof is really on the side of materialism. Consciousness holds everything to be like itself, until it is proved to be different. Everything is spiritual until shown to be material.

of the presence and working of something which is without the mechanism of things, and whose energy cannot be reduced to any physical equivalents. We noticed the historical growth of a revelation, which it is difficult to account for as a spontaneous generation of nature. We traced the processes of the manifestation of a divine life with man. We have seen in the development of a progressive revelation the evolution of a power greater than natural forces, and working out its benign results according to a higher law. The natural evolution of the Semitic stock does not contain the whole development of the history of Israel. We then beheld, standing among men, one whose generation no natural science can declare, whose Person is a wonder, and whose life is a miracle, if this world and the powers of this world are all of the universe; but whose advent is hardly a surprise, and whose work is a unity, if we view it in relation to a divine order, and as the culmination of a supernatural evolution of nature. We beheld in that consummation of the creation the beginning of a new reign higher than the dynasty of man, the ushering in of a new kingdom of a constitution beyond the earthly which it shall supersede, even the kingdom of heaven. We have listened to the prophecies of the final glory of that kingdom, and find in them the worthy end and consummation of the whole divine process, or supernatural evolution, of the creation—of nature, life, and human history. So far as we can read from the face of this present world the story of its own past, and the probabilities of its future, we learn that it has not always been, and that it cannot last forever. We discover in the present visible nature the signs that it is but a part and moment of a diviner whole. The scene cannot be, as we have repeatedly said, the demonstration of the Unseen; but the more we learn of nature, the more confidence we may have in the spirit's affirmations of faith. We have seen that this world is unfinished, and this apparent or visible nature incomplete—its evolution a contradiction and destruction of itself—unless we believe that it is continuous with a supernatural realm, and a preparation for that which is perfect, which is to come.

This conclusion will at once be subjected by many to the reproach of dualism, and it will be said that evolution excludes the supposition of a twofold development of the creation. But, as matter of fact, we find a twofoldness in experience which we may hide from ourselves for the moment under some mask of words, but which we cannot obliterate so long as we are thinking men. We do not make, we simply recognize, the dualism which exists in the constitution of nature. There are two kinds of force, two lines of law, two orders of development, two processes of evolution,— body and mind, nature and spirit, earth and heaven. We secure only a fictitious unity when we ignore either kind of being, or seek to reduce either to the terms of the other. The desire to reduce the universe to a unit, is the *ignis fatuus* of much positive science. It lures rash scientific speculation into extremes of folly. Haeckel's boastful monism, for example, or claim that he has reduced all things in heaven and earth to one kind of protoplasmic matter, involves the double absurdity of asking the human mind to commit suicide, and also of attempting to bring nature into subjection by beating the very breath of life out of it. Science, then, would have to perform the office of undertaker to a dead world. Nature, however, is not a mere collection of specimens preserved for our dissection; and philosophy still has a higher task to fulfil than to keep the doors of a museum-world. There is an "inner life of things," and a unity of the spirit in the creation. We have followed, in our discussion, the course of a twofold development, and found in nature and history repeated and manifold signs of a double evolution—a supernatural as well as natural law, and order, and growth;—but the two are one in their origin, their aim, and their end. The supernatural evolution, whose signs and evidences we cannot deny, is not a work of spiritual power against nature; rather we have conceived of it throughout as a *connatural* evolution—a development with nature, and through nature, of something which is more than nature; the result or goal of which is a new nature, the second nature, the glorified creation, the new heaven, and new earth of the Scriptures. The unity is real, the dualism which we observe apparent. The dualism exists in time, and to our finite intelligence; the unity is in eternity, and to the mind of the Omniscient. A monistic theory is conceivable only when we bring in the idea of the living God as the everywhere present Spirit, and eternal unity of the creation. The oneness of all things amid infinite diversity is a truth of the Spirit. All the sciences seek for this unity, but religion alone finds it. When Comte proposed as the end of positive science the reduction of all phenomena to one law, he really brought back again the banished age of theology. The one comprehensive formula for all existing things is—God. By Him all things consist. The unity of the creation is a truth of the Godhead. The science of the senses may knock in vain for this truth to be opened to it, but the poet finds it revealed wherever he looks. It is not a lesson of biology, but a truth of life disclosed to the living soul. He who possesses what Wordsworth called "the first great gift, a vital soul," who has "the feeling intellect, reason in her most exalted mood," becomes the true seer, the interpreter of the thought of God hidden in nature's heart. The divine secret of existence which the logic of Mr. Mill could not break open, which the science of the Royal Academy cannot torture to confess itself in its laboratory, is the truth pervading all things, which the feeling intellect of Wordsworth discerned, and the sense and the mystery of it made him the great poet of nature's spiritual aspects and prophetic moods. To the poet's vital soul nature wore an expression of divinity on her very face.

> "The unfettered clouds and region of the heavens;
> Tumult and peace, the darkness and the light;
> Were all the workings of one mind, the features
> Of the same face, blossoms upon one tree;
> Characters of the great Apocalypse,
> The types and symbols of Eternity,
> Of first, and last, and midst, and without end."

We need never hesitate, therefore, to bring old faiths into new light. Our spiritual life can suffer and grow pale only if we shut it out from the increasing light, and leave it to grow in the darkness. The clear shining of knowledge may dissipate a thousand fancies which we have mistaken for realities; but it shall bring to faith health, and vigor, and renewed life. While many run to and fro, and knowledge is increased, Christianity cannot be preserved as a cloistered virtue, or a scholastic art; but out in the breezy world, under the open sky, rejoicing in the light, its strength shall not be abated, nor its eye grow dim. Reverently and humbly, but nothing doubting, the Christian apologist of to-day may follow wherever new paths of knowledge seem opening to our approach; and though he goes down into the depths, or wanders through realms of strange shadows, and endless confusions, nevertheless, after he has traversed all the spheres into which thought can find entrance, if he remains true to the spirit sent for his guidance, his better self,—like Dante following Beatrice from world to world—he shall find himself at last by the gates of Paradise, walking in a cloud of light, full of all melodious voices.

THE END.

THE RELIGIOUS FEELING.

BY

Rev. NEWMAN SMYTH.

One Volume, 12mo, cloth, - - - - - $1.25.

In this volume Mr. Smyth has it for his object to formulate the religious feeling as a capacity of the human mind, and to vindicate its claims to authority. He sets before himself at the outset the task of convicting sceptical philosophy out of its own mouth. The work is thoroughly logical, and displays a familiarity with the most recent German thought which is rarely to be found.

CRITICAL NOTICES.

MR. JOSEPH COOK'S opinion of "*The Religious Feeling:*"
"A fresh, keen book, copies of which I wish were scattered broadcast throughout the land:" and, in a letter to the author, "I admire exceedingly the familiarity you exhibit with the latest scientific literature. The reverent spirit with which you treat all Christian truth, the elegance of your style; the searching originality of many a page in your volume, insure it a lasting, and, I hope, a wide usefulness."

"The argument in its clearness, force and illustrations, has never, to our knowledge, been better stated. Mr. Smyth has brought to his work a clear, analytical mind, an extensive knowledge of German philosophical thought, and an intellectual familiarity with the later English schools. He does his own thinking, and writes with perspicuity and vigor."—*The Advance.*

"Upon his own field of metaphysical and moral philosophy he displays a degree of clear, acute, and analytic reasoning which is of a high order and exceedingly effective, both in demolishing the semi-materialistic philosophy of Darwin and Spencer, and in demonstrating the spiritual nature and supernatural origin of the human soul."
—*Chicago Interior.*

"We welcome this volume as a valuable contribution to that type of thought in the vindication of theism which is specially demanded at the present time. The discussion throughout evinces much reading and vigorous thought, and is conducted with marked candor and ability."—*New Englander.*

"We can cordially recommend the reader to follow the author through his entire argument, for it is both brief and clear. The book will form a help to many perplexed minds, and it epitomizes very satisfactorily some of the best results of conservative German thought."—*Cincinnati Gazette.*

"This very interesting book is always eloquent and suggestive. What makes it especially noteworthy, seems to us its significance in relation to our day."
—*New York World.*

"The argument contained in these pages is eminently satisfactory. It is one of the best answers to Darwin and his followers we have ever met with."—*The Churchman.*

⁎ *For sale by all booksellers, or will be sent, prepaid, upon receipt of price, by*

CHARLES SCRIBNER'S SONS,

NOS. 743 AND 745 BROADWAY, NEW YORK.

Lange's Commentary,

CRITICAL, DOCTRINAL, AND HOMILETICAL.

TRANSLATED, ENLARGED, AND EDITED

BY

PHILIP SCHAFF, D.D.,

PROFESSOR IN THE UNION THEOLOGICAL SEMINARY.

This is the most comprehensive and exhaustive Commentary on the whole Bible ever published in this or any other country. It will be completed in 24 large royal octavo volumes. Twenty-two volumes have already appeared, and the remaining two are now in press.

The German work, on which the English edition is based, is the product of about twenty distinguished Biblical scholars, of Germany, Holland, and Switzerland, and enjoys a high reputation and popularity wherever German theology is studied.

The American edition is not a mere translation (although embracing the whole of the German), but, to a large extent, an *original* work; about one-third of the matter being added, and the whole adapted to the wants of the English and American student. Its popularity and sale has been lately increasing in Great Britain.

The press has been almost unanimous in its commendation of LANGE'S COMMENTARY. It is generally regarded as being, on the whole, the most useful Commentary, especially for ministers and theological students—in which they are more likely to find what they desire than in any other. It is a complete treasury of Biblical knowledge, brought down to the latest date. It gives the results of careful, scholarly research; yet in a form sufficiently popular for the use of intelligent laymen. The Homiletical department contains the best thoughts of the great divines and pulpit orators of all ages, on the texts explained, and supplies rich suggestions for sermons and Bible lectures.

The following are some of the chief merits of this Commentary:

1. *It is orthodox and sound*, without being sectarian or denominational. It fairly represents the exegetical and doctrinal *consensus* of evangelical divines of the present age, and yet ignores none of the just claims of liberal scientific criticism.

2. *It is comprehensive and complete*—giving in beautiful order the authorized English version with emendations, a digest of the Critical Apparatus, Exegetical Explanations, Doctrinal and Ethical Inferences and Reflections, and Homiletical and Practical Hints and Applications.

3. *It is the product of fifty American* (besides twenty European) *Scholars*, from the leading denominations and Theological institutions of the country. Professors in the Theological Seminaries of New York, Princeton, Andover, New Haven, Hartford, Cambridge, Rochester, Philadelphia, Cincinnati, Alleghany, Chicago, Madison, and other places, representing the Presbyterian, Episcopal, Congregational, Baptist, Methodist, Lutheran, and Reformed Churches, have contributed to this Commentary, and enriched it with the results of their special studies. It may, therefore, claim a national character more than any other work of the kind ever published in this country.

8vo, per vol., in sheep, $6.50; in half calf, $7.50; cloth, $5.00.

₊ *The above book for sale by all booksellers, or will be sent, post or express charges paid, upon receipt of the price by the publishers,*

CHARLES SCRIBNER'S SONS,

743 AND 745 BROADWAY, NEW YORK

Faith and Rationalism.

By Prof. GEORGE P. FISHER, D.D.,

Author of "The Beginnings of Christianity," The Reformation," Etc.

One Volume, 12mo, Cloth, $1.25.

"This valuable and timely volume discusses ably, trenchantly and decisively the subjects of which it treats. It contains within small limits a large amount of information and unanswerable reasoning."—*Presbyterian Banner*.

"The book is valuable as a discussion of the mysteries of faith and the characteristics of rationalism by one of the clearest writers and thinkers."—*Washington Post*.

"The author deals with many of the questions of the day, and does so with a freshness and completeness quite admirable and attractive."—*Presbyterian*.

"This singularly clear and catholic-spirited essay will command the attention of the theological world, for it is a searching inquiry into the very substance of Christian belief."—*Hartford Courant*.

"This little volume may be regarded as virtually a primer of modern religious thought, which contains within its condensed pages rich materials that are not easily gathered from the great volumes of our theological authors. Alike in learning, style and power of descrimination, it is honorable to the author and to his university, which does not urge the claims of science by slighting the worth of faith or philosophy."—*N. Y. Times*.

"Topics of profound interest to the studious inquirer after truth are discussed by the author with his characteristic breadth of view, catholicity of judgment, affluence of learning, felicity of illustration, and force of reasoning. . . . His singular candor disarms the prepossessions of his opponents. . . . In these days of pretentious, shallow and garrulous scholarship, his learning is as noticeable for its solidity as for its compass."—*N. Y. Tribune*.

---

* *The above book for sale by all booksellers, or will be sent, prepaid, upon receipt of price, by*

CHARLES SCRIBNER'S SONS, PUBLISHERS,

743 AND 745 BROADWAY, NEW YORK.

Prof. F. Max Muller's Works.

LECTURES ON THE SCIENCE OF LANGUAGE.

By F. MAX MULLER, M.A., Fellow of All Souls College, Oxford.
FIRST SERIES:—Comprising those delivered in April, May, and June, 1861. One vol., crown 8vo, half calf, $4.50; cloth, . $2.50
SECOND SERIES:—Comprising those delivered in February, March, April, and May, 1863 *With thirty-one illustrations.* One vol., crown 8vo, half calf, $5.50; cloth, ... $3.50

From the Atlantic Monthly.

"Easily comprehensible, and yet always pointing out the sources of fuller investigation, it is ample, both to satisfy the desire of those who wish to get the latest results of philosophy, and to stimulate the curiosity of whoever wishes to go further and deeper. It is by far the best and clearest summing up of the present condition of the science of language that we have ever seen, while the liveliness of style and the variety and freshness of illustration make it exceedingly interesting."

CHIPS FROM A GERMAN WORKSHOP.

By F. MAX MULLER, M.A., Fellow of All Souls College, Oxford. Reprinted from the Second Revised London Edition, with copious Index. Vol. I. ESSAYS ON THE SCIENCE OF RELIGION. Vol. II. ESSAYS ON MYTHOLOGY, TRADITIONS, AND CUSTOMS. Vol. III. LITERATURE, BIOGRAPHY, AND ANTIQUITIES. Three vols., crown 8vo, cloth, per vol., $2.50; the set in half calf, . . $13.50

From the New York Evening Post.

"This book of Prof. Müller would afford no end of interesting extracts; 'Chips' by the cord, that are full both to the intellect and the imagination; but we must refer the curious reader to the volumes themselves. He will find in them a body of combined entertainment and instruction such as has hardly ever been brought together in so compact a form."

LECTURES ON THE SCIENCE OF RELIGION.

WITH PAPERS ON BUDDHISM, AND A TRANSLATION OF THE DHAMMAPADA, OR PATH OF VIRTUE. By F. MAX MULLER, M.A. One vol., crown 8vo, half calf, $4.50; cloth, $2.00

From the Chicago Evening Journal.

"The thoroughness of its method, the vigor and clearness of its discussions, and the extensive learning wrought into the text of the work, give it the high character which commands for such a production the rank and authority of a standard."

THE ORIGIN AND GROWTH OF RELIGION,

As illustrated by the Religions of India. By F. MAX MULLER. One vol., crown 8vo, $2.50.

There can be no doubt that this volume will be welcomed by all earnest and thoughtful minds.

*** *The above books for sale by all booksellers, or will be sent, prepaid, upon receipt of price, by*

CHARLES SCRIBNER'S SONS, PUBLISHERS,
743 AND 745 BROADWAY, NEW YORK

www.ingramcontent.com/pod-product-compliance
Lightning Source LLC
Chambersburg PA
CBHW032010220426
43664CB00006B/199